david g. clark
colorado state university

william b. blankenburg
university of wisconsin

you & media

mass communication
and society

canfield press ✝ san francisco
a department of harper & row, publishers, inc.
new york   evanston   london

The authors thank the following for permission to use various passages and quotations:
Columbia Journalism Review, for passages from William A. Hachten, "Journalism and the Prayer Decision," Fall 1963 ᶜ.

H. Doyle Harvill, The Tampa Times, for passages from a letter of April 20, 1970, to the authors.

National Council of Teachers of English, for passages from David Boroff, "Television and the Problem Play," in TV as Art, copyright 1966.

Public Relations News, for "Case Study No. 1311, Reaping PR Benefits From an Awards Program," Vol. XXVII, No. 33, August 16, 1971.

Public Relations Quarterly, for passages from "The Adversaries and the News Ethic," by William B. Blankenburg, Vol. 14, No. 4, 1970.

You and Media: Mass Communication and Society

Copyright ᶜ 1973 by David G. Clark and William B. Blankenburg

International Standard Book Number: 0-06-382507-4

Library of Congress Catalog Card Number: 73-1481

73 74 75 10 9 8 7 6 5 4 3 2 1

Acquisition, editing, and interior design by Brian K. Williams

Cover design by Joseph Fay

to andy

contents

preface

The purpose of this book is to examine in detail the values underlying the relationship of mass communications and society in the United States. Most of us see the mass media from only one point of view. We see the end product—the content. And we may think we are the ultimate decision-makers regarding what we read, watch, or listen to. But whether we admit it to ourselves or not, we are the objects of the aspirations, the constant planning, sometimes even the scheming, of media proprietors for the attention only we can give, and for which they receive their reward.

Furthermore, during the gathering, wrapping, and presentation of this content for our ultimate approval, the media make decisions that have enormous influence on our lives but of which we know very little. They set our priorities for discussion of the day's events with our friends. They tell us what to eat, what to wear, what opinions are socially acceptable, what actions are likely to be successful. They alert us in the morning, guide us during the day, and soothe us at night.

If you do not believe this, try to put aside the media for three or four days. You will become a stranger in your own land. Try to persuade your friends to follow your example. Be prepared to become an outcast. Be prepared, also, for ultimate failure, because it is impossible today to isolate oneself completely from the media for very long. In June of 1971, a stone-age tribe of 27 men, women, and children was discovered living in caves in a rain forest on the Philippine Island of Mindinao. They had never seen an outsider. Their language had no words for weapon, anger, hostility, or war. By October 1972 the tribe —the Tasaday—had been visited three times by a network television crew. They knew about helicopters, bolo knives, hiking boots, cameras, and tape recorders. And they were the subjects of an hour-long NBC documentary. Sad as it may seem to "civilize" such gentle folk, had not worldwide attention been focused on them through the media, they might have been left alone, to be overrun shortly by logging interests and settlers. As it was, the Philippine government stepped in and declared their area a sanctuary.

It is true for us, as it is for the Tasaday, that what we don't know can kill us. And the great role of the media in today's world is to tell us just that: what we don't know. How the media do that and how well they do it is everybody's business. Which is why we have tried to write this book from the standpoint of the "mass" in the mass communication process.

Hardly anyone can pose such a task for himself and not become immediately aware of subjects that must be omitted. We have, for example, said little about the influence of the American media upon the rest of the world. The American Century has been announced in large part by means of content produced for consumption in the United States, but distributed world-wide as well. And evidence suggests that the search for media markets will expand, not contract. In 1972, India's population approached 500 million while television sets in that country numbered fewer than 10,000. Two facts such as these are the stuff of dreams for U.S. media proprietors. But despite the fact that we have not been able—in limited space—to address the topic of international communications, a reader of this book can discover the values that may govern subsequent developments.

Much of the same sort of reasoning can be applied to other areas we have slighted. For example, we have touched but in passing upon that great and varied staple of rural and small-town communication, the weekly newspaper. Our omission owes not to a lack of fondness for the weekly, which is sometimes romantically viewed as the mother of all mass communication, but to a realization that—from the consumer's point of view—the weekly is a relatively minor ingredient of the media mix. The 8500 weeklies in this country have about 8.5 million circulation *weekly,* whereas dailies have about 60 million *daily.*

So we ask the teacher and implore the student to use our book as we have intended it to be used. It is a book with a point of view, meant to be argued with, and written for thinking people who will want to pursue its many subject areas more deeply. There is no such thing as the last word on mass communication, nor will there ever be. What is possible is constant searching and sifting to identify the driving forces that make the media move as they do.

Even for the person most committed to a career in the media, and we hope that many who read these words are so dedicated, the skeptical approach we have taken is valuable. Nothing is more certain than change, and changes are taking place and will continue to come as the new technology arrives. If we apply old methods, old techniques, old definitions, we will repeat the mistakes of the past without learning from them. But if we can somehow open our minds, look at the past for what it can teach us, and look at the new for what we may do that was never before possible, there is hope for the improvement of our world.

There are signs of awakening, but there must be more. Within the past decade, an acceleration of change has occurred on a number of fronts in our society: race, education, foreign relations, rights of women, economics, life styles—the entire fabric of existence. But too often there has been an arrogance in the value systems the media have espoused. With a few exceptions, those have been of an upper-middle-class mercantilism, and they have operated as if those values were universal, fixed, not subject to change.

As a result, we seek to take the reader through the establishment of those media values, to show the reasons why they evolved into what they are, to explain how they are changing, and to suggest ways the bombardment of useless values in the meantime may be survived.

We would do more. We hope to suggest in the last section of our book ways in which changes beneficial to the media and the audience may be undertaken. We hope to do these things without antagonism toward the media. We firmly believe that the media represent, in today's mass society, a kind of second government for all Americans, in which the best hopes of men may be aired, and furthered, for benefit of all. And we would have no other system.

D.G.C.
W.B.B.

a mass communication system at work

the name of the game is preselection

Why'd You choose such a backward time and such a strange land?
If You'd come today You would have reached a whole nation.
Israel in 4 B.C. had no mass communication.
—Judas, to Jesus, in "Jesus Christ Superstar"

Oh, Lord, won't You buy me a color TV?
Dialing for Dollars is trying to find me!
—Janis Joplin, in "Pearl"

Content is the reason we the audience devote so much of our time and money to the mass media. Why buy a radio except to hear music and news? Why subscribe to a newspaper except for the information it brings on so many subjects? We may think of ourselves as having freedom to select what we want from among a nearly infinite number of choices. But as consumers of content, we encounter it as the final product of a series of steps we only vaguely perceive. Long before the news account arrives, before the magazine story is printed, the movie script filmed, the book published, the performance scheduled, even the performer contracted, a process known as preselection has made far-ranging effects upon content as we eventually will receive it. Let us begin this examination of mass media values with an example of content, and see where we are led.

a star is preselected

She came up from the smoky, humid refinery town of Port Arthur, Texas, one of the children of the middle class who were themselves classless and homeless in their own country in the early 1960s. She drifted, first to Austin, always that least inhospitable of Texas towns, then westward along the trail the homeless have always moved in this country—to California.

The migration of the 1960s was different from the two previous treks in recent times. This was no move toward the war plants, and no escape from a drought-ridden heartland. This time the drought was in the soul, and the promise of the new land was not full employment but fulfillment of self. And in her search, Janis Joplin went to the classic hunting ground: the Haight-Ashbury.[1]

When she arrived, the Haight itself was in the process of being discovered, of converting from a lower middle class neighborhood near San Francisco's Golden Gate Park into the hippie, drug culture, flower child (all terms applied by the mass media) capital of the dropout world. Over the next few years the Haight would see its importance grow until San Francisco authorities would wring hands in public over an expected summer onslaught of 50,000 youths from all corners of the earth, and then just as suddenly would fade away from ills brought on by those complaints common to movie stars and advertisers—overexposure and overcommercialism.

Janis went the full route of drugs, and an Austin friend remembers her having been treated in a San Francisco hospital before returning, after a year or so, to Texas. Always, however, whatever anchor she had in life was not drugs, not family, friends, or religion, but music. For awhile she hung around the University of Texas, working as a keypunch operator, and playing her autoharp and singing at local bars and coffeehouses. She once won two bottles of Lone Star beer in a talent contest involving her and the bluegrass band she worked with. She had, then, a style that was strictly traditional, strictly country, as befitted one of her southeast Texas pine-woods origin.

Between that time and the October Sunday in 1970 when her road manager found her dead of an overdose of heroin in a Los Angeles motel room, she acquired style, a reputation, fame, riches, a following of millions, in just about that order. She did not find lasting happiness, contentment, fulfillment, or peace.

She did learn, as many before her, that folk heroines are discovered, packaged, advertised, distributed, and purchased in this society (as in any other) pretty much the same way as automobiles, detergents, foreign and domestic policies, universities, Heisman Trophy winners, and vaginal sprays. And if she, or Jimi Hendrix, or Otis Redding, or Marilyn Monroe, or Humphrey Bogart, or Ernest Hemingway, or Vincent van Gogh were to come back, she and they and countless others would see that once the image is established, once the trend is set, the actual existence of the person is no longer essential. The product takes on a life of its own. Alive, someone said, Lenny Bruce was a problem. Dead, he's a property.

For Janis Joplin, discovery was slow in coming. In fact, the odds were against discovery coming at all. One nationwide contest involved 13,000 rock groups competing for a chance to be noticed. Every year thousands of adolescents leave the junior high bands and the drum and bugle corps to branch out into the music they feel is uniquely their own. It isn't, but they think so. An outfit called Glass, from Port Townsend, Washington piled into a Volkswagen bus and went to Los Angeles to be discovered. They spent a week trying to convince more than 20 A & R men (Artists and Repertoire) from the recording companies that Glass should be put under contract. At week's end, back in Washington, the chief songwriter reported what he had learned. "I was really surprised that the record companies weren't concerned about the human aspects of making music. The whole industry seems to be turning into one big machine to turn out money."[2]

But perhaps a larger truth is that Glass got its chance to be discovered. The 300 or so recording companies work hard at discovering new talent. They send their A & R men around the country literally begging for new talent, shopping constantly. They survey what they see, and report back, and go again. And still the process has much sheer chance involved. Janis Joplin had been performing around San Francisco for some time with a band called Big Brother and the Holding Company. They had even made one, disastrous, record for a Chicago company which could not even get around to releasing it. But in her case, luck and recognition came in the forms of the 1967 Monterey Jazz Festival and Clive Davis, of the Columbia Broadcasting System.

By then she had dropped her bluegrass style, her quiet style, her Odetta style, her blues style, and who knows how many other styles. By then she was stomping and screaming in *her* style, which she had developed not shrewdly or calculatingly but in self-defense against the electronic upheaval that went on behind her while she sang. (In 1970 more than $215 million worth of organs, and nearly $160 million worth of fretted instruments were sold in this country—part of the sales which helped put the music instrument business over the $1 billion mark for the first time.[3])

Here's how Ralph J. Gleason, former San Francisco *Chronicle* jazz critic, now interpreter of the rock scene for *Rolling Stone* magazine, described Janis at Monterey:

"There she was, this freaky looking white kid from Texas on stage with all the hierarchy of the traditional blues world, facing an audience that was steeped in blues tradition, which was older than her ordinary audience and which had a built-in tendency to regard electric music as the enemy.

"The first thing she did was to say 'shit' and that endeared her right away. Then she stomped her foot and shook her hair and started to scream. They held still for a couple of seconds, but here and there in the great sunlit arena, longhairs started getting up and out into the aisles and stomping along with the band. By the end of the first number, the Monterey County Fairgrounds arena was packed with people writhing and twisting and snaking along in huge chains. It was an incredible sight."[4]

Clive Davis, then vice president, shortly afterward president of Columbia Records, also thought so. "Janis and contemporary music shot out of Monterey together in 1967 and I was fortunate to be there. I will always be personally grateful to her as she more than anyone else at Monterey made me intensely aware and excited about the new and future direction of music."[5]

Clive Davis was being a little modest. As a producer for one of the largest record companies in the country (Columbia's contract talent included Bob Dylan; Simon & Garfunkel; Blood, Sweat and Tears; and many more), he held something very much like instant fame in his hands. Janis Joplin, Big Brother and the Holding Company created their sensation at Monterey, and drifted right under the searching eye of Clive Davis.

It is a familiar pattern. Elvis Presley, whose records have sold more than anyone's, *anyone's* (250-plus million), was moving his southern lady fans to most unladylike reactions quite awhile before Arnold Shaw, scouting for the Edward B. Marks Music Corporation, encountered a Presley recording on a Memphis label during a trip to Nashville. "I was not familiar with the artist, who sounded like a Negro blues-shouter, but who also sang with a nasal quality characteristic of hillbilly white," Shaw reported later. The mixture had a curious drive and sensuality for him, though he was a little puzzled. "To be candid, I could not make out most of the lyrics."[6] At the urging of Presley's promoter, the now-famous Colonel Tom Parker of Nashville, Shaw took some disks back to New York and called them to the attention of a midwest deejay who did a Saturday show in New York. Reluctant to experiment in the big time, the disk jockey decided to try them out over his daily shows in Cleveland. Within days he was on the phone exclaiming, said Shaw, that he had never had such fantastic responses to any records he had ever programmed. It wasn't long before Ed Sullivan called. But Sullivan, who was afraid that he had correctly read the meaning of Presley's pelvic motions and that the audience would be shocked (he had and it wouldn't), had the cameras shoot from the belt up during the new star's three brief appearances. Even worse was Presley's spot on the Steve Allen show, which was locked in a rating battle with Sullivan. Allen had him come on in white tie and tails, top hat, and cane. If Elvis voiced any objections to that kind of monkey-suit behavior being forced upon him, they have not come down to us, and were certainly not listened to, and he was too well mannered a young man to argue. Nevertheless, the "real" Presley could not be framed from only the waist up. When it became clear not only that the audience would go along but was in fact far ahead on that road, he was allowed almost as much freedom on camera as on the concert stage.[7] And away he went. "Presley pictures don't need titles," a Metro-Goldwyn-Mayer executive said in awe a few years later. "They could be numbered and they would still sell."[8] So began Presley's reign (a long one as such things go) as king of the rock pile. When the Beatles, during one of their early visits to Hollywood, stopped by to pay homage, Presley's ranch manager was so sure of his boss's position that he did not bother to learn their names. He simply addressed them as "Hey, Beatle!" They answered, too.[9]

economics is the tie that binds

Problems of communication are not limited to those caused by the generation gap between rock stars. As the economic (or establishment) go-betweens between musicians and their publics, recording companies must face and solve severe problems. Mike Curb, the president of MGM Records and himself a young man, issued a plaintive lament about what happens. Hard-drug rock stars, he said, "come into your office, wipe out your secretary, waste the time of your promotion people, show no concern in the recording studio, abuse the equipment, and then, to top things off, they break up!"[10]

A partial solution to this collision of two cultures is known as the company freak. He is decorative, but he has a function. A fellow freak described Billy James, one of the first of the genre, shortly after James had left Columbia and gone over to Elektra: "this charming, barefoot dynamo, running around the office, sitting on the floor, putting his feet up on the walls. And the room is full of kids coming in and out, hanging out, receiving solace, advice, encouragement." It should be added that the particular freak doing that talking is an English major who spent several years editing college textbooks.[11]

Despite the difficulties which the producers and the artists encounter in reaching understanding, there is always the common bridge of economics arching across tastes and distastes. To militant blacks, the networks may be symbols of the white power structure. ("The revolution will not be brought to you by Xerox in four parts without commercial interruptions," declares the young black poet Gil Scott-Herron. "The revolution will be live."[12]) But Columbia Records was happy to distribute an album of 15 talks by the late Malcolm X ("The Chicken and the Duck Egg" and "We Want to Collect on Our Investment," among others). And in 1971 RCA thought it saw a market for an album on the memorial services for the late Whitney Young, head of the National Urban League, which was to receive all the profits.[13]

Indeed, sometimes the producer communicates the economic message far too clearly to the artist. That seems to have been the conclusion of the top rock impresario, Bill Graham, whose Fillmore West and Fillmore East operations formed the kernel of rock music germination in this country for six years. Graham finally got disgusted and decided to close his forums, which frequently had provided public exposure for many groups which subsequently became famous. As the rock stars began to capitalize on their new fame, and charged up to $50,000 for a week's stand, Graham found it harder and harder to fill his theatres at those prices, and fell victim to the revolution he had helped start.[14]

So with discovery, or observation, the event becomes fixed, successful, and ready for frequent repetition. If no one had stood in the aisles at Monterey to dance for Janis, she might conceivably have changed her style again. But they did, and Columbia Records saw, and reportedly soon paid a quarter of a million dollars to the Chicago record company just to get the Holding Company's contract and the unreleased record. Columbia bought, and what it bought was the Joplin image and performance at Monterey. Innovations in style might come, but later. By the time of her death, the two albums she had made for Columbia both had grossed more than $1 million on the manufacturer's level. The style remained the same, though in her last album, issued shortly after her death, there were signs of a more subdued style emerging.

But with success she was locked in. Not just into a singing style, but a life style, whether she wanted it that way or not. Chances are she did at first, and chances are just as good that later she hated it, wanted to break out. But she was typed, and the public expected the image. So she fed it. The Southern Comfort trademark (though she switched to gin and vodka a year or so before she died). The feathers in her hair, the satin and velvet, the rings and bracelets (enough, said *Rolling Stone,* for a Babylonian whore). Cursing the cops. Making bad jokes about drugs the way mindless nightclub comics kid about booze to their boozy audiences. And doing other things, privately, like reading Thomas Wolfe's *Look Homeward Angel* and other serious books, "but don't tell anybody."[15]

Partly to further the Joplin claim as heiress to the blues title, she and several Columbia executives bought a gravestone for Bessie Smith, who had gone unmarked since 1937 at Sharon Hill, Pennsylvania. "The greatest blues singer in the world will never stop singing," read the inscription.[16]

Thus the image was preserved and additions were made and the whole thing was cultivated by everyone who had a hand in it, especially interviewers and editors seeking to spark up their copy: "Mamas, Lock Up Your Sons—Here Comes Janis!"; "Passionate and Sloppy"; "Singer With a Bordello Voice"; "Janis Joplin Philosophy: Every Moment She Is What She Feels"; "Janis Joplin: The Voodoo-Lady of Rock."[17]

And when some took the put-on too seriously, took the heavy drug advice (as she herself did, unable to separate the reality from the image much of the time), there were the public relations efforts to counter the bad publicity. Dr. David E. Smith, founder and director of the Haight-Ashbury Medical Clinic, testified to the positive steps the recording industry had taken to help the clinic treat, in three and a half years, 50,000 drug users without government aid. Janis and the Holding Company gave three benefits to support the clinic, he reported, not to mention "regular support from the music industry," including $5,000 from the Monterey Pop Festival.[18]

who's in charge here?

In this model of a mass communication system we're building, we've identified so far three members: the talent or raw material, the talent scout-agent-reporter-observer, and the policy maker, who determines for the company how the resources will be allocated. Will the network buy westerns, situation comedies, or cops and robbers? Will we send the camera crew to cover this or that demonstration? Shall we record this sound or that? What is the competition doing? And, when the "trend" has about run its course, is it time to move on to something else?

As content begins its progression from isolation to mass attention, something approaching complete control of the system resides in the policy makers. As they choose what will be recorded, filmed, written about, published, and otherwise processed for sale to the public, they are as often as not dominated by economic considerations to the exclusion of all others. Columbia Records would not have shelled out for the contract with Big Brother and the Holding Company had there not been a very good chance of recovering that money through later record sales. The Beatles would not have spent nearly $50,000 to record "Sergeant Pepper's Lonely Hearts Club Band" had they not, under their Apple label, controlled all three steps. The economic advantages that come to one who can provide the talent, "discover" it, and make the policy decisions involved in exploiting it are so obvious, in fact, that sometimes people go a little out of their way to refine their control still further.

Back in the late fifties, an attractive, clean-cut young man named Dick Clark was very much an institution among teen-age Americans. Clark had made a number of television endeavors for the American Broadcasting Company, but the most successful was "American Bandstand," a daily, low-budget show televised from Philadelphia. The format was simple. Clark played records and interviewed recording stars. The recording stars performed and the audience, composed of teen-agers, danced. "I seek to provide wholesome recreational outlets for these youngsters whom I think I know and understand," was the way Clark put it when he was asked to testify before a Congressional subcommittee.[19] As it turned out, he knew and understood a good deal more than youngsters.

For one thing, Clark understood that if he had his own song publishing and recording company or companies, contracted his own performers, made his own policy decisions, and then played the results on his own nationwide television show, a lot of the inefficiency and plain bad luck could be removed from the marketplace. So he organized several publishing and recording companies, and during a period of two years played on his television show just over half the records of his companies an average of 15 times. Sixty-five percent of these records were played before they received any national rating at all in the "Top 100" charts of *Billboard* magazine, which conducts nationwide popularity ratings. By pushing records and songs in which he had property rights in this manner, he was able to have at least one song, and often more than one, in the "Top 100" list in all but 10 weeks in a 116-week period.[20] And there was absolutely nothing whatever illegal about what he did. His intelligence had simply devised a better way of doing what many record producers were engaged in at the time: paying cash to disk jockeys for playing records on the air. That was not illegal either, then, though it pretty soon became so.

But imagine 14-year-old Janis Joplin, settling down after school and on Saturdays before a television set to watch "American Bandstand," and listening to the smooth Mr. Clark explain how this next song is going to be one of the top hits of the coming weeks, so give it a good listen. And interviewing the artist and discovering all kinds of interesting things about his life. And slipping in, too, a suggestion to go down to the record store and get this latest one while it's hot. Fourteen-year-old Janis certainly had no reason to doubt Dick Clark's sincerity.

During the rise of so-called underground newspapers in the late 1960s, it became recognized that one of their steadiest income sources was the record industry, which sought to reach prospective buyers in the dropout world. Consider a full-page ad that ran in Milwaukee's *Kaleidoscope* (on the same date in 1968 as the famous picture of John Lennon and Yoko Ono without a stitch—not counting appendectomy scars—staring out at a war-torn world). The ad shows six young men (two of them black) sweating it out in a holding cell, the floor of which is littered with protest signs. Also on the floor is a portable phonograph, and the young men appear lost in contemplation of the music it is playing. "But the Man can't bust our music," asserts the copy. "The Establishment's against adventure. And the arousing experience that comes with listening to today's music. So what? Let them slam doors. And keep it out of the concert halls." Nothing can stop you from listening to the ear-stretching and transfixing sounds, continues the copy, of Bach played on the Moog Synthesizer, Edgar Varese on chains and sirens, and—revolutionary among revolutionaries—Leonard Bernstein conducting Charles Ives' *Holidays* Symphony. For who is lining up with the readers of *Kaleidoscope* against the Establishment and the Man, but Columbia Records?[21] These approaches of the music recording industry may seem crass and cynical to some, though others defend such practices as legal, hence not immoral, and in fact quite businesslike. But persons who speak grandly of the role music will play in the construction of the coming new world seem by contrast somewhat naive. For instance, in his *The Greening of America,* Charles A. Reich sang of the cultural revolution thus: "The new music is, first of all, incredibly important because it's the chief language and means of communication for the people of this new consciousness, particularly young people. The kids have discovered a new means of communication, like extrasensory perception. We don't have to send each other messages through the mail because we have a magical network of communications, and the chief vehicle of that is music."[22]

But if the system is not as natural and spontaneous as Reich suggests, neither is it as artificial as Dick Clark would have made it. There are some further steps in the process which complicate it and which occasionally help bring diversity as well.

people have some say, though the public has little

The first of these steps is the competitive process by which content emerges from the recording studios, the reporters' typewriters, the film companies, the screening rooms, and the editorial offices. Competition tends to produce likeness, and competitors do their level best to extinguish their competition, but as long as different people make decisions, the opportunities for differences to occur will exist.

Consider the final gatekeeper of the recorded music industry —the disk jockey. When payola was king, he would play what he was paid to play. That is, if he were lucky enough to work in one of the top national markets, those metropolitan areas that are used to set the musical tastes of the rest of the country. If not, then he played what other people were paid to play, and which came to him via the "Top 100" list in *Billboard* or some similar magazine. At any rate, the choice was pretty much his, as it is now—though at some radio stations the choices are now made by computer.

But the deejay has little direct control over what the record distributor brings around for him to choose from. Most of those 300 or so recording companies have a regional distributor who spends a good deal of time trying to get records played on the air by disk jockeys. Mike Alhadeff is one such distributor. In his mid-twenties, outgoing, aggressive, he has been employed by ABC Record and Tape Sales for two years. His territory is Seattle, Washington, one of the top markets. ABC is a subsidiary of the American Broadcasting Company. Alhadeff cultivates disk jockeys, takes them to lunch, and does his best to get the new records played on the air.

"Every day, records come in the mail from my labels—Mercury, London, and Parrot. I am required to listen to them all, which could be and has been up to 25 a day."[23] Alhadeff then chooses a few which he thinks have the best chances for success at a particular station, and sets out. He must visit the dozen stations regularly, for his competitors are on the road, too.

Once the disk jockey has been approached, ABC Record and Tape Sales must begin a second step. Supplies of the new records must be distributed to the retail stores, so purchasers can find the song after they've heard the record on the radio. Most of the big discount stores prefer the record distributors to function as rack jobbers, which means the distributors stock the shelves themselves, the same way the bread truck driver keeps fresh loaves on supermarket shelves. In a business where a record can come from nowhere to lead the best-seller list in a week, speed is essential. Although the distributor has virtually nothing to say about the content of the product, he is nevertheless one of the most important links in the system, for without him nothing could be sold.

Or, more accurately, it could not be sold in the volume and at the speed necessary to make the industry profitable. During his 1971 trial for his part in the My Lai slayings, "The Battle Hymn of Lt. Calley" lay around southern discount stores for months collecting dust. But with the lieutenant's conviction, interest perked up, and Plantation Records of Nashville had its biggest hit since Jeannie C. Riley's "Harper Valley PTA." In one four-hour period, 140,000 orders for the record came in, and inside a week more than a quarter of a million requests to buy were registered.[24] But, as all merchants know, a sale is not completed until delivery is made, and the record purchaser is a notoriously shifty character in his desires. Therefore, enter the record wholesaler with his emphasis on large-scale, rapid distribution. Enter, too, the imitators hoping to cash in on a profitable development. Within hours following Calley's conviction, Capitol Records was "alerting" radio stations to a forthcoming "cover" version to be recorded by Tex Ritter. The competition might thus take advantage of the valuable groundwork done by the original promoters and, given an efficient distribution, capitalize on other people's promotion.

When Janis's posthumous album, *Pearl,* was released three months after her death, Columbia Records took no chances that the record might not succeed. Despite the fact that the Joplin–Jimi Hendrix rock-and-roll way of death legend was still going strong (a Philadelphia poster company had run off a hundred thousand posters of Janis since her death, and a San Francisco tattoo artist was needling the "Janis Joplin Heart" at $10 each), Clive Davis assigned large funds to the promotion campaign. Full-page ads in the trade magazines (to alert the deejays who might not be on the distributors' routes), fulsome announcements in college newspapers, displays in record store windows. Davis even allowed himself to be interviewed for a mild muck-raking by NBC of how the Joplin image was being exploited after death. "I don't think any album sells itself," Davis told "First Tuesday" interviewer Tom Pettit. "We will do it tastefully, but we will certainly bring the resources of Columbia Records behind the album, just as if Janis were alive." *Pearl* was released while the manufacturing of half a million albums was still underway. It shot to the top of the sales lists, and by the end of six months was still in the top 50 best-selling albums. By then one million copies had been sold, netting a profit of around $1 per album.[25]

enter scavengers, bootleggers, and pirates

Such profit possibilities tend to bring, besides the "cover" jobs issued by other recording companies, a form of competition that is very hard to fight: tape bootlegging or piracy. Due largely to the inadequacy of a copyright law that was written in 1909—well before electronic copying devices, both sound and visual, were developed—such piracy has blossomed into big money, since the bootleggers pay no royalties to the artists, bear no original production costs, and have the legitimate owner doing the publicity work for them.

Some states have laws against such operations, but the absence of specific Federal protection until 1972 made it difficult to prevent pirates from operating through discount houses, auto stereo centers, and the like, across state lines. One such operation was tracked from California to Arizona, where investigators found 150,000 tape cartridges, 17 winding machines, duplicating equipment, wrapping and labeling machines, along with 100 full-time employes using sophisticated quality-control techniques. There was even a catalog, from which more than 400 songs could be ordered. And like any big-time operation in the recorded music industry, the pirate company had an elaborate distribution system, using telephone answering services in various cities to take orders. One agent for a number of song publishing companies brought suit in Wichita, Kansas against four major oil companies, seeking to fix responsibility on them for allowing service station operators to sell bootleg tapes in that area.[26]

Estimates of the scope of record piracy are guesswork at best, but by mid-1971, publishers and recording companies that had legal rights to music being bootlegged, and that consequently had spent much time and effort tracking down their unfair competition, had worked out what they considered a realistic estimate. One-third of all recordings sold were bootleg, they said. If that were true, it would mean $500 million a year.

who or what is out there buying, listening, reading?

By now you will have been telling yourself that we have left out the very key ingredient of the mass communication process, the element to which all the effort is directed—in short, the audience. Indeed, it is true that much of the process seems to ignore the audience, even though a great deal of lip service is paid the notion that the audience is the final judge of what is acceptable and what is not. Possibly a major reason why the audience tends to be ignored has to do with the lack of knowledge about who and what the audience is. The multimillion-dollar popular music industry, for example, operates on all levels with little real understanding of just who buys the records and why.

Behavioral science has only recently begun to investigate the composition of the various mass media audiences. Much of the findings so far seem rather pedestrian in nature—that blacks would rather, when given a choice, listen to a soul station than to top 40 music, that southern white teen-agers listen to country and western music a lot, that as audience groups do become identified, radio stations develop music formats to attempt to reach them.

One of the more interesting findings so far has had to do with the comprehension, or lack of it, with which the audience receives the message. Despite the voiced concern of government, industry officials, and others over the communication of drug lyrics, the startling fact seems to be that although teen-agers listen to drug lyrics and social protest music, they do not understand what is being said. A survey of 1200 high school students in Detroit, Flint, and Grand Rapids, Michigan, uncovered just that fact. Fewer than 30 percent of the subjects of a confidential questionnaire were able to write out correctly the "message" supposedly contained in four controversial hit "protest" song lyrics. Asked directly what attracted them most to a song, a large majority ranked sound ahead of meaning.[27] No doubt such findings are as disquieting to lyricists as they are comforting to those who saw revolution following every performance of the Beatles. A pessimist might ask, however, just what would be the consequence should millions of teen-agers actually begin to grasp the meaning of the songs they hear daily and purchase frequently.

critic: "the media are to blame for ... "

The ambiguity of the system—the unresolved questions of whether people are influenced, and if so, just exactly in what ways—tends to make it an easy target for those who wish to fix blame for things they don't like. Conspiracy theory includes rock. The editor of the British leftist magazine *New Statesman* charged the rock music industry (including, presumably, the Beatles) with being part of a plot by the commercial wing of the Establishment to exploit the gullible young and keep them subservient and stupid:

Their huge faces bloated with cheap confectionery and smeared with chain store makeup, the open sagging mouths and glazed eyes, the hands mindlessly drumming in time to the music, the broken stiletto heels, the shoddy stereotyped "with-it" clothes: here, apparently, is a collective portrait of a generation enslaved by a commercial machine.[28]

So the left accuses the right of using rock as an opiate of the masses. And the right has similar notions about the left. Professor Joseph Crow of Pacific Western College lectured extensively on the point during the height of the Beatles' reign:

The high quality of their recent recording almost scientifically creates a mood for them to push home the message in their songs. I have no idea whether The Beatles know what they are doing or whether they are being used by some enormously sophisticated people, but it really doesn't make any difference. It's results that count, and The Beatles are the leading pied pipers creating promiscuity, an epidemic of drugs, youth class-consciousness, and an atmosphere for social revolution. What The Beatles begin is imitated, and often expanded upon, by literally hundreds of other groups who in turn reach tens of millions of people.[29]

For persons accustomed to taking their explanations of cosmic forces with just a bit more complexity, these theories are too simple. Nevertheless, they have a certain plausibility. Or, as Frank Zappa, holder of a master's degree in music, but better known as leader of the Mothers of Invention, puts it: "If the right kind of beat makes you tap your foot, what kind of beat makes you curl your fist and strike?"[30]

Those two factors—uncertainty about just who the audience is (all we know is that it is large, mostly young, and seems to like the music), and ignorance of the effects the music has—bring both the fear and the reality of government intervention.

media: "we are not! but just to be on the safe side ... "

In the face of mounting criticism of the rock music industry as encouraging drug use, elements within the industry began action on two lines. First and most obvious was the recording and release, with appropriate publicity, of anti-drug messages, such as songs and one-minute spots to be played on the same stations that had made famous the suspect songs. "Speed kills," said Zappa in his spot, "so if you want to be dead in five years keep on using it." Grace Slick of the Jefferson Airplane, herself a highly publicized marijuana user, and a number of other rock stars took part in the campaign, which by its very existence tacitly acknowledged the belief by the music industry in its power to persuade its audience to follow a course of action. Numerous anti-drug songs had been recorded in the past—including Jimi Hendrix's "Red House," Canned Heat's "Amphetamine Annie," and the Byrds' "Artificial Energy"—all without the publicity that was now cranked out to underscore the anti-drug theme.[31]

The second course of action was for some of the recording companies to attempt to wash their hands by unloading a few of the more open drug users among their recording artists. This form of self-regulation, coming after substantial criticism and publicity, could not escape the cynical charge that it resulted more from fear of possible legislation than from any strong conviction, no matter how strongly voiced, that the industry should clean up its own house. MGM Records' Mike Curb put the argument in its classic simplicity—the way it has been put by the movie industry, the advertising industry, and other industries that have faced, or imagined themselves to be facing, government regulation of some aspect of their affairs. "MGM will not be used to further the use of drugs," Curb announced. "It's important for a company run by young people to take this action rather than some senators in Washington." The action he referred to was MGM's release of 18 acts—alleging drug use—from contract following the drug deaths of Janis, Jimi, and Al Wilson of Canned Heat.[32] Curb pointed out that a morals clause in the MGM contract—a descendant of the old movie contracts of the 1920s when the private lives of the stars were scandalizing them out in Kansas and the movie companies had to tone things down—allowed MGM to take action. And he thus implicitly admitted that MGM all along had possessed the power to regulate its artists had it wished to do so.

When the threat of government intervention did come to the recording industry, it came indirectly, as befits control imposed in a First Amendment area. The Federal Communications Commission, which does not have jurisdiction over the recording industry but does over the thousands of broadcasting stations that use recordings, simply announced that stations would be held accountable for knowing the content of the songs played on the air. This was not as simple a thing to know as it might seem, since the nature of language frequently permits more than one meaning to be taken. When the seniors at Monroe High School in Iowa chose "Bridge Over Troubled Water" to be played at graduation, the local newspaper editor claimed it was a "drug" song. Her reason? The lyrics, "Sail on silver girl ... Like a bridge over troubled water I will ease your mind," meant to her a reference to a hypodermic needle. To the students, the words had to do with friendship, and the dispute was resolved by recourse to the Des Moines drug center, which had never had anyone come in after being hooked by that song.[33] But does the Beatles' "A Little Help From My

Friends" mean one's pills or one's friends? And how are mere disk jockeys supposed to keep up with every change in the code language used by the drug culture? That's what broadcasters wanted to know, but the FCC in its cumbersome, bureaucratic, and sensible way insisted that *somebody* in the straight community ought to know what the lyrics meant, and since broadcasters had the legal responsibility, the job was theirs.

Naturally, the broadcasters sought to pass on the responsibility to the record makers. They in turn threatened with loss of their indispensable outlet to the mass public, went into their routine to convince all—government, broadcasters, and public—that in fact they were highly opposed to drug lyrics, and had been all along.

what we really need is a new trend

But perhaps what had changed was not public arousal, government intervention, or recording company self-restraint. Perhaps the times had simply changed, the trends shifted, the fads worn out. Jesus was just around the corner.* Last week's top single artist had dropped to seventh this week and would be 30th week after next. *Pearl* was up longer than most, but went off the top 50 list after 40 weeks. When he spoke of reporters covering the primary campaign in 1968, Senator Eugene McCarthy described the mass media well. Reporters, he said, are a little like blackbirds on a fence. One comes in, and pretty soon another, then a whole flock. And then one flies off, and pretty soon they all fly away. He was describing not merely reporters looking for a story but all the mass media, looking for an audience.

for further reading

Eisen, Jonathan. *The Age of Rock: Sounds of the Great American Cultural Revolution.* 2 Vols. New York: Random House, 1970.
Hirsch, Paul M. "Sociological Approaches to the Pop Music Phenomenon," *American Behavioral Scientist,* Vol. 14, No. 3, January/February 1971, pp. 371–388.
Landau, Deborah. *Janis Joplin: Her Life and Times.* New York: Paperback Library, 1971.
Shaw, Arnold. *The Rock Revolution.* New York: Crowell-Collier, 1969.

---

*He arrived, of course, via "Jesus Christ Superstar" and by early 1972 was well into the mainstream of the recording industry, as shown by these releases: "Truth of Truths" (Oak); "Rock Requiem" (Verve); "Divine Hair—Mass in F'" (RCA); "Rock Mass for Love" (Decca); "The Survival of St. Joan" (Paramount); and a lot more. Possibly the Coming was stopped in its tracks by a Scots Guards bagpipe version of "Amazing Grace."

part
1

the
environment
and the
media

presenting mass communication

men, messages, and machines

Where once priests and kings decided what the populace would hear, the
proprietors of the mass media now decide.
—Ben H. Bagdikian

Just before noon on November 6, 1455, a gloomy Johann Gutenberg
slumped into the refectory of the Barefooted Friars, which served as
the courtroom of the city of Mainz. Gutenberg was no stranger to
lawsuits.[1] Sixteen years earlier, in Strasbourg, he won a case that had
endangered his secret experiments with soft metals and wooden
presses. Still earlier, in 1436, he had twice been sued: by a shoemaker
for defamation and by a young woman for breach of promise.

He also had money trouble. Though of patrician birth, Gutenberg spent all he had on his research—and on his extensive wine cellar

(420 gallons in 1439). He had an income, but it was hard to collect. At one point he kidnaped the city clerk of Mainz in an effort to force the city to pay 310 guilders in overdue rents and annuities. Not surprisingly, he became a persuasive and prolific borrower. In 1438 he negotiated an illegal loan from the parish of St. Thomas in Strasbourg, and six years later he cajoled a relative into cosigning a note for 150 guilders.

Now, in 1455, he was in court again, this time for defaulting on the largest loan of his career—1600 guilders in principal and about 400 more in interest. This was a phenomenal amount. In those days, 2000 guilders could buy 250 oxen or several large farms. The plaintiff was Johann Fust, a Mainz lawyer and gold merchant. Like Gutenberg, Fust knew something about metallurgy, and he was impressed with Gutenberg's experiments in casting metal types and his schemes for printing religious tracts.

In 1450 Fust had loaned Gutenberg 800 guilders at 6 percent interest to carry on the work, and two years later the inventor tapped Fust for another 800. By then Fust had no illusions about Gutenberg's business ability, but he was still intrigued by his printing contraptions and the profits to be made from them. Fust could have foreclosed the first loan in 1452 and acquired the equipment that was collateral, but he didn't know how to operate the machinery. So he agreed to the second loan on condition that he be made a working partner.

The partnership was instructive to Fust, both technically and economically. He could see that Gutenberg's works in progress—missals and psalters—were attractive and marketable, but also painfully slow in production because they required several different fonts of type. Probably at Fust's urging, Gutenberg switched to another sure-fire product, one that needed only a single size of type: a Bible.

By 1455 the Bible was nearly completed, far behind schedule, and Gutenberg was in court, threatened by foreclosure while at the very threshold of success. If Gutenberg won, he could complete the project, repay the debt, and share the profits. For Fust it was winner take all. Fust now understood the skills of printing, and he knew he could rely on Gutenberg's assistant, a former scribe who was named Peter Schoeffer.

It wasn't a long trial. Schoeffer testified against his master, and Fust won. Schoeffer soon afterward married Fust's daughter, became his partner, and together they completed the famous Gutenberg Bible. Gutenberg went bankrupt, was given a pension by the Archbishop of Mainz, and died in 1468. But his contribution—the casting of movable types—immortalized his name.

Gutenberg's invention had its beginnings about 5000 years

earlier when an Egyptian sharpened a stick and drew symbols in clay. These pictures were attractive, had a certain durability, and, most importantly, could partially take the place of spoken communication. Over the centuries, the Egyptians evolved picture-symbols of things, ideas, word sounds, syllable sounds, and ultimately letter sounds. The Egyptians mixed these symbols, much to the exasperation of the tradesmen of Phoenicia, who about 1200 B.C. impatiently dropped the Egyptian picture signs and kept only the more compact symbols for individual sounds of speech. What was good for business—in this case an alphabet—was good for Phoenicia.

Written communication has some enormous virtues. It can do things the communicator himself cannot do: transcend time and space. Both capabilities were needed in the expanding Mediterranean societies. Merchants, priests, and rulers all had use for communication that did not rely on fallible memory. Written communication extended their senses and their power.

But extended communication is not quite "mass" communication if by the term we mean exposure of verbal messages to a large, dispersed audience within a fairly short period of time.[2] For mass communication, mankind needed fancier tools than styluses, papyrus, and dyes. Mass communication awaited machines, which in turn awaited developments in technology. The inventions came, and still come, and every innovation affects people individually and socially. It has been a long trek from pictographs to alphabets to printing to photography and electronics. Today we are awash with media whose scope can barely be sketched. In America alone we have all this:

1. A television industry with 691 commercial and 198 educational stations reaching 95.5 percent of American households, about half of which have color sets.

2. A cable television industry with about 2750 operating systems reaching about 6 million homes and 18.5 million viewers.

3. A radio industry with 4368 AM and 2711 FM stations reaching 336 million sets, of which about 95 million are located outside the home.

4. A motion-picture industry with four dominant studio/distributors and numerous others, releasing about 270 films a year to approximately 10,300 "four-wall" and 3700 drive-in theatres, whose annual receipts are about $1.25 billion.

5. A record industry producing about 7000 single and 4000 album titles a year, with a retail value of about $1.7 billion.

6. A magazine industry of about 10,000 periodicals, producing 2.5 billion copies, most of them special interest, with annual receipts of about $3 billion from sales and advertising.

7. A newspaper industry composed of about 1750 dailies and 9000 weeklies. The dailies produce over 63 million copies a day and have annual advertising receipts of more than $6 billion.

8. A book publishing industry of about 1600 publishers who bring out 25,000 new titles and 12,000 new editions a year for total annual receipts of about $2.9 billion. There are about 80,000 retail outlets for paperbound books, and 10,000 that also sell hardcovers; the U.S. has about 24,000 libraries.

9. A telephone system of about 120 million sets carrying 490 million conversations a day over more than 600 million miles of wire.

10. A postal service that handles about 87 billion pieces of mail a year through approximately 32,000 post offices.

11. An outdoor advertising industry that has about 231,000 poster and 35,500 paint "standard" units throughout the nation.[3]

the machine in the middle

Structurally, at least, the most important feature of mass communication is the insertion of a machine into the information process. Yet we rarely give it a second thought, because for most people the machine is not an end in itself, but merely a means for learning about their more distant environments. And one can flip on a television set or pick up a newspaper without brooding about semiconductors and hertzian waves and points and picas.

What are the major characteristics of the mass communication machines?

1. They permit a few senders to transmit duplicate messages to many receivers at the same time, or nearly so. The most spectacular example occurred on July 21, 1969, when astronauts Neil Armstrong and Edwin E. Aldrin, Jr., spoke from the moon to a worldwide audience estimated at nearly one billion people. That same year, mass communication machinery enabled CBS to bring "The Beverly Hillbillies" to 13.5 million U.S. households in a typical week; Hugh Hefner to titillate us with over 5.2 million copies a month of *Playboy;* and the Beatles to sing for us from 5.3 million records of "I Want To Hold Your Hand."

2. Mass communication machines are better at sending than receiving. Out of the billion people who watched the astronauts only a handful of technicians—and the President—could talk back to them. Readers and viewers of more ordinary mass communication can talk back only in limited ways, usually without the precision and effectiveness of interpersonal communication.

3. The machine cannot reproduce everything that happens. Someone once queried the New York *Times,* "If you publish 'all the news that's fit to print,' how come there's so much more news that's fit to print on Sundays?" The answer is that advertising supports more editorial space on Sundays, and the *Times*—or any other medium—covers only as much as space, money, time, energy, and perceptiveness allow. Something gets left out, and in terms of a universe filled with events, almost everything gets left out. Whoever runs the machine must make selections.

4. *The machine requires money to build.* Neil Armstrong said as he set foot on the moon, "That's one small step for man, one giant leap for mankind." The cost of that message—including getting Armstrong to the moon to say it—figures out to a little more than $2 billion a word. Fortunately, the cost was spread among many taxpayers (though some would argue otherwise), and the Apollo 11 mission yielded much more than words (some would dispute that, too). Descending abruptly from the moon to an urban cellar, we find that an underground newspaper can be established for about $2500 in equipment—which is still a lot of money for those who are inclined to be underground publishers.[4] (Some basement newspapers achieved penthouse economics; between 1965 and 1969 the Los Angeles *Free Press* grew to a circulation of 95,000 and a reputed gross income of $1 million.) Above ground, a small daily newspaper will have as much as $1 million tied up in equipment, and a large one $25 million or more.[5] The average-sized daily, with 36,000 circulation, may have $1.25 million in presses and another $300,000 in typesetting equipment. All told, its tangible assets may total nearly $4 million. The average television station has $1.93 million in physical assets. And, since the cost of producing mass communication is considerable, it is natural that those who have invested large sums will strive to protect their investments.

5. *Mass communication machines require skilled managers and technicians.* In a large medium, few if any people know how to operate every piece of the machine from, say, linecasting to press operation. Even if they do, many hands are required, and a social organization grows around the machinery and has communication problems of its own. The average daily newspaper has about 200 employes, not counting supporting workers in the wire services, paper industry, and other allied trades. The complexities of the machinery demand intelligence, aptitude, and training. The minimum requirement for technicians is literacy, and this alone is enough to exclude 40 percent of the world's adult population from significant roles in mass communication production.

6. *The machine requires considerable financial support.* The owner is willing to take short-term losses in anticipation of later profits or as a means of attacking competition, or for tax purposes. But an average-sized daily has total annual operating expenses of around $4 million, including $1.5 million in payroll, and a publisher would have to be a very well-heeled zealot to support losses of that scope for very

long. Ultimately the audience must pick up the tab, and this it does both directly and indirectly. In the case of books and motion pictures, the arrangement is fairly straightforward, but other media are supported more circuitously. It costs about $120 a year to place a daily and Sunday newspaper in a household and only one-third or less of this comes directly from the subscriber. The television viewer pays no subscription unless he connects to a cable television system. Thus enters a third entity—government or advertising—which extracts funds from the consumer and redistributes them to the media. In this country, advertisers channel most of a newspaper's revenues and virtually all of broadcasting's. To acquire this support, a mass medium must perform a two-way selling job. It sells its basic content to an audience, then sells the audience to the advertiser.

tending the gates of communication

The process of mass communication pivots on the machine and consists of gathering raw material, processing it for machine reproduction, and distributing the results to the audience. This system does not have unlimited capacity. It is especially constricted in the middle, at the machine, where someone must choose what will be reproduced. This person, invisible to the audience, might answer to the title of news director or managing editor or executive producer. Social scientists have conveniently tagged them all with the title *gatekeeper.*

It's a mistake to assume that there is but one gatekeeper in every mass communication system and that the sun rises and sets at his whim. Available content is reduced to manageable proportions by a long series of filters, as demonstrated earlier by the structure of the popular-music industry. It begins with the first person who notices an event and decides whether to pass it along as a message. This early bird might be a reporter, a talent scout, or a creative person who recognizes a new idea in his own head. Obviously talent scouts reject much of what they find; similarly, reporters select only what's important, and individuals who discover something in themselves don't always tell about it.

If the early perceptions are passed along, they will eventually be judged by editors of various kinds who stand just in front of the machine. The most frequently studied gatekeeper is the telegraph editor of a daily newspaper who decides which among hundreds of wire-service news stories warrant transmission to the local audience; there are equivalent gatekeepers in every medium.

Even after the machine has done its work, the gates can be squeezed a bit by distributors. In the late 1960s, Ancorp National Services, Inc., the largest newsstand retailer in the country, refused to sell certain magazines and newspapers because those publications would not purchase advertising poster space on its stands. Since Ancorp held a retail monopoly at several Eastern rail, air, and bus terminals, many potential customers could not buy copies of *Newsweek, McCall's, Time, Life, Fortune, Reader's Digest,* and other publications for various periods of time. However, the magazines were available by subscription. The lesson is that gatekeeping can occur at many points—ultimately with the reader or viewer—but the gatekeepers in front of the machine are of particular significance because once something is mass produced it is usually available in some way. This fact is well known to people who want to keep something out of the channel.

At first glance, the gatekeeper's job looks much like that of a censor. Certainly the editor-gatekeeper shunts aside more material than the bluest-nosed guardian of morals. True, an editor will occasionally make deletions on grounds of taste, but as a rule his attitude is positive and he makes choices for purposes of transmission, not for the sake of suppression. He thinks in terms of what the audience wants and needs rather than what it shouldn't have. If he had his way, practically all of his raw material would be passed along to the reader. But the mass communication system doesn't have the capacity for this.

So the gatekeeper must operate under such constraints as the amount of time, money, and tools at his disposal; the quality and availability of raw material; his own traits, skills, knowledge, and values; legal and social pressures, including those coming from government, advertisers, and his fellow professionals; and the desires of his large, unseen audience.

One limit on his ability to choose is the richness or slenderness of his material. Shortages are most often evident in artistic media, where producers, directors, and publishers frequently lament a dearth of talent. This is less a problem in the popular arts, where "talent" can be manufactured and heavily merchandised (the Monkees, for example), and in the news media, where wire-service and staff reporters shower the editor with much more copy than he can use. An editor might complain that "there's no news today," but he only means there are no super-spectacular stories. When the news editor of an average daily arrives at work, he is confronted with 50,000 words of copy, mostly accumulated from teletype machines. In the next six or seven hours before deadline he will be blessed with 60,000 more. He and his associates must judge it all and throw away four-fifths of it for lack of space.

If the gatekeeper is the executive producer of a half-hour network news program, he will have hundreds of stories, or tips for stories, available from the wire services, his own staff, and affiliated stations.

He must begin to make story decisions early in the day. His newscast will have time for less than 4000 words—perhaps eighteen or so stories —and he will be faced with two and one-half hours of news film that must be cut to about eight minutes.

The gatekeeper must budget his time and resources. Should the film be shot in the studio or on location? What's available at what cost? Should we send a reporter to the legislature today? A cameraman? Or should we just rely on the wire services?

And, inevitably, inexorably, there are deadlines. If the newspaper's presses don't roll on schedule there will be overtime to pay, heavier traffic for the delivery trucks, and the distinct possibility that the paper will not get into the home before Dad switches on the TV news and Mom begins preparing their supper. Broadcasting schedules are even more precise. David Brinkley once remarked, "The work is endlessly interesting but it is confining. Every night, rain or shine, sick or well, news or no news, you have to be in the studio at six-thirty-oh-oh-oh-oh. Broadcasting is the only thing done by human beings that is always punctual. The *only* thing."

Within the confines of time and technology and available content, the gatekeeper will also be influenced by his own personality and his orientation toward his audience, his colleagues, and society in general. Like everyone else, gatekeepers come equipped with their own tastes and tempers, shaped by their social environments. Just how deeply the national mood can affect mass communicators can be seen in the spate of pro-Russian movies that issued from Hollywood during World War II, followed by a rash of anti-Communist films during the Cold War. Nor are the gatekeepers of news immune from cultural values. The popular Chicago *Daily News* columnist Mike Royko delightfully demonstrated how male chauvinism infects news coverage. If the media treat news of men and women the same, Royko asked, why haven't we seen a political story like this:

GRANDFATHER IN RACE FOR MAYOR; OPPOSED BY YOUNG SINGLE MALE

Richard J. Daley, a well-rounded but fashionably dressed grandfather, today launched his campaign for an unprecedented fifth term as mayor.

In his first campaign speech, the 5-7 father of seven pointedly avoided mentioning his opponent, lean dark-haired Richard Friedman.

At a press conference, Daley outlined his reasons for running again, and was then asked if he thought a man could be a father and husband while pursuing a political career. He said:

"Naturally, I'm a father and husband first, but my wife has always encouraged me to be a career man. . . . "

Daley, who combs his hair straight back, wore a crisp blue suit with ankle-length trousers. . . .

It's hard for a journalist, or anyone else, to overcome deep-seated attitudes, but as a professional he tries to be aware of his biases. When he succeeds, which is not always, he is still likely to be attacked by persons who have no reason to be other than partisan. In his famous Des Moines speech in 1969, Vice President Spiro T. Agnew took aim at network newsmen and charged "this little group of men" with living and working "in the geographical and intellectual confines of Washington, D.C., or New York City"—communities, he said, that "bask in their own provincialism, their own parochialism. We can deduce that these men thus read the same sources. Worse, they talk constantly to one another, thereby providing artificial reinforcements to their shared viewpoints." In response the networks hastened to point out the diversity of birthplaces among their newsmen and saluted them for their fairness. But, unwittingly, Agnew provided a test of their susceptibility to pressure. A study that compared newscasts before and after the Vice President's Des Moines speech indicates that the newscasters increased their proportion of attributed sentences and decreased the number of sentences that made inferences about the news. In other words, they played it cooler.[6]

Advertisers are also reputed to exert influence on gatekeepers, and the casual reader of automotive and movie magazines, and the real-estate or travel pages of newspapers, is struck by peculiar coincidences in advertising and editorial content. On November 19, 1970, a television newsman of WXOW-TV in La Crosse, Wisconsin, reported on the Heileman Brewing Company's annual stockholders' meeting. He concluded his account with a fervent "Congratulations to Heileman on its first 100-million-dollar year," which was directly followed by a commercial for Heileman's Old Style Lager. In one of its last desperate years the *Saturday Evening Post* promised to put Henry Ford's picture on its cover in exchange for $400,000 worth of advertising from the Ford Motor Company. The Bergen (New Jersey) *Record* once editorialized strongly against a supermarket chain that had been fined 12 times in seven years for selling hamburger that contained illegal amounts of fat. But for all its wrath, the editorial omitted the name of the supermarket chain.

Generally, however, direct influence of advertisers on the information media is much overrated. Editors and advertisers are typically unaware of exactly what the other is up to, though in small cities, especially, they tend to share an attitude of boosterism. But there are also tough-minded editors like Thomas Pew of the small (10,000 circulation) Troy (Ohio) *News,* who expose shoddy merchandising on the local scene. Pew argues, "If the reader trusts the paper and feels it will counter any misleading advertising, the advertiser actually gets more money for his dollar from the paper."

Entertainment media are something else. In the heyday of radio and the early years of television, advertising agencies bought time slots from the networks, packaged their own programs, and didn't much worry about boundaries between entertainment and salesmanship. Today more than 90 percent of network series are sponsored by more than one advertiser, and instead of seeing the star of the show glide suavely from a song to a commercial, we often find such collisions as this, heard in the summer of 1971: "This portion of 'Ice Palace' has been brought to you by Sani-Flush." Network ownership of programs and multiple sponsorship has put a little more distance between advertiser and producer. Yet they still stalk the same bird, the Mighty Greenback, and their paths are usually parallel.

Surely many readers and viewers couldn't care less about the entanglements of advertising, entertainment, and information. Some are suspicious when they coincide, and others, oddly enough, are incensed when they don't. In 1971 the New York *Times* tried to clarify matters with this editorial:

> A number of readers have written The Times objecting to our editorial of March 10 denouncing the Ali-Frazier fight, in view of the large amount of space this newspaper had devoted to the subject on its sports pages and in promotional advertising during the preceding few days.
>
> To suggest that The Times coordinate the stories and pictures in our news columns with editorial policy is to show a misunderstanding of the function of a newspaper as we see it. The Times's principle of total separation between news and editorial opinion means not only the exclusion of editorial comment from news stories. It also means an unremitting effort to dissociate the method of presentation of news events (and The Times's own promotion of its coverage of those events) from our editorial views as expressed on the editorial page of The Times.
>
> Thus, if a world's heavyweight boxing championship is adjudged by the news editors of The Times to be a valid item of news, i.e., if it is of interest to the readers of The Times, then it must be covered in this newspaper as thoroughly as The Times's facilities and expertise permit; and our readers and prospective readers may well be told about that coverage through promotional advertising. The editorial stance of The Times on this or any other subject is and should be totally irrelevant to the news judgment on how much space to give the story, or whether to give it any space at all. The fact that The Times may editorially disapprove of professional boxing—incidentally, a position we have expressed many times in the past—has literally nothing to do with The Times's coverage of professional boxing.

The influence of the owner of a medium upon the gatekeeper can be profound, for good or ill. An often quoted study by sociologist Warren Breed of social control within newspapers showed that unwritten news policies do exist and are transmitted among employes largely by osmosis. Even so, a venal publisher will have to buck some lofty journalistic ideals held by his staff—and in this decade many working journalists are learning to nip occasionally at the hand that feeds them. A stellar performer can call many of his own shots. When San Francisco columnist Herb Caen returned to the *Chronicle* from the *Examiner* in the late 1950s, he was alleged to have taken 40,000 subscribers with him. A publisher hesitates to tamper with that kind of popularity. On June 25, 1971, the ABC Evening News covered the dedication of a small dam near Humboldt, Iowa. This was not a very startling event, but the dam was dedicated to a citizen named Joe Reasoner. ABC anchorman Harry Reasoner, a native of Humboldt and nephew of Joe, thought it was worth reporting, and did so with great charm.

The fondness of the audience for a personality is not lost upon media executives. Producers of network news programs have learned that ratings are affected much less by the quality of news than by the wryness of Brinkley or the affability of Cronkite. When Huntley and Brinkley of NBC moved ahead of Douglas Edwards of CBS in the early 1960s, CBS dumped Edwards for Walter Cronkite. Then during the 1964 political conventions Cronkite was still behind Huntley and Brinkley, and he was replaced by Bob Trout and Roger Mudd. They fared even worse in the ratings, and Cronkite returned—unruffled, of course. As it turned out, Cronkite overtook Huntley and Brinkley three years later—even though the anchormen themselves could see few fundamental differences in quality of their coverage.

Thus the audience looms large in the mind of the gatekeeper as he roots through his material, buffeted by social and professional forces and pressured by technology. The surpassing irony is the insulation of the gatekeeper from his audience. Unlike the reporter or ad salesman, the news editor is chained to his desk during most of his seven- or eight-hour day. He is frequently at work during the hours that ordinary people devote to socializing or watching TV. If the reader is unhappy about the choices the editor makes (and the reader has scanty knowledge of what gets left out), he usually complains to a higher editor or a reporter or the publisher. If a readership survey is conducted, it is usually for the benefit of the advertising department, not the editor, and emphasizes the most flattering findings. If the gatekeeper is a television producer with an audience of 20 million, he is even further removed from the rank-and-file audience.

questing the great big audience

What should come out of the machinery of mass communication? Put yourself in the role of the gatekeeper for a moment, and you decide. Will you choose the finest in art, poetry, drama, and literature? Maybe you find artistry a trifle boring. You wonder whether there'll be an audience of any size. And will there be enough art for today and tomorrow and all the days to come? Genius and its appreciators are rare. And remember: your machinery is big, expensive, and mortgaged. The boss is not in business for the sheer hell of it. Will you provide up-to-the-minute news and learned discussions of politics, science, and religion? Yes, but don't make it too heavy. People have enough troubles of their own. Besides, they may not understand intellectual content. Advertising? Yes—all you can get, provided it's paid for and not in absolutely wretched taste. Light entertainment? Lots of it. You have an embarrassingly strong appetite for it yourself, and so do most people. It's attractive, inoffensive, and durable.

Until the early media—books and newspapers—became truly massive, they appealed to small, literate, homogeneous, and fairly well-to-do audiences. Editors were socially and intellectually close to their customers. They enjoyed a mutual loyalty that ordinarily persists today only among small, specialized media.

Then early in the nineteenth century both the audience and the tools of printing grew in size and complexity. To attract a larger following, an editor added more diverse and popular content. The "penny press" of the 1830s found an eager market for gossipy local news, sensation, and human interest. Earlier newspapers, printed in limited quantities for specific audiences, concentrated on commercial and political information. Though more frolicsome than their predecessors, the mass newspapers of this period did not discard politics and commerce but instead baited more hooks.

Newspapers are still reluctant to delete popular content—an announcement that a trifling comic strip will be discontinued usually provokes grumbles from some segment of the audience. So the trick is to keep the old strip and find space for the new one. In 1967 the Associated Press Managing Editors Association surveyed its members for their perceptions of change in editorial content over the preceding decade. The study concluded, "Many if not most of the changes have moved in keeping with the social changes in the complexion of the nation." However, the report added, "Little has actually been dropped since 1957, but a great deal has been cut or condensed."

Resistance to change is understandable. Somewhere out there is somebody who wants or needs his piece of content. Every item will be read by someone, though few will read all.

Print journalism is not the only medium that hesitates to make major changes. Television, for all its churning of programs, has found staple commodities in action-adventure, situation comedy, musical variety, and sports. Nor is rock music radically different from other forms of popular art, according to *New Yorker* critic Ellen Willis, who observed after Woodstock:

> What cultural revolutionaries do not seem to grasp is that, far from being a grass-roots art form that has been taken over by businessmen, rock itself comes from the commercial exploitation of blues. It is bourgeois at its core, a mass-produced commodity, dependent on advanced technology and therefore on the money controlled by those in power. Its rebelliousness does not imply specific political content; it can be—and has been—criminal, Fascistic, and coolly individualistic as well as revolutionary.

The bulkiness of mass communication has put a distance between the gatekeeper and his audience. This and the costliness of production have made him cautious about innovations. He may not know his customers well, but he knows what they have bought in the past—and he guesses they will buy more of the same in the future. The gatekeeper must operate to some extent from a stereotype of his audience and, in the case of popular entertainment, he can tailor-make content to suit that image. A fan-magazine editor sitting in a Madison Avenue office might conjure up a vision of his typical reader—perhaps a would-be groupie in Beatrice, Nebraska—and commission a hack writer to dash off 1500 words about unrequited love among the amplifiers. Chances are it has sold before and will sell again and again. Or film producers note the success of *The Wild Angels,* and within the next three years we are treated to *Devil's Angels; Born Losers; The Glory Stompers; Bike Boy; Angels from Hell; Run, Angel, Run; Hell's Angels; The Savage Seven; The Mini-Skirt Mob; Hell's Belles;* and *Hell's Angels '69.* It's all but impossible to trace the innovator, if there is one, because all mass-oriented entertainment bears a family resemblance. The ancestor of the cycle flicks may have been Marlon Brando's *The Wild One,* made in 1953—or *The Great Train Robbery* of 1903 because it was an outlaw-adventure film. Or *Oedipus Rex,* 429 B.C.

If an attentive gatekeeper espies a sufficiently large subgroup in the massive audience, he can make a special attempt to capture it. Hot-rod and surfing magazines arose as the result of editorial alertness and enterprise. At the same time the big general magazines—*Collier's, The Saturday Evening Post, Look, Life*—had their function displaced by television, which is much more efficient at being all things to all people. So, in general, the larger the medium the less special (and perhaps more banal) its content.

The outpourings of all the media cascade upon us in a perpetual torrent. There's really no escaping it, nor should we particularly want to. There are treasures amid the trash. When John Steinbeck was touring Montana he encountered a young man of 20 who felt he was "just rotting" in his home town. Steinbeck questioned him and found he subscribed to *Time* and *The New Yorker*. "You don't have to go anywhere," Steinbeck said. "You've got the world at your fingertips, the world of fashion, of art, and the world of thought right in your own back yard."[7]

Most of what we know has come to us through the media. Practically everything we know about what goes on outside our home town—and much of what happens within it—has been mediated. Sometimes the flow is multi-stage: a friend may read or view information and then pass it along to us in conversation. Political communication and influence, especially, is regarded as having two or more steps, one of which involves the media.[8]

The effects of the media monsoon are varied and sometimes momentous, and we'll talk about them at length in later chapters. For now suffice it to say that one person's good news is another's bad, one person's beauty and truth are another's hokum and bunkum; and mass communication has stood accused of homogenizing society and driving it asunder—at the same time.

censorship: fervor and futility

But it keeps on coming, the good and the bad, because all of us, like the youth from Montana, have a need for extended communication if we are to have even the faintest notion of what's happening in society or the world. The leaders of society are among the first to feel the need for mass communication. Tribal chieftains convene ceremonial gatherings and are patrons to balladeers and scribes and entertainers. It is no surprise to learn that in 1511 the city of Rimini lured a printer named Niccolo Brenta away from Venice with a 15-year exemption from taxes and free housing for his family and printing equipment. Subsidies and special privileges—some of which were the antecedents to copyright—were not uncommon during printing's first century. Nor is it surprising to find that in 1955 citizens of the sparsely settled but TV-hungry plains of central South Dakota donated a transmitter and tower to a commercial broadcaster from Sioux Falls—just so they could receive one channel. The fact that people of this country are willing to pay for communication at the rate of nearly $700 per household per year confirms the demand.

Because they are important to society and because their effects are mixed, the media attract control. Even mass communicators themselves demand such controls as copyright. (Their inspiration, as in other things, may have been Fust and Schoeffer, who didn't mind a monopoly so long as it was theirs; and in 1466, after printing spread to other cities, they pirated an edition of St. Augustine's *The Art of Preaching* from a Strasbourg printer.) Less appetizing then, as now, is censorship, which is the first control that occurs to even the most thick-headed social chieftain. The first known censorship trial after the invention of printing occurred in Cologne in 1478, when the city council attempted to suppress the *Dialogus Super Libertate Ecclesiastica,* written by a local clergyman who needled the council for reducing subsidies to priests. This was largely a civil political matter, but soon the church was to become the foremost censor. In 1485 the archdiocese of Mainz (which 20 years earlier had pensioned Gutenberg) took notice of printers' "thirst for glory and greed for money" and issued a mandate for prepublication censorship as well as suppression of undesirable books already in print. The Archbishop appointed as censors the faculties of the universities of Mainz and Erfurt.

It especially galled His Excellency that "thoughtless and ignorant men have dared to translate learned texts into incorrect and vulgar German and by doing so they have caused misunderstanding." Echoes of those sentiments can be heard after nearly 500 years. "The purpose of my remarks tonight is to focus your attention on this little group of men who not only enjoy a right of instant rebuttal to every Presidential address, but more importantly, wield a free hand in selecting, presenting and interpreting the great issues of our Nation," said Vice President Agnew in his 1969 Des Moines speech.

Selection, presentation, and interpretation are what mass media do by their very nature. The effects are ordinarily beneficial to society, but sometimes not. Society must risk the bad to receive the good. However, not everyone is willing to accept these risks, and persons with power sometimes act to constrict the flow of communication. The communication machines are vulnerable to outside pressure for at least two reasons. First, they have a need for support, and they are subject to taxation and other regulations. Second, the sheer bulk of mass-communication machinery usually requires fixed production sites. Powerful transmitters and big presses are not portable; they can be located by censors and pressure groups. (Even so, the operators of underground newspapers and clandestine radio stations in occupied countries have found ways to elude their pursuers.)

Censorship almost invariably fails. In December 1964, New York City won the longest and most expensive obscenity case in its history. Lenny Bruce was found guilty of giving "obscene, indecent, immoral, and impure" performances in a Greenwich Village nightclub. From then on, he was barred from the stages of New York. But within a few years Times Square was pocked with peep shows, triple-X movie houses, pornographic book shops, and in 1971 Bruce was the subject of a Broadway play and two films. In the 15th and early 16th centuries the Roman Catholic Church, despite its vast organization and close links with civil authority, was unable to halt the printing that fueled the Reformation. Early censors failed even though they were quite capable of burning at the stake a bookseller, Mace Moreau, in Troyes, France, and of condemning the Parisian printer Antoine le Sot to be hanged, strangled, *and* burned. Martin Luther was an early fighter against censorship (he had, after all, a vital need to communicate), but in 1525 he asked the Duke of Saxony to prohibit the writings of his enemy Andreas Bodenstein von Karlstadt—with little effect. If there was a market for mass communication, printers cheerfully swallowed their ideology and published what would sell.

The need to communicate is a powerful force upon senders and receivers alike. The need can be altruistic or selfish, virtuous or unwholesome. Either way it eventually succeeds over suppression.

for further reading

Bagdikian, Ben H. *The Information Machines: Their Impact on the Media.* New York: Harper & Row, 1971.

Bailey, George A., and Lawrence W. Lichty. "Rough Justice on a Saigon Street: A Gatekeeper Study of NBC's Tet Execution Film," *Journalism Quarterly,* 49 (Summer 1972), pp. 221–229; 238.

Dexter, Lewis Anthony, and David Manning White, eds. *People, Society, and Mass Communications.* New York: The Free Press, 1964.

Emery, Edwin. *The Press and America: An Interpretative History of Journalism,* 3rd ed. Englewood Cliffs, N. J.: Prentice-Hall, 1972.

Gieber, Walter. "Across the Desk: A Study of 16 Telegraph Editors," *Journalism Quarterly,* 33 (Fall 1956), pp. 423–432.

Lyle, Jack. *The News in Megalopolis.* San Francisco: Chandler, 1967.

McMurtrie, Douglas C. *The Gutenberg Documents.* New York: Oxford University Press, 1941.

Ogg, Oscar. *The 26 Letters.* New York: Crowell, 1948.

Rivers, William L. *The Mass Media: Reporting, Writing, Editing.* New York: Harper & Row, 1964.

Schramm, Wilbur, ed. *Mass Communications,* 2nd ed. Urbana, Ill.: University of Illinois Press, 1960.

Small, William. *To Kill a Messenger: Television News and the Real World.* New York: Hastings House, 1970.

man's need
to communicate

how do you know you're alive?

The need to communicate is as strong as the need to eat, sleep, or love.
—Lorenzo Milam

When New York City dailies were closed by a strike for 17 days, sociologist Bernard Berelson and a team of interviewers seized the opportunity to ask New Yorkers what they missed by not having newspapers. As expected, most said they sharply felt the loss of serious news about current events. But there were other reasons, too, and not all of them were rational. Some readers felt out of touch with other people; some sensed a loss of prestige because they weren't well informed; a few felt insecure. Said one respondent, "If I don't know what's going on next door, it hurts me. It's like being in jail not to have a newspaper."

Readers also missed the sheer pleasure of reading. And many regretted the loss of entertainment and advertising.[1]

Though individuals can cope for some time without their media (people say they go on vacations to get away from the news, but they still take along their transistor radios), it is impossible that a modern society could function more than briefly without its media, so interwoven are they in the fabric of civilization. As Ben H. Bagdikian has observed, "News is the peripheral nervous system of the body politic."

Just why communication is important can be seen in the major tasks it performs. Several years ago Professor Harold Lasswell proposed that communication has three prime functions: surveillance of the environment to call attention to threats and opportunities; correlation of the various parts of society in making a response to the environment; and transmission of the social heritage to later generations. In briefer terms, communication serves variously as sentinel, organizer, and teacher. No society exists without these activities, whether performed by individuals or institutions. Furthermore, modern media are also rich in entertainment and advertising, and two more important functions can be perceived in mass communication: to provide escape from the grind of everyday living, and to oil the wheels of commerce.[2]

why we depend on communication

In its broadest sense, communication means interaction with our physical, biological, and social environments. We are terribly dependent on these interactions, for without them we cannot know whether we are in danger or safe, despised or loved, hungry or satisfied.

This need for communication with our environment is so basic that most of the time we don't realize we have it—or that we are fulfilling it. Zoologist Desmond Morris tells of a study of 466 Madonna-and-child paintings done by artists of different eras. Of the paintings, 373 showed the baby being held on the mother's left breast. Why? Because that is where the heart is, and the mother's heartbeat is the most comforting communication an infant receives. In fact, Morris continues, the *unborn* infant depends upon that steady, rhythmic sound to tell him all is well. Nor do we abandon our need for this subtle form of reassurance when we grow older. We simply convert it into, among other things, a love for music. Not for nothing, suggests Morris, has the rock music industry developed in a time of great stress for the young.[3]

All animals have to be in sensory communication with their physical and biological surroundings to find food, protect themselves, and to reproduce their species. A loss of sensation—the inability to hear a predator, for example—can mean loss of life. Similarly, to be lost from primitive social communication—from the pack, the herd, or the tribe—is to be condemned to death. The human animal is fairly adaptable to his environment, but even for humans, to lose touch—literally or figuratively—is to die a kind of death.

It was a long evolutionary leap from basic sensory communication to the kind of symbolic communication known as language. To the extent we can date the birth of *Homo sapiens,* mankind has taken virtually its whole life to invent it. (Nature, of course, has all the time in the world.) Not that man set out to invent language; he had more fundamental things to do. But when his survival was enhanced by abstract communication, and well after his brain was large enough to make sense out of sensation, he elaborated on his gestures, grunts, and grimaces.[4]

Consider the luck of the primates. In their 70-odd million years of existence, they have resided in flimsy but versatile bodies governed by fair-sized brains. Only within the last million years, the Pleistocene epoch, did the primate brain triple its size to what we like to regard as human proportions. En route to human status, which is usually characterized by scientists as the ability to reason and to make tools (which, come to think of it, is what scientists do for a living), our primate forebears found safety in trees, and their hands grew skillful at grasping. These skills demanded the controlling services of an enlarged brain, and brain and hand developed together. As the glaciers receded and the epochal droughts arrived, those primates who developed legs adequate for walking and running upright, and who retained the skills of hand, were able to rove widely for food. Within the last 70,000 years their brains and skills developed enormously (compared with previous change), spurred by the relatively rapid climatic changes of the Pleistocene. The herd instinct, which might at this stage be politely entitled family affinity, was complicated by glimmering value judgments.

Much of this is speculation born of enigma. We can only guess the extent to which prehistoric man communicated with words or other abstractions. He did not begin jotting down his communication symbols until only an eye blink ago in time. True, the Cro-Magnon man, about 30,000 B.C., embellished his caves in Lascaux and Altamira with stunning portraits of animals and hunters, and these paintings suggest symbolic thinking—a prerequisite to language—but art and record-keeping came much later.

About 12,000 years ago, Neolithic man developed tools that enabled him to kill animals from a safe distance. He also invented pottery to hold water, fashioned protective clothing from fibers and skins, and, most notably, made the rational discovery that plants grow from seeds.

Thus after having been shaped for so long by his environment, man was now prepared to fashion his own immediate surroundings. He no longer had to travel light, fast, and nervously. He could build a home. His new life was not exactly leisurely, but neither was it as frantic as foraging. He now had the opportunity to practice the more abstract chores of which the mind is capable: architecture, logic, myth, government, keeping records. Whether he knew it or not, he was beginning to construct a complicated social environment that would soon include art, literature, mathematics—and taxes, landlords, and mothers-in-law. Living increasingly by his wits, he departed the toils of nature and enmeshed himself in social networks whose filaments are communication.

what it means to lose communication

It's as true for modern man as it was for his primal ancestors: losing communication is a kind of dying, and that's why we shun the loss. To understand the need for communication, consider its absence.

Eldridge Cleaver describes Folsom Prison: "The heavy steel doors slammed shut with a clang of finality that chilled my soul. The first time that door closed on me I had the same wild, hysterical sensation I'd felt years ago at San Quentin when they first locked me in solitary. For the briefest moment I felt like yelling for help, and it seemed that in no circumstances would I be able to endure that cell."[5]

The Russian physicist Alexander Semyonovitch Weissberg, jailed during Stalin's Great Purge, recalls Kharkov prison in 1937: "Gradually the loneliness closed in. Later on I was to experience situations which amounted almost to physical torture, but even that seemed preferable to absolute isolation."[6]

But you don't have to go to prison to experience isolation. Expelled from the Black Muslims, Malcolm X found himself "in a state of emotional shock. I was like someone who for twelve years had an inseparable, beautiful marriage—and then suddenly one morning at breakfast the marriage partner had thrust across the table some divorce papers. I felt as though something in *nature* had failed, like the sun or the stars. It was that incredible a phenomenon to me—something too stupendous to conceive."[7]

Malcolm X found consolation in his family and his personal beliefs, but others have had no one to turn to. They have been trapped in a social—and sometimes sensory—void. Admiral Richard Byrd spent six months alone in a hut beneath the snow in the Antarctic. He had looked forward to quiet and solitude, but found confinement, endless monotony, and "a tremendous need for stimuli from the outside world . . . sounds, smells, voices and touch." Before long, he experienced nightmarish hallucinations.[8]

It's a mark of human gregariousness that psychologists didn't formally study sensory and social deprivation until quite recently. Many of the experiments stemmed from a concern for the men who would be tucked away for long periods in atomic-powered submarines and orbiting spacecraft. In the earliest experiments, volunteers were enclosed, one at a time, in darkened, sound-proofed chambers. With their eyes covered with goggles, their hands and arms enclosed in cardboard tubes, many of the volunteers could stand the isolation for only a few hours. Most soon lost track of time and some lost touch with themselves. Many underwent hallucinations: one saw a series of eye-glasses staring down at him. Another envisioned golden toadstools growing from bare red earth, with bright sunlight glinting from their stems in hues of yellow. Another saw herself as a spoon stirring slowly in a glass of iced tea. She felt for her legs; they were making wide, stirring motions.

The severest punishment society can impose upon a deviant person is complete sensory deprivation: the death sentence. Scarcely less severe are solitary confinement, banishment, and ostracism. The strongest sanction of the Roman Catholic Church is—note the word—excommunication.

All of this suggests that the mind needs a certain amount of sensory input to maintain its health, just as the body needs food and exercise to remain in condition. When starved of stimulation the mind tends to invent its own, sometimes to the extent of hallucination. Just how much stimulation is required varies widely among individuals. Some tolerate solitude, some have the force of will to keep their heads together, and some need rescuing from isolation and monotony. Fortunately, most of us never lack for sensory inputs—the opposite is usually true. But this, too, can be a problem.

coping with the glut of messages

If there is such a thing as too little stimulation, there is also too much. Songwriter Roger Miller is right: you can't change film with a kid on your back. Sensory bombardment can be serious. It is a key to what author Alvin Toffler calls "future shock"—mental and physical distress resulting from more stimulation than the human system can bear.[9] He gives as examples soldiers who are overwhelmed by the many alarming stimuli of battle; travelers who are plunged into the manifold sights and sounds of strange lands and thus suffer culture shock; and executives who are pressed from all sides by demands for decisions. The apparent effects of sensory deprivation and sensory overload are frequently similar: anxiety, apathy, impaired judgment, strange visions, and something akin to schizophrenia.

It has been estimated that through simple observation of his surroundings the average urban person can receive 100 bits of information a minute—a "bit" being defined as a unit of information that provides enough data for a decision between two equally likely alternatives.[10] Thus during a 17-hour day of browsing in his environment, a person could receive just over 100,000 bits of information.

No one can pay attention to, much less assimilate, more than a fraction of the messages available to him. *We are selective, both consciously and unconsciously.* Professional gatekeepers do some sifting for us, but we are also our own gatekeepers.

Indeed, we operate a series of gates. To be completely successful, a message must be noticed, understood, remembered, and acted upon. Most of the millions of messages around us fail at the first gate because we exercise selective attention. (And we don't always select rationally or even consciously.) We also misunderstand, to varying degrees, many messages because our interpretations of them are also selective. And even if we accurately perceive messages, we may forget them—especially those that are unattractive. Then too we may not choose to respond to a message, or not know how to respond.

We ignore most of the stimuli around us because we lack the capacity to handle them, because they are weak, or because they are unfamiliar and uncongenial. Has anyone not daydreamed during a dull lecture or averted his eyes from a scene of horror? Sometimes tuning-out can take peculiar forms, as witness this note in the *Cornell Alumni News:* "Correction: The November 1970 *News* reported the death of N. Kim Hooper '61. The *News* has now learned that Mr. Hooper reported his own death in order to stop the flow of alumni mail. He is, in fact, alive and well in Berkeley, Cal."

We also tune in what we particularly want. Amid the babble of a noisy party we gleefully eavesdrop on the scandalous conversation behind us as we stare thoughtfully across the room. And we rapidly scan and discard hundreds of headlines in a newspaper, stopping to pursue those stories that somehow intrigue us.

The way we select depends on many things, including the nature of the message, its source, the setting in which the communication takes place, and our particular needs. Always involved are the attitudes and knowledge we have previously acquired from parents, friends, groups, and society in general. We cannot help but assimilate certain social values, because we are socially dependent from birth; throughout life we are rewarded for performing according to the expectations of other people. The dues we pay in exchange for any kind of affiliation include a certain amount of conformity.

It has been argued that language itself is more than a tool, it is social instruction. One does not learn a language without learning the many things—some of them laden with cultural biases—that words symbolize. A theory of linguistic relativity was proposed several years ago by the scholars Sapir and Whorf. They compared various languages and found that each is attuned to its particular culture. They discovered, for example, that Eskimos have more word-symbols for snow than have persons who live in temperate climates, and thus the Eskimo is able to perceive snow more subtly than is an Apache. According to Whorf, this means that "no individual is free to describe nature with absolute impartiality but is constrained to certain modes of interpretation even while he thinks himself most free . . . all observers are not led by the same physical evidence to the same picture of the universe, unless their linguistic backgrounds are similar, or can in some way be calibrated."[11] To some people linguistic bias is a nasty trick. Abbie Hoffman warned his followers not to "internalize the language of the pigs."[12] Female delegates to an Alternative Media Conference in Austin, Texas, complained of "language discrimination" and proposed dropping all masculine and feminine pronouns in favor of unisexual replacements based on the Latin root *vir,* meaning "man." Some suggestions: *ve* for *he* or *she, verself* for *himself* or *herself.*[13]

Just as our biases lead us to tune out many unfamiliar and distasteful messages, they also color the way we understand the communications that we do accept. For one thing, we find it convenient and efficient to construct pigeonholes and fit things into them in a process called stereotyping. It's a kind of attitudinal shortcut about which Walter Lippmann wrote many years ago: "For the most part we do not first see, and then define, we define first and then see. In the great blooming, buzzing confusion of the outer world we pick out what our culture has already defined for us, and we tend to perceive that which we have picked out in the form stereotyped for us by our culture."[14] And so, quite often, we casually consign new information about people, objects, and ideas into preconceived categories.

just between you and me

Mr. Spock, the long-eared First Officer of the Starship Enterprise on TV's "Star Trek," had the knack of "mind-melding": he could merge his thoughts with those of others, and the exchange of meaning was exact. Here in the real world communication is easily derailed. Two humans of similar backgrounds can share messages, but the transfer of meaning is never perfect because no two persons are the same in every respect—if they were, they'd have no need to talk to each other.

Spock simply laid hands on his fellow communicant, and that was that. But after we compose a message for someone else, we have to let go of it, and whoever picks it up will interpret it according to his own mental framework. Messages are sometimes caught by the wrong handle. At the 1971 annual meeting of the New York Times Company, a stockholder asked whether the *Times* was going into the "cassette business." The chairman understood her to say "sex business," and there was momentary bedlam.

In face-to-face conversation, two persons can supplement the verbal channel by using facial expressions and gestures. The listener nods his understanding, providing "feedback"—signaling that the message is getting through. If the message is not succeeding, a quizzical expression, a blank look, or a yawn can inspire redundancy, a backing-off for another run at communication.

The story is told of a South American diplomat recently arrived in the United States who had not quite mastered English. Asked at a party if he had children, he replied "No," and added haltingly: "You see, my wife, she is inconceivable." The other person looked puzzled. "No," he continued, "she is unbearable." Finally the diplomat beamed. "She is, how you say, impregnable." His listener understood. The notion of infertility was familiar to both, and thanks to a little feedback and some redundancy, the meaning came through.

But if frames of reference do not jibe, the intended and received meanings may be grossly different. In September 1952, the New York *Post* charged that vice presidential candidate Richard M. Nixon was the beneficiary of a secret $18,000 fund donated by California businessmen. Many of General Eisenhower's key advisors urged him to dump Nixon from the ticket. Thomas E. Dewey suggested that Nixon go on television to explain himself to the public, and Eisenhower postponed making a decision on retaining his running mate until he saw the effects of the broadcast. On September 23, Nixon, with his wife at his side, went before cameras in the El Capitan Theatre in Hollywood and delivered his now-famous "Checkers" speech, so called because of his affectionate reference to his dog Checkers. Nixon defended his honesty and appealed to Republicans to support him. The speech was an enormous success. About 55 million viewers—at that time the largest audience ever—watched his appeal, and nearly two million people sent letters and wires of support to the Republican Central Committee. The rest, as they say, is history.

Nineteen years later a film of the speech was exhumed by an enterprising young New Yorker and shown in a theatre together with several experimental and protest films. Again the speech was hugely successful, but this time as comedy. Those who attended—most of them under 30—roared with delight at Mr. Nixon's reference to his wife's "respectable Republican cloth coat."

The message of the "Checkers" speech had not changed, but the context had—the time, the place, the audience were considerably different in 1971, and so was the response to the message.

not by words alone ...

In 1960 the television networks proposed a series of joint appearances by presidential candidates Richard Nixon and John Kennedy. Several of Nixon's supporters, including President Eisenhower, urged him not to participate, arguing that Kennedy, who was comparatively unknown, should not be given undue exposure. But Nixon did not want to appear afraid of a fight, and he remembered the triumph of "Checkers." Arrangements were made for four "Great Debates."

Kennedy came to the first debate on September 26 tanned, rested, and well primed by his staff. Nixon, however, was extremely tired and underweight. As he got out of his car at the studio he struck his knee painfully against the door. Both candidates were offered the services of a CBS make-up expert, and both declined. Nixon applied a bit of Max Factor "Lazy Shave" to his jowls.

On the tube Nixon appeared pale and haggard. Afterward his mother called to ask if he wasn't feeling well. Kennedy, in contrast, looked fresh and healthy. Before the remaining three debates Nixon availed himself of makeup, but the impression had been set. A Gallup poll indicated that 42 percent of Americans thought Kennedy had the best of the television debates, while 30 percent thought Nixon won. The remainder called it a draw or couldn't make up their minds.

This proves the impact of TV, but it also reveals the power of nonverbal communication. The peculiar fact is that people who followed the debates on radio, rather than television, thought Nixon had won them all.[15]

Television and radio carried exactly the same words of the candidates, but there are more cues in a message than words. TV bore information that Nixon never intended to provide.

Messages rarely travel alone. Their fellow passengers may interfere with communication or enrich it. In electronics, the term "noise" is used to describe an extraneous signal on a channel, and engineers try to squelch it. (After the first debate, Nixon was careful to use makeup.) Two persons conversing in a busy hallway will raise their voices, speak more slowly, and repeat themselves if necessary to overcome the interference.

But there is much more to nonverbal communication than

"noise." It is the very medium of painters, sculptors, dancers, and musicians. The inflections of speech and the typography of written words are nonverbal enhancements of verbal messages. Status symbols comprise a silent language—or so the owners hope—and sales of Cadillacs and fashionable clothing flourish. In some societies illiterates have been known to buy the tops of fountain pens in order to wear them as a sign of writing ability.

It has been estimated that up to 80 percent of all communication is nonverbal. A British scholar once figured that there are some 700,000 meaningful human gestures. The forms of wordless messages are endless: photographs, traffic lights, costumes, giggles, blushes, ulcers, handshakes, and so on. The late J. Edgar Hoover was said to have tested his agents for nervousness by noting their sweaty palms while shaking their hands.

Even things that do *not* happen can be communicative. Inspector Gregory of Scotland Yard asked Sherlock Holmes if he had any clues in the theft of a race horse and Holmes invited his attention to "the curious incident of the dog in the night-time." Gregory was baffled: "The dog did nothing in the night-time." "That," replied Holmes, "was the curious incident."

problems of persuasion

The response we make to a communication largely depends on what is already in our heads. This holds for persuasive messages as well as those that seek only to inform or entertain. Every message must run a series of hurdles, and it should be apparent by now that the receiver is not passive.

What the persuader wants to do is to guide or reinforce or change our behavior. Sometimes he does this for our own sake—as is the case of the earnest evangelist or parent or friend—and often for his own benefit. In the latter case he says "vote for me," "buy my product," "think my way." At base he says "help me," but if he's smart he'll phrase it as "help yourself." The shortest route he can take is through an understandable and believable message that invites a person to do what he is already inclined to do—a message that offers ways to satisfy a need without disturbing the receiver's values or his relationships with his social environment.

If these conditions are right, the desired response may occur almost automatically. Let's say a friend has resolved to goof off and wants some company. About 3 o'clock of a sultry afternoon he drops by and says, "I'll buy you a beer." We're out the door like a shot—if our friend has made good on his promises in the past . . . if we haven't just quenched our thirst . . . if beer has previously satisfied us . . . if we have no qualms about alcohol or leaving our work ... if we're not afraid of being seen entering a tavern in the middle of the afternoon. Then we're in the tavern, and an oily-looking stranger sidles up and mumbles that he wants us to contribute to the New Hitler Fascist Club. Now, *he's* got a problem.

If the persuader anticipates difficulties he can resort to three general strategies:

1. He can modify the message, channel, or the messenger. As noted earlier, the audience takes cues from all three. If possible the persuader will tailor the message to fit the customer, taking advantage of existing attitudes. He'll also overcome interference by selecting the clearest channels, using more than one, turning up the volume, or repeating himself. He may try to jam other channels so that counterarguments cannot get through. Or he may employ auxiliary channels to augment his messages. The leading purveyor of canned music makes this claim: "Muzak subscribers receive the right music at the right time to offset fatigue, tension, boredom and monotony."

The persuader might also hire a special messenger—one who is attractive or prestigious or particularly believable. Sears, Roebuck could have chosen any of a thousand announcers to introduce its low-phosphate detergent, but it shrewdly lured former Interior Secretary Stewart Udall, a well-known conservationist, to deliver the pitch.

2. He can try to manipulate the mental processes of the receiver. If the process is already in motion and headed in the right direction, the persuader has only to supply the right answer to the customer's needs. Happy is the car salesman who is approached by a sweet old lady, checkbook in hand, who asks whether she should take the red one or the green one. A customer inside the store is worth a hundred outside the door. Not surprisingly, phonograph record distributors offer inducements to store managers to display certain labels prominently.

If the receiver is headed in the wrong direction, or not going anywhere in particular, the persuader has more work to do. He has to run the full course of making his message seen, understood, remembered, and acted upon. The disinterested receiver is likely to be a skeptic. The persuader may attempt to create new needs and quickly offer the right satisfactions. Little wonder the word "new" so often appears in advertisements. It suggests that here is something to which old judgments don't apply; the persuader can hope the checking process will be short-circuited. Similarly some persuaders are inclined to operate on young people, to instill the right attitudes well before it comes time to buy. Consequently the manufacturers of cars, typewriters, sewing machines, and other products make their wares available to schools free or at low cost. This is persuasion for the long haul, guiding the process from the beginning, not waiting for the customer to wander through the door.

The persuader may also resort to emotional appeals to circumvent logical processes. Presumably one has only to shout a threat at the receiver and he will grasp the offered straw. This may work for bandits, but without physical coercion the receiver may simply repress or avoid the message and never hear the solution. If he does listen, he might not understand. Several years ago a toothpaste manufacturer placed advertisements that warned, "Beware of Pink Toothbrush." You can avoid bleeding gums, he said, by using my toothpaste. Sure enough, many customers began asking their druggists for pink toothbrushes.

Another technique is role-playing. If a person can be induced to take a public position on an issue, even if only play-acting, he will tend to accept that position. Indeed, the more pleased he is with his own eloquence, the more likely he is to internalize the position. Thus an advertiser asks us to praise his product in 25 words or less.

Or the persuader may show the receiver that he is at odds with himself—and then offer a solution. Considerable research has evolved from the theory that people try to keep their attitudes in balance. Suppose an individual develops a deep interest in ecology, especially in regard to air pollution. He joins the Sierra Club, campaigns for reforms, and generally develops views favorable to conservation. He also owns a much-loved, oil-burning 1959 Buick. One day a friend points out that his commitment to clean air and his affection for the smoky old Buick don't square with each other. The ecologist-motorist now experiences a tension that psychologists call "dissonance," and he wishes to reduce it. The friend is in a nice position to persuade by offering a solution. He suggests an overhaul for the Buick and advises leaving it at home on weekdays in favor of a bicycle. This tactic of dissonance reduction doesn't always work. As in the case of threats, the message can be avoided, a decision deferred, or the conflict rationalized away.

3. *The persuader can modify the social environment.* In an experiment that relates to dissonance theory, a psychologist asked a student to match, for length, a line he had drawn on the blackboard with three other lines. Unknown to the student, seven of his classmates were confederates of the experimenter. Announcing their judgments about the line, the seven stooges responded with wrong—but unanimous—opinions. The naive student was faced was an objective truth—and a group of friends solidly agreed to the contrary. The experiment was repeated with 50 different naive subjects, and there was a marked tendency among them to agree with the group and not to believe their own eyes.[16]

We all belong to groups of varying size, formality, and significance: families, fan clubs, political organizations, and so on. From our groups we have received a variety of social and psychological rewards, and we repay them with loyalty. A persuader may use these ties. "Everybody's doing it," he says, dropping a few names we respect and identify with. He might also induce our school to show his film, or have our classmates sell his wares, or tell our children to ask mom and dad to buy his product.

Breaking our ties is difficult for the persuader. Maybe he will merely try to distract us from checking his signals against group norms as he slips us the message. Perhaps he will direct us to a different group, just as a court paroles a juvenile delinquent to a solid citizen. Nazi concentration camps were tragic laboratories in the techniques of provoking deviant behavior by separating individuals from familiar groups and transplanting them into new and highly controlled surroundings. According to psychologist Bruno Bettelheim, himself a prisoner in Dachau and Buchenwald, the Nazis attempted to reduce prisoners to an infantile state and then rear them anew: "The prisoners lived, like children, only in the immediate present. . . . They were unable to establish durable object-relations. Friendships developed as quickly as they broke up. . . . A prisoner had reached the final stage of adjustment to the camp situation when he changed his personality so as to accept as his own the values of the Gestapo."[17]

Even in a highly controlled situation such as a prison camp many persons firmly maintain their values. In normal life, a persuasive communicator lacks the powers of coercion and isolation to control the minds of his subjects. He may, however, take advantage of stress and isolation when they occur naturally, as when confidence men prey upon new widows.

These three grand strategies are presented separately, but really they go together. Perceptions of message characteristics and the social environment reside in the head of the receiver together with his personality and his processes for sorting things out. A persuader can huff and puff and blow the house down, and still there will be a good many people going about their own things. As psychologist Raymond Bauer puts it: "The audience selects what it will attend to. Since people generally listen to and read things they are interested in, these usually are the topics on which they have a good deal of information and fixed opinions. Hence the very people most likely to attend to a message are those most difficult to change; those who can be converted do not look or listen."[18]

In brief, the receiver of messages is a seeker. He largely chooses what he wants, and uses what he accepts for his own purposes. He seeks because he has a need to interact with his environment. This picture of the communication process replaces the fading snapshot of the receiver being bowled over by messages from a designing persuader. But as we sit down to a congratulatory banquet to salute our self-determination, let us remember that there is a menu. We choose what we want, all right—from what's available.

The great menu-makers of our time are the media of mass communication. And to them we now turn our attention.

for further reading

Berelsen, Bernard, and Gary A. Steiner. *Human Behavior: An Inventory of Scientific Findings.* New York: Harcourt Brace Jovanovich, 1964.

De Fleur, Melvin L. *Theories of Mass Communication,* 2nd ed. New York: McKay, 1970.

Hall, Edward T. *The Silent Language.* New York: Fawcett, 1959.

Innis, Harold. *The Bias of Communication.* Toronto: Toronto University Press, 1951.

Maccoby, Eleanor E., Theodore M. Newcomb, and Eugene L. Hartley. *Readings in Social Psychology,* 3rd ed. New York: Holt, Rinehart and Winston, 1958.

Mehta, Ved. "Onward and Upward with the Arts: John Is Easy to Please," *The New Yorker,* May 8, 1971, pp. 44–87. A witty analysis of conflicting theories (and scholars) of language.

Parry, John. *The Psychology of Human Communication.* New York: American Elsevier, 1968.

Ruesch, Jurgen, and Weldon Kees. *Nonverbal Communication: Notes on the Visual Perception of Human Relations.* Berkeley, Calif.: University of California Press, 1961.

Schramm, Wilbur, and Donald F. Roberts. *Process and Effects of Mass Communication,* 2nd ed. Urbana, Ill.: University of Illinois Press, 1971.

Smith, Alfred G., ed. *Communication and Culture: Readings in the Codes of Human Interaction.* New York: Holt, Rinehart and Winston, 1966.

Tax, Sol, ed. *Evolution After Darwin.* Vol. II: *The Evolution of Man.* Chicago: University of Chicago Press, 1960.

broadcasting

the great salesman

One of the myths about American television is that it operates as a cultural democracy, wholly responsible to the will of the viewing majority, in terms of the programs that survive or fade. More aptly, in the area of entertainment mainly, it is a cultural oligarchy, ruled by a consensus of the advertising community.
—Les Brown, *Television: The Business Behind the Box*

What it all comes down to is what Shakespeare said. The show's the thing.
—Robert Wood, President, CBS Television Network

During the annual promotional campaigns of the pre-1971 television season, NBC viewers received a frequent image of John Chancellor, the anchor man of the NBC Nightly News, pushing a new kind of news program for the upcoming season. It was the "Quarterly Report," a documentary review of the past three months' events, and it would be aired four times during the coming year. To hear (and see) Chancellor tell it, "Quarterly Report" was going to be some kind of show. Xerox would sponsor.

Days after the premiere, Xerox announced how it felt about the program when it refused to make a second copy.

A little background on this incident illuminates the nature of commercial broadcasting in the United States. First of all, the Xerox Corporation's ad agency, which proposed the idea, let its basic assumptions show a little too obviously. The agency recommended the title of "Corporation US" for the show, which would have, according to the proposal, this rationale:

> In a very real sense the United States is a corporation with virtually all its citizens shareholders. Whether these shareholders have voting rights or not affects how well the corporation runs.
> Corporation US competes in a complicated, full-paced and often deadly marketplace. The success of its corporate life—the freest possible society—and its survival in the marketplace depends on the response of its citizen shareholders. . . .

According to *Variety,* before the show landed at NBC it was offered to CBS, which declined it. "We turned it down because it violated several of our basic policies," a CBS News spokesman was quoted. "Xerox insisted on having its name in the title as presenting it. They wanted to editorialize, and they wanted a good deal to say about the nature of the broadcast." That was okay, apparently, with NBC, except that the network balked at the name of the program, and "Quarterly Report" was taken instead, since it connotes a business orientation more subtly than either the original title or another substitute, "Corp-US-All."

At any rate, the first program was so bland and so filled with noncontroversial material that the shareholder got no inkling whatsoever of "where he stands and where he's going," as the proposal promised he would. Xerox, styled by *Variety* as "once the picture window in the video home of the brave" for its earlier, fearless support of controversial programs, had editorialized all right, but in reverse, steering clear of the expression of any opinions. The result was dullness, perceptible to audience, network, and sponsor. Viewers left in droves, and so did Xerox.[1]

This brief episode in the continuing struggle of broadcasting to find happiness and fulfillment in the sophisticated world of show business permits four statements to be made:

• Broadcasting has always been big business, with definite assumptions about the superiority of its value system.

• Broadcasting is the great salesman of materialism in mass production society.

• Like any great salesman, broadcasting bends over backward not to offend the customer.

• There are exceptions to every rule.

No matter how pessimistic we may get over such matters as the overcommercialism of broadcasting or its failure to reach consistently high program quality to match its excellent technical standards, we should not overlook the exceptions, nor should we forget that in the brief 50-year history of commercial broadcasting, the medium has gone from almost complete altruism to commercial blitzkrieg, tempered at times by instances of important public service. Change is almost certain to continue.

a seagoing postman

In its beginnings, radio was by far the least mass oriented of the mass media.[2] For more than a decade after the Italian Guglielmo Marconi in the mid-1890s first sent Morse code without wires across a few hundred yards of his father's estate, wireless was considered to have a very serious drawback: unlike with the telephone, everyone could listen in. Despite this handicap, the new device's obvious application to maritime and naval needs aroused the interest of the English, eager to support any new communications development to bring the far-flung British Empire closer. The result of their interest and Marconi's need for money was the formation in 1897 of the Wireless Telegraph and Signal Company, Ltd., soon shortened to simply British Marconi. The company set out to acquire patents, then manufacture and lease transmitting and receiving sets for use on ships going out of sight of land. Partly the idea was to enable the shore to tell the ships where to head for last-minute cargo pickups; partly the need was military, to allow war vessels to communicate out of sight and in fog; and partly, in those preradar years, wireless was needed for safety.

In 1899, Marconi equipped two U.S. ships to report back to newspapers on the progress of the America's Cup Race. The result was a world sensation, but the new company still had slow going. In 1901 the U.S. Navy briefly considered adopting wireless, discarding the homing pigeons that had served so faithfully for so long. The birds won, partly because the foreign-owned Marconi would only rent, not sell, its equipment, but also partly because pigeons don't talk, whereas wireless blabs to the whole world.

Nevertheless, wireless telegraphy did have enough to recommend it for various military services to be interested. Offsetting the fact that anyone might listen in was the great advantage that the thing would work in the dark, in the fog, and at distances greater than mere line of sight. For awhile, amateurs with a poor sense of humor broadcast fake distress calls, fake orders to naval vessels, and—when chided for their pranks—responded with curses and obscenities. The Russo-

Japanese War of 1904 marked the first wartime use of radiotelegraphy, and not only by combatants, for the *Times* of London employed wireless to flash back news reports. But an iceberg floating where it had no business being probably did more than anything else to focus public, and commercial, attention on radio.

The Cunard liner *Titanic,* touted as unsinkable, struck the iceberg on her maiden voyage in 1912. While she was taking two and a half hours to go down, the liner *Californian* was a mere 20 miles away. She might easily have reached *Titanic,* but her radio operator had turned off his set and gone to bed. As it was, the first ship to arrive on the scene, *Carpathia,* had learned of the disaster by means of radio. A young Russian immigrant, David Sarnoff (who later became more famous as guiding spirit of the Radio Corporation of America), was working as a wireless operator for American Marconi, a subsidiary of the British firm. At his station on the East Coast of the United States, Sarnoff heard *Titanic's* call for help and relayed it. Finally *Carpathia's* operator heard, and the ship responded. The dimensions of the tragedy —1513 lives lost along with the greatest ship of the day—prompted the U.S. Congress to enact a law requiring ships going out of sight of land to have radio transmitting and receiving equipment.

Use of radio by ships and military stimulated its commercial development, but the years before World War I were filled with a number of lawsuits as radio manufacturers sought to resolve questions of just who owned what invention, and as speculators tried to turn quick profits in the new industry. In England, government officials bought large blocks of British Marconi stock, then started rumors that the British Navy was about to go heavily into wireless equipment. As the price of stock rose, the officials sold out, making considerable profits. The scandal had its repercussions in the United States, as Lee De Forest, inventor of the vacuum tube, found himself accused of defrauding the public through the mails. After a lengthy trial, the inventor was acquitted, but to raise money for his defense, he had been forced to sell his invention for much less than it was worth to American Telephone and Telegraph, which thus gained complete rights to what would be the most important single device in the development of voice broadcasting. The federal judge lectured De Forest severely upon his acquittal, telling him to give up all pretense of being an inventor, and to get "a common garden variety of job and stick to it."

nationalization poses problems and a solution

Patent disputes and stock scandals were shoved into the background by World War I, and when the U.S. entered the war, the radio industry was nationalized. During the war, with all the patents under control of the Navy, substantial improvements were made, raising problems of access to them after the war, since they had come under what normally would be considered illegal use of the patents. Furthermore, voice broadcasting was clearly at hand.

One invention developed and owned by the General Electric Company was so advanced that only one peacetime customer existed. This was the Alexanderson Alternator, which permitted vastly increased transmitter power, and the only company with sufficiently developed resources to use it was British Marconi. While at the Paris Peace Conference, President Woodrow Wilson learned of the approaching sale and became alarmed at the prospect of British Marconi resuming domination of the wireless field. Wilson sent an emissary to GE, asking them, on patriotic grounds, not to sell the alternator. GE agreed.

government as partner or bystander?

At this point, two questions clearly posed themselves in this country: how was the great potential of radio to be tapped, and who was to do the tapping? The answer to the second would, in effect, answer the first. Thus, in 1919, two alternatives arose. One was for the U.S. government to continue as a partner in some kind of semi-public monopoly for the administration of all forms of broadcasting. This, in fact, was the plan endorsed by Owen D. Young, then vice president (later president) of GE, and by Franklin D. Roosevelt, then assistant secretary of the Navy, among others. But among the older heads in government were some who feared the creation of a broadcasting trust even with government as a partner—since much of their efforts in the past 20 years had been against trusts. Something of a debate developed within government, and before it could be resolved, the electrical companies decided to go ahead with the second alternative.

The major American companies—GE, Westinghouse, AT&T— got together with smaller companies and pooled their radio patents. They then bought out the U.S. subsidiary of British Marconi and established a company to hold the patents and handle sales. They titled this company, accurately but unimaginatively, the Radio Corporation of America.

At that point ended whatever role the government might have played in the early development of commercial radio in this country. Other countries might and did establish noncommercial radio systems as their major forms of broadcasting. But it would be 50 years before the U.S. government would begin systematic support of noncommercial broadcasting.

So the answer to the question of who would develop broadcasting was answered by big business: it would. The question of how broadcasting would be developed took a little longer, but not much. Voice broadcasting had been a reality at least since 1906, but radio manufacturers wore blinders—they thought of radio primarily as a point-to-point form of communication. As a result of this peculiar blindness, men of real vision, like David Sarnoff, had to lead their superiors along very patiently. Sarnoff in 1916 was assistant traffic manager of the largest radio firm in the U.S., American Marconi. "I have in mind a plan of development which would make radio a 'household utility' in the same sense as the piano or phonograph," he wrote his boss. The sale of a million of these radio music boxes at $75 each, he added, could bring in as much as $75 million a year. His proposal was received as visionary if not radical, and nothing was done about it. But in 1920, American Marconi belonged to RCA, and so did Sarnoff, and he renewed his suggestion. This time he was listened to. The electrical companies began the large-scale manufacture of radio receiving sets. They would sell these at the same time they sold their transmitters. The broadcaster, a department store, for instance, would buy a transmitter, put on some kind of programs in the evenings, and encourage the public to come in and buy a receiver.

It worked. Fantastically well. On January 1, 1922, the Department of Commerce counted 28 broadcasting stations in the U.S. One year later there were 538.

But a momentary hitch developed. With that many stations on the air, people could now choose what they wanted to hear, and a demand grew for better talent. Professional entertainers were the logical answer, but they expected pay. How to get the money to pay popular artists? A new system was needed. But a tax on sets might restrict sales, and there was a scarcity of great public benefactors who might come forth and endow radio. That left the unthinkable—invading the sanctity of the home with a crass commercial pitch. But would the public stand for it?

It fell to that great capitalistic enterprise, AT&T, to provide the final answer to the questions who was to pay and how. Using the softest, gentlest sell imaginable, a real estate operator delivered a 15-minute talk over the AT&T station in New York, WEAF, at 5:15 P.M., August 28, 1922. Something about Hawthorne Court, a new system of tenant-owned apartments in Jackson Heights. Fresh air, freedom from constraints of city life. Nathaniel Hawthorne, one of America's greatest fictionists, would have loved it. As a result, the Queensboro Corporation sold a few apartments, created no public outcry of indignation, and enshrined itself in the hearts of every station manager and advertising agency in the country.

The rest is certainly not silence. What happened next was a scramble so desperate for the available remaining frequencies that broadcasters finally went on a vast claim-jumping spree. If you had a frequency that was affected by poor atmospheric conditions, you simply announced you were changing to a better frequency, and changed. The only law dealing with commercial broadcasting in the early 1920s said merely that anyone could get a license to broadcast if he met three requirements: he had to be a U.S. citizen, he had to have a transmitter, and he had to ask for a license.

So while American broadcasting was undergoing its final shakedown in the mid-1920s, and was setting the structure that we have in essential respects today, government played no role at all as a representative of the public. Within a half-dozen years, RCA had formed up its National Broadcasting Company with two networks, the Red and the Blue (which in 1943 was sold for $8 million to the man who made Lifesavers candy, and became known as the American Broadcasting Company). The Columbia Broadcasting System was established as a program procurement agency and was on its way to becoming a large network. The advertising agencies were adding radio specialists who could write for the ear. In Kansas, a shady doctor with a shadowy medical background was transplanting goat glands into middle-aged men to try to rejuvenate their sexual vigor, and he was making a fortune selling his operations and patent medicines over his radio station. Elsewhere quacks were hawking cancer cures, telling fortunes, praising God and damning chain stores, and generally behaving as if the whole thing were some kind of carnival.

government as referee

Finally, elements of the broadcasting industry in favor of more orderly development prevailed, and government entered the field as assigner of frequencies and regulator of the more flagrant abuses. The Federal Radio Commission, established in 1927, and superseded in 1934 by the Federal Communications Commission, sought to represent the public interest in broadcasting insofar as that interest could be recognized. In some ways it was immediately successful. Broadcasting stations were created to reach the far corners of the country. Fortune telling and other obvious exploitation of poor and ignorant were eliminated. But the communication policy thus established was a short-range one: to correct abuses of the moment and to ensure that all the country might be reached by broadcasting. The FCC rarely consciously looked ahead to the distant future, or tried to influence broadcasters to meet much more than minimal standards of public interest, convenience, or necessity.

Indeed, the FCC's limited efforts to assure that the public interest was served by broadcasting often had the opposite result. Here are two examples. In the fall of 1971, an effort to return some programming control from networks to local stations during television's prime evening hours went into effect. The "prime time access" rule required that a few hours a week of prime evening time be left for local stations instead of networks to fill. The idea was that local stations would use the time for news and public affairs programs, for shows that featured local performers, and for granting television access to local concerns during peak viewing periods. But with few exceptions, the local autonomy resulted not in new and different programs but in an upsurge of reruns, rented by local stations from the syndication firms owned by the networks. Prime-time television, observed *Time,* is a well-balanced ecological system: it continually recycles its waste products.

The second example is perhaps more serious, since FCC policy appears partly to blame for the lack historically of broadcaster involvement in significant public issues. In 1939, a company known as Mayflower Broadcasting Corporation sought to take over the license of John Shepard III, whose station was WAAB, in Boston. Mayflower argued that Shepard had used his radio station to carry editorials upholding causes he espoused and to support candidates for political office. The argument was that a radio station was so influential because of its power to reach vast numbers of listeners that it should not be allowed to broadcast opinions of its license-holder. The case took two years to wind its way through the Commission, which in 1941 declared that "the public interest can never be served by a dedication of broadcasting facility to (the licensee's) own partisan ends. . . . A broadcaster cannot be an advocate."[3] The FCC renewed Shepard's license, but the lesson was plain to all broadcasters. Licensees might allow other persons to air opinions, but should not do so themselves. Thus newspapers, comprising the other large voice in the local marketplace of ideas, were left alone with the right to editorialize. In a time when newspaper competition within cities was declining to nearly zero, the public interest was not well served by the FCC. The Mayflower decision was so criticized, in fact, that eight years later the Commission reversed its stand. This time editorializing was permitted in language if not in spirit: "overt licensee editorializing, within reasonable limits and subject to the general requirements of fairness . . . is not contrary to the public interest."[4] The requirements of fairness referred to included the obligation to seek out opposition to the licensee's opinion. No one seemed to know exactly what the FCC meant by seeking out opposition, and hardly anyone cared to try to find out. After all, if a station editorialized, there was always the possibility that the FCC might decide at the end of the three-year license period that the public interest had not been well served, and renewal might be denied. The easiest course was to go on as before, saying nothing and trying not to offend the customers or the government. Even by the 1970s, only about one-half the broadcasting stations in the U.S. admit they editorialize, and many of these editorialize infrequently. About one-fifth editorialize daily.

So, instead of broadcasters developing a vigorous tradition of speaking their views on public issues, as have newspapers, something very much the opposite resulted. And broadcasters often resembled sheep huddled together, afraid to be different, fearful of everything but the search for the big audience.

In television, according to the former vice president of audience measurement at NBC, Paul Klein, the effort to find the largest share of the audience results inevitably in what he calls the Least Objectionable Program: not what you want to watch, but what you're left with after rejecting all the other programs.[5]

How else, asks Klein, can we explain the substantial guilt most people have about watching television? If we watched because we actually wanted to see a particular program, we wouldn't feel guilty about it. Instead we watch, says Klein, from boredom, to escape from our lives, or for similar reasons, and we choose our "favorites" by eliminating the most objectionable. It's all a plot, contend some critics of broadcasting (and of the mass media generally), to *fix* the attention without *engaging* the mind. For if the program really engaged our minds, we would be much less receptive to the commercial than we are now.

Whether or not such assertions are true, and they most certainly are not true on the occasions when broadcasting lifts itself to the heights it is capable of, there is unquestionably extreme competition at a low-grade level.

In October 1959, a new series began on ABC-TV, which was slogging along as an also-ran network behind NBC and CBS. By mid-April of 1960, the series was the most popular on the air, and also the most violent. The program was "The Untouchables," and its success set off a trend in crime and violence programs on all networks. In the fall of 1960 a group in Los Angeles surveyed one week of nighttime television and counted 144 murders, 143 attempted murders, 52 "justifiable" killings, and found incidents of lesser violence too numerous to count.[6] The group noted, too, that ABC used film clips of its most violent scenes as promotional spots throughout the day.

Nor was the turn to violence a passing thing. In studying a sample of 183 programs for 1967 and 1968, University of Pennsylvania communications researcher George Gerbner found that 81 percent contained some kind of violence. ABC's technique in competing against the other two networks became known as "counter-programming." If NBC and CBS had competing comedies, ABC tried to "knock them off" with a sharply contrasting western. But the action had to be plenty active, as this report from a Hollywood script supervisor to the ABC-TV vice president in charge of programming shows:

> This is loaded with action. Many exciting scenes.
> Opens right up on a lot of action—a running gunfight between two cars of mobsters who crash, then continue to fight in the streets. Three killed. Six injured. Three killed are innocent bystanders.[7]

But as combat veterans often relate, horror eventually gives way to boredom in the face of repeated experience with brutality. Soon even ABC was having difficulty finding new methods of shocking. "I wish," said the producer of "The Untouchables" to the writer, "you could come up with a different device than running the man down with a car, as we have done this now in three different shows. I like the idea of sadism, . . . "[8]

The contest in violence was entered, willingly or not, by the other networks. CBS countered ABC's counter-programming with a dictum of three parts: "broads, bosoms, and fun." And with its two competitors going more heavily into "action" programs, NBC followed with entries of its own.[9]

Yet the whole race is cyclical. Studies have shown that the process operates something like this. A network comes up with a program that seems a great success. It may be period violence, as "The Untouchables" was with its stories of Chicago gangsterism in the 1920s. It may be violence under the cloak of current "law and order" concerns, such as "Dragnet," "Hawaii Five-O," or "The FBI." It may not be violence at all, but country comedy, such as "The Beverly Hillbillies," "Petticoat Junction," and "Green Acres." If it is successful, the other networks imitate it, taking some 12 to 18 months to enter the field. Competition in kind ensues until either the programs begin to lose audiences or until public revulsion sets in, usually in the form of a Congressional or other governmental investigation. In 1968, for example, ABC-TV announced it had "reiterated ABC's long-standing policy to prohibit the use of violence for the sake of violence." The memorandum was sent after the network heads had become "aware of a substantial change in the emotional climate in the country regarding the portrayal of incidents of violence on television."[10] What generated the publication, if not the formulation, of the memorandum was a request of the National Commission on the Causes and Prevention of Violence, which was itself formulated after the assassination of Dr. Martin Luther King and Senator Robert Kennedy.

By the time any investigation gets around to collecting assertions that the programs may be harmful, the novelty of the trend has worn off anyway, and the networks seem rather relieved not to have to continue in the same vein. They point with pride to their new efforts, which tend to be advertised as "relevant" to whatever social problems are currently up for discussion. Just as the final research reports on the effects of television violence were going in to the National Institute of Mental Health's Project Television and Social Behavior in late summer of 1971, the networks announced completely revised children's programming schedules for that fall. *Variety* was thus prompted to observe that the nets thus might claim the research was completely invalidated, since it was based upon old programming.[11]

However, networks have never yet admitted, not even in such roundabout fashion as this action would seem to indicate, that they feel their programs stimulate antisocial behavior. All they will admit for the record is that violence attracts viewers. A study of Saturday morning children's television done in May and June of 1970 revealed that networks were programming a commercial every 2.8 minutes. To keep the young viewers tuned in for these commercials, networks were relying heavily on violence. Seventy-one percent of the stories featured at least one instance of human violence.[12]

At any rate, the public furor has always in the past died down after awhile, and a season or two later someone produces a show of great immediate success, and the whole cycle begins anew.[13]

Broadcasting at the network level thus may be seen as a kind of three-cornered play in which the participants are the networks, the public, and government. Most of the time, the active players are the networks, wrestling among themselves for the attention of the public, which only rarely asserts itself. For all the complaints voiced by broadcasters about government interference, they remain mostly free to compete as they wish.

but there has to be a winner— and losers

With this kind of competition, there has to be some kind of referee. There is, and it is not the Federal Communications Commission. It is the A. C. Nielsen Co., which has been described by Les Brown, television and radio editor of *Variety,* in his *Television: The Business Behind the Box,* as the next greatest influence after the networks on television today. Every fall, everyone connected with television, from network head to actor in a new series (and even a good many viewers), await the judgment of the Nielsen ratings. Stars burst into light or flicker into darkness, heads of vice presidents don crowns or roll in the halls, Mercedes Benzes are ordered or put up for sale.

The Nielsen rating system offers no criticism or advice, no helpful hint about just what went wrong, no suggestion that maybe next week's show will be more to the public's liking.[14] The ratings report only facts, and mighty thin facts at that: how many out of 1200 homes had TV sets turned on to what channels during a certain time period. Twelve hundred homes, chosen as carefully as possible to be representative of the nearly 200 million Americans able to receive television. Twelve hundred homes, each with a little box, an Audimeter, attached to the TV set, so that every time the set is turned on, the time and channel are recorded on slowly moving 16mm film. Not who or what is watching; just the fact that the TV set is on. Does the family have a baby (or an insomniac dog) who won't sleep unless he hears the human voice? Then perhaps his preference for Johnny Carson instead of the late movie registers as 70,000 faithful viewers of the "Tonight Show." Do the Nielsen families ever go out at night and leave the TV turned on to discourage prowlers? If they do, then thousands of Americans are logged in as fans of one particular network—the one the set was tuned to when it was turned on as electronic watchdog. But though the set is on all evening, the number it represents might go from 40,000 up to 70,000 and then back to 50,000. Why? Because the number of turned on sets among the sample of 1200 is constantly varying. Presumably all over America people are turning the TV on and off all evening.

Periodically, the householder in the Nielsen sample takes the film from the little box on his TV set, sends it in, and the information on it is computerized along with the rest of the sample. Soon the data emerge in the form of two numbers for each show: a rating, which is a percentage of the total possible audience, based on households; and a share-of-audience, which is a percentage of the actual sets in use. A rating of 17 generally is considered satisfactory in prime time evening hours, and this means that 17 percent of all TV households in the sample of 1200 were tuned in to that program. (That is, a maximum of 204 households tuned in!) A share of 30 is generally considered minimally satisfactory, since that means that just under one-third of all sets on were tuned to that program, and consequently that the network is barely mustering its share of a three-network field.

To counter fears that once a family is designated an Audimeter family, it will attempt to influence network TV by tuning its set in some deliberate way, Nielsen shifts its Audimeter boxes at the rate of 20 percent a year, so no household remains in the sample more than five years. Families get 50 cents a week for cooperating, and in addition receive gifts, which they select from a catalog. Naturally, Nielsen helps out with repair costs on the TV set. An inoperative set does no one any good, least of all the networks who set their commercial rates on the basis of their Nielsen ratings.

Nielsen has another sample of 2200 households which do not use the Audimeter but which keep diaries of viewing time by all family members. In this way, networks learn whether viewers are old or young, rural or urban, educated or not, and so on. The Nielsen ratings system is the dominant one in broadcasting, but there are others, among them Pulse and the American Research Bureau. Methods used range from asking viewers to keep diaries of their watching to the telephone coincidental survey, when phone calls are made during the time when shows are on the air, and listeners are asked what the set is tuned to at that instant. Significantly, neither Pulse nor ARB nor Nielsen asks whether viewers like what thay watch, and why. Such questions are deemed irrelevant by the ratings firms and by the networks as well. If you began asking people if they *liked* what they watched, you'd be starting all kinds of trouble for yourself.

The shakiness of this whole system and the degree to which the networks are committed to it was well illustrated back in 1966. A young man named Rex Sparger apparently approached the producer-husband of actress Carol Channing just before her TV special was to be aired. Sparger wanted to do some "audience research" for the show, *during* the show, and Miss Channing's husband hired him for the sum of $4000. Sparger had been an investigator for a House Commerce Subcommittee during a probe of TV ratings a couple of years before. According to charges made later, during the course of his subcommittee work he had obtained a list of some homes in the Nielsen Audimeter sample. He is supposed to have sent a letter and questionnaire to 58 of these homes in Ohio and Pennsylvania, asking the householders to watch the show and fill out the questionnaire. He enclosed three dollars for their trouble, and promised another five dollars upon return of the completed questionnaire. Sparger later said he was doing it for a book exposing the ratings system; Miss Channing's husband denied doing it to try to get Miss Channing a series on TV; and A. C. Nielsen, who had got wind of the whole thing before the show went on the air and deleted the 58 homes from the sample, was sufficiently scared to file suit against Sparger for $1.5 million. The network involved said it knew nothing about it. What it probably meant was it didn't want to know. One referee is enough. Having more than one means disagreements, so why bother?[15]

do viewers *really* get what they want?

Regarding the assertion that in broadcasting the salesman rarely dares offend his customers, the question to ask is—which customers? The answer must be, the *paying* customers. In Jackson, Mississippi, television station WLBT was, for a long time, systematically excluding blacks from consideration either as performers or as viewers. The Office of Communication of the United Church of Christ showed that WLBT was doing such things as cutting off network scenes of whites attacking black civil rights demonstrators, deleting a preview promotion for "Bonanza" showing that a black man was to be starred in the next Sunday's show, and totally ignoring needs of black viewers in selecting local programs. All this and more in an area where blacks made up more than 40 percent of the viewing audience. They were customers, all right, but not the ones who bought time on the air. The practice had gone on for so long that it clearly had the acquiescence of the local advertisers.[16]

Such shenanigans have been the rule rather than the exception at most levels of broadcasting. A National Educational Television documentary of exploitation of the poor by certain banks and banking practices was ruled off the air in a number of localities, apparently for fear of offending bankers as a group.[17] When ABC made plans to televise regionally the 1970 football game between the State University of New York at Buffalo and Holy Cross, the Student Association of Buffalo designed a half-time program to express their views on the Vietnam war, racism, and industrial pollution. Learning of the program, ABC refused to carry the half-time activities, and instead panned around campus scenery. A complaint filed later with the FCC charged that one of the students planning the show had been told by the ABC sports producer that the telecast was a business enterprise, that companies were buying commercial time, and that those sponsors would not appreciate a half-time show that alienated potential customers.[18] Better to avoid discussion of public affairs entirely than to risk upsetting the audience prior to the commercial.

doing right—and paying the price

Occasionally broadcasters do provide exceptions to their general rule of not giving offense. Usually the exceptions are provided by the same organizations who most often bear the brunt of criticism for submitting to dollar pressure, the networks. Having larger advertiser constituencies, the networks have less to fear in reprisals than do local stations, and sometimes they realize it. A good example is the CBS documentary "The Selling of the Pentagon," first broadcast on February 23, 1971. A highly critical examination of public relations efforts by the Department of Defense to win support for its policies, the program's commercial spots were bought by Procter & Gamble (two minutes), American Home Products, Allstate, S. C. Johnson (all one-minutes), and Holiday Inn and Pontiac (half-minutes). The program created such a furor in and out ot government that CBS reran it in March. Though all the publicity almost guaranteed a greater audience the second time around, none of the original advertisers bought time. In fact, only two commercial positions could be sold at all by CBS (spots went to Midas Muffler, Del Monte, Mobil, and Beechman).[19]

Among other charges the program made against the Defense Department were that the Pentagon was spending $190 million a year to propagandize the American public, that it was sending teams of "traveling colonels" around the country to argue in favor of U.S. military presence in Vietnam, and that it was staging expensive firepower demonstrations for key local business and community leaders. The debate that ensued, with Vice President Agnew, Congressional supporters of the Pentagon, and critics of CBS on the one side, and network supporters on the other, involved not whether the Defense Department does these things and whether they are proper, but the editing techniques employed by CBS in preparing the program. The Investigations Subcommittee of the House Committee on Commerce summoned Dr. Frank Stanton, president of CBS, and supoenaed all film and scripts involved in the show's production. Stanton refused to provide more than films and scripts of the versions actually aired; the subcommittee voted to seek a contempt of Congress citation against him, which the House of Representatives resoundingly refused to do.

Question: If you as the manager of a business, and responsible to stockholders, were put to this kind of trouble and expense, would you do:

    a. more of the same?
    b. less of the same?
    c. about the same?
    d. all of these?
    e. none of these?

If your answer is b, then rate yourself as network managerial potential. While the debate of "The Selling of the Pentagon" raged, April 24 peace rallies in Washington and San Francisco featuring hundreds of thousands of demonstrators were (1) ignored by ABC, (2) given 42 minutes after "The Game of the Week" and 15 minutes after "The Saturday Night Movie by NBC, and (3) given one hour in the middle of the afternoon by CBS. But the Pentagon did not seem unduly chastened by its "exposure" on television. Screening Vietnam action film for newsmen early in Demember 1971, Pentagon spokesmen declared the footage showed the Ho Chi Minh Trail under attack by U.S. planes. When newsmen noticed some of the camera angles were from the ground, and challenged the film's authenticity, an investigation showed it was shot in Florida.

When an individual broadcaster tries to break out of the pattern of commercialism that prevents the industry from reaching its potential, he may find himself on the outside of his community looking in. Ralph Blumberg, the operator of station WBOX in Bogalusa, Louisiana, found himself in that situation not long after he decided to do what he could as a local broadcaster to implement the law of the land. Specifically, Blumberg agreed to work with the U.S. Department of Justice's Community Relations division in 1964. The objective was to work out peaceful integration and thereby head off trouble in the form of clashes between militants, both white and black.

Blumberg and half a dozen other Bogalusa leaders—ministers, lawyers, the newspaper editor—agreed to sponsor a speech by Brooks Hays, former Arkansas Congressman and prominent Southern Baptist. But the Bogalusa Ku Klux Klan began to agitate against the meeting, calling Hays a Communist, and vowing to tag anyone who attended his meeting an "integrationist," to be dealt with "accordingly by the Knights of the Ku Klux Klan." Blumberg felt that if the community could be informed of such preposterous charges and threats, the Klan would be stopped in its tracks.

So he began to broadcast editorials over his radio station. From that point forward his life became a terror. Threats were made openly to him and to his wife. The station would be dynamited, he was told. His family would be killed. So would he. His car windows were broken, his tires slashed, and after he decided to publicize his fight nationally, six high-powered bullets were pumped through his transmitter house. Still he refused to knuckle under. Let his own words tell the story:

> We decided to stay and fight for two reasons. First, if we could keep our doors open long enough with outside help, perhaps the local merchants would eventually come back with us and we could start operating normally again. Secondly, if we let them put us out of business without a fight, then every radio station, TV station and newspaper in small communities in America would be vulnerable to this same type of attack. Nobody would ever stand up and be heard for fear of economic reprisal, and small communities are where this racial problem seems to be most prevalent.

Blumberg stayed, and watched his advertisers drift away. By the middle of March 1965 he was down to six sponsors. His lease was canceled, and he had to move his studio to a mobile home four miles out of town. Finally, he became so frightened that he sent his family to relatives in St. Louis, and remained to carry on the fight alone. Contributions from outside the town amounted to about $9000 in a six-month period, but that, finally, was not enough. Broken economically but not in spirit, Blumberg sold out and took a job in New York as a news editor for CBS. The new WBOX owners were a chain that operates stations throughout the South. The programming plan they announced they would follow consisted of 100 percent country and western music. Are you listening, KKK?[20]

for further reading

Arlen, Michael. *Living Room War.* New York: Viking Press, 1969.

Barnouw, Eric. *A Tower in Babel: A History of Broadcasting in the United States.* Vol. I—to 1933. New York: Oxford University Press, 1966.

————. *The Golden Web: A History of Broadcasting in the United States.* Vol. II—1933 to 1953. New York: Oxford University Press, 1968.

————. *The Image Empire: A History of Broadcasting in the United States.* Vol. III—from 1953. New York: Oxford University Press, 1970.

Brown, Les. *Television: The Business Behind the Box.* New York: Harcourt Brace Jovanovich, 1971.

Friendly, Fred W. *Due to Circumstances Beyond Our Control.* New York: Random House, 1967.

Kendrick, Alexander. *Prime Time: The Life of Edward R. Murrow.* Boston: Little, Brown, 1969.

McGinniss, Joe. *The Selling of the President 1968.* New York: Trident Press, 1969.

the movie business

what hath Eadweard Muybridge wrought?

Men are now beginning their careers as directors by working on
commercials—which, if one cares to speculate on it, may be almost a
one-sentence résumé of the future of American motion pictures.
—Pauline Kael

The most poignant aspect of art in movies is not its rarity or ambiguity
but the fact that it is economically unnecessary.

"The deal, that's all this business is about," a contemporary
producer told author John Gregory Dunne. "What's available, when
can you get him, start date, stop date, percentages—the deal, it's the
only thing that matters. Listen, if Paul Newman comes in and says he
wants to play Gertrude Lawrence in *Star!*, you do it, that's the nature
of the business."[1] Money and prestige and power: "Glamour, recognition, V.I.P. treatment by airlines and restaurants, access to beautiful

women, power to hire and fire, and all the other goodies offered by the Bitch are constantly waved before the twitching noses of ambitious men," says Ingo Preminger, producer of *M*A*S*H.*[2]

Nor is it necessarily art that lures millions to the movies every week. The audience has an itch for pleasure, and the industry has a two-hour cure. The cure is not free. The average cost of moviegoing is $1.30 a person and rising (in 1950 the average was 44 cents). Still, this is not very much for an individual to pay, but it does add up to about $1,250,000,000 a year (not counting popcorn) and is a considerable prize.

With this much money at stake, movies are nothing if not big business. A typical Hollywood film costs about $12,000 a minute to shoot, and probably no single artisan except a clumsy diamond cutter can expend at that rate. Even in Hollywood it requires a group effort. There are probably a few people who still believe that actors make up their lines and actions as they go along, and certainly there is a coterie of critics that expounds a theory holding the director as author of films. But movies are collaborative, and while the director may dominate the actual filming, he is not always present at either the beginning or the end of a movie's making.

the producer and his problems

The man who does worry about the film from start to finish is the producer (who may also be his own writer, director, or actor). Too simply stated, his role is to acquire options on a story and talent, secure financing from a film distributor or other backer, shepherd the project to completion, and place it in the hands of the distributor, who passes it on to the exhibitor and through him to the audience. And at that point the producer has time to pray that a share of the public's dollars, like spawning salmon, will find their way upstream.

The producer mentioned here is a so-called "independent." He is under no continuing contract to a studio. In Hollywood's economically gilded days, before network TV became the dominant entertainment medium and when the major studios initiated most of their own films, a Vice President in Charge of Production (such as Irving Thalberg or Darryl Zanuck) would buy stories and assign a contract producer to serve mainly as a budgetary watchdog. Now the studios are primarily distributor-financiers who themselves turn to bigger lenders for capital.

Most of today's producers are free-lance packagers. The producer begins by seeking a story, and if it is presold to the audience, sure-fire, so much the better. A best-selling book, he reasons, is a good story, and even if it isn't a good story it has some publicity value. *Sex and the Single Girl* was purchased for over $100,000, and it mattered little if nothing was retained for the film but the title. Charles K. Feldman purchased Mary McCarthy's novel *The Group* for $162,500. Miss McCarthy is an outstanding author and critic but not a boff in the stix, so Feldman sank more than $50,000 into publicity for the book even before he found backing for a filmed version—in fact, his promotion of the book was designed to make it more attractive to a distributor. Once production began, Feldman took the title of executive producer and hired Sidney Buchman as producer-screenwriter, and Buchman in turn hired Sidney Lumet as director. Together they selected a cast.[3]

Like other mass-media gatekeepers, the producer and his associates operate under several pressures, most of them rooted in money. There is less *ars gratia artis* (MGM's slogan) than *ars gratia pecuniae* (Stan Freberg's). If one lays out $5.5 million for the movie rights to *My Fair Lady,* one is inclined to cast Audrey Hepburn, at the peak of her drawing power, instead of Julie Andrews, who is huge in New York but unknown in Bloomington. No matter that Miss Hepburn can't sing; she can move her lips to the voice of Marni Nixon, who can.

The goal of the producer is to assemble as many marketable elements as he can without giving away too much of the expected revenue. Most actors will work for a flat amount, and extras for a daily rate, but stars demand a piece of the action, as do big-name directors and writers. This is largely an effect of the breakdown of the old studio system and of taxes. In one of several panicky reactions to television in the 1950s, the major studios cut loose their leading contract performers and directors to save money when theatre attendance declined. After years of comfortable peonage, such actors as Gregory Peck found themselves in demand by independent producers who were short of cash but long on negotiation. Some stars, perceiving in themselves hitherto unrecognized talent, also turned to directing and producing. The star with unlimited faith in his own drawing power could foresee that a percentage of profit would far outrun the few hundred thousand dollars of a flat contract. (Some were expensively deflated.) The percentage deal also had the virtue of deferring income over a period of years, which was advantageous for tax purposes. Even though a performer such as Elizabeth Taylor could command a million-dollar fee, it was worth her while to spread it over several years. It was also wise for a star to establish his own corporation, the tax on which is about 50 percent rather than the 90 percent on personal income of star magnitude. The star might also find it wise to invest in tax-free municipal bonds, in trust funds in the Netherlands Antilles, in cattle ranching, or to move to Switzerland, where income taxes are low and the sky is clear.

All of this has been both a joy and a bane to the independent producer. He is faced with a wide array of free agents, some of whom will put up their own money; however, the more talented or popular they are, the larger the slice they will demand. Moreover, some ask for a percentage of the gross revenues—that is, a slice off the top—instead of the net profits. This increases resistance from the distributor-bank-roller who is accustomed to being first at the trough for his 30 percent. The exhibitor, too, takes his off the top, and the producer, who set the film in motion, can suffer the nightmare of seeing his movie rake in cash that never quite filters down.

As *Variety* has noted, the U.S. film business is one of the few industries where the manufacturers get only 40 percent of the gross volume returned from the market. The rule of thumb is that a film must gross two and one-half times its production cost in order to break even. Little wonder that stars began to seek a percentage of the gross rather than the net—and in some cases, a guaranteed minimum. If the star guesses right—as William Holden did when he contracted for ten percent of the gross of *The Bridge on the River Kwai* to be paid at the rate of no more than $50,000 a year—he will find himself too old to walk to his Tyrolean bank by the time all the returns are in.

Because the negotiations for talent and financing are so convoluted and subject to renegotiation, many projects die young. Even after production begins, some projects abort. Star Elliot Gould and producer Jack Brodsky, who were partners for *Little Murders,* had a falling-out during their next effort, *A Glimpse of the Tiger.* The outcome was reported with bemusement by *Variety:* "Project was revived briefly last month when Barbra Streisand apparently agreed to step in, although it wasn't clear whether she would take the role vacated by her estranged husband (thus requiring a script revamp) or take the Kim Darby part. Peter Bogdanovich was inked to direct the revived 'Tiger' and Ryan O'Neal was reported set to appear opposite La Streisand. Production veepee John Calley reports all is off now and pic costs will be charged off to Brodsky-Gould productions."[4]

Naturally a producer would prefer docile actors such as Clark Gable or Rock Hudson, but only if they were also good at the box office. The tempestuous or neurotic or finicky star can wreck a tight production schedule. With upwards of a million dollars at stake, the producer wants a quick and steady pace. Fortunately for him, participation in profits has inspired some previously "difficult" stars to new heights of efficiency. Once he formed his own company, Sinatra became known as "one-shot Frank."

Because of high costs, a shooting schedule is established in advance of filming and it is difficult if not impossible to reshoot a scene if a blunder is noticed more than a few days after the original take. By then the sets may have been dismantled and some actors released. A few repairs can be done to the sound track; "looping," or post-recording an actor's speech for dubbing in place of the original words, is common practice. But the filming itself is done out of sequence in order to make the most economical use of sets and performers. Actors are called only for those days in which they are needed, and a supporting performer may never see the full script. Even the stars, who do have full scripts, must rely on the director and editor to build their fitful performances into a coherent role.[5] The point is that movies are not continually reworked for perfection prior to editing. Often the producer and director are no better than their cutter, or editor, who is never better than the skeins of film handed to him. Some directors' contracts call for complete artistic control, right through the final editing. This was the case with Dalton Trumbo, who filmed his own book, *Johnny Got His Gun.* Other directors don't care or don't have time or are rushing off to another film, as Pauline Kael points out in her account of the filming of *The Group.* If the shooting has been fast and loose, the editor is left to make a silk purse out of a sow's ear or other portions of ham.

x, as in sex

As in the other mass media, the pressure the movie communicator most wants to feel is that of the audience, and typically this is the most difficult pulse to locate. The moviemaker can be assured that *somebody* will buy a ticket to anything he releases, but what he wants, and economically needs, are several million somebodies. Like other entertainers, he pays close attention to past successes. The initial choice of story and talent are crucial, and in this the producer can be guided by his artistic judgment or, more likely, what he believes are universal appeals and upward trends. Hence the rashes of films about spies, motorcyclists, soulful youths, chapfallen cowboys—a good many of them writhing in sex, violence, slapstick, or soupy romance.

The producer knows the potential audience is young and full of juice. So do such organizations as the National Catholic Office for Motion Pictures (née Legion of Decency), the Department of Films of the Lutheran Council, and the Code and Rating Administration of the Motion Picture Association of America. The latter is best known for its G, PG, R, and X branding irons, which leave their marks on movie advertisements. (A "G" movie is judged wholesome enough for anyone, while an "X" film is closed to young people, usually because of its sex, violence, or language. "PG" and "R" are intermediate gradations that suggest parental guidance and accompaniment, respectively.) Adopted in late 1968, this system was borrowed from the British, who many years ago established a "U" (for universal), "A" (not suitable for children), and "X" (adults only) scheme that was designed to stave off rigid external censorship. By mid-1971 the U.S. rating system was under crossfire. Religious groups thought the industry's censors were too lax and producers felt they were too strict. When black filmmaker Melvin Van Peebles' *Sweet Sweetback's Baadasssss Song* was rated "X," he added the words, "By an all-white jury." Other producers complained that the censors didn't understand that sex and violence were integral to their artistry—which didn't stop the same producers from making cuts in exchange for more liberal ratings.

The moviemaker will try to stimulate the public pulse with advertising ranging from the grandiose ("A Motion-Picture Event as Epoch-Making as the World Events It Portrays") to the bizarre ("He Had a Teenager in His Cabana and a Hot Contessa Dating Him on Her Husband's Grave"). The 1971 movie *Willard* did heavy business, thanks to a campaign that featured a leaping rat. This was no accident. In pretests in Scranton and Wilkes-Barre, the rat advertisements out-pulled ratless ads by 50 percent. Less successful were the first adver-tisements for *Wild Rovers,* which depicted Ryan O'Neal smiling and hugging William Holden as they shared a horseback ride. The public, not sure what it was in for, stayed at home. MGM quickly switched to a new campaign that reassuringly promised "*Wild Rovers* is full of two-fisted action." Occasionally, deeper surgery is required. When John Huston's *Freud* languished at the box office it was reissued as *The Secret Passion.*

Not all movie advertising is acceptable to newspapers; some have policies against advertising X-rated films, and many will doctor the illustrations. The exhibitor agrees to changes because an advertis-ing blackout can be lethal to receipts. Therefore, some distributors obligingly offer two versions of a film ("One strictly horror, the other the very last word in sex," announced King Film International, regard-ing *The Night of the Damned*) and some will provide two sets of adver-tisements. A 1970 film entitled *Fornicon* also traveled more quietly as *F: The Pattern of Evil.*

Free publicity and commercial tie-ins are also sought. A good share of the film personalities who appear on TV's nighttime talk shows are there to promote their newest product. Expensive campaigns are waged to win Academy Awards, and stars are arm-twisted into attending premieres around the world. In recent years, all publicity has become good publicity, and when Elizabeth Taylor and Richard Burton enacted their most passionate scenes away from the set of *Cleopatra,* they did not hurt the film. In the wonderland of Hollywood, even secrecy is publicity: Marlon Brando's performances in *Guys and Dolls* and *The Godfather* were shielded during production in order to tantalize the press and public. Tie-in promotions are mutual back-scratching between the moviemaker and other businessmen. Arthur P. Jacobs, producer of *Dr. Doolittle,* signed about 50 licensing agreements with manufacturers who would make *Doolittle* toys, lunchboxes, T-shirts, dog food, and cereal. Despite all this, the $18 million *Doolittle* won a tepid response from moviegoers.[6]

As the *Doolittle* experience indicates, a vast amount of huckstering does not necessarily wring a proportionate number of tickets from a lukewarm and distant audience. The early successes of Hollywood owed a great deal to the novelty of film, and perhaps also to pioneer directors and producers who, fresh from the garment district, were closely attuned to the tastes of the mass audience. The modern critic Dwight Macdonald has observed: "Hollywood is in the middle of a barbarically provincial non-city, three thousand miles from our cultural capital. . . . It is as if all British films were made in Tanganyika. My modest proposal for improving the quality of our films is that the industry move back to where it started from, namely, Fort Lee, New Jersey, a short bus ride from civilization."[7]

Actually, the center of Hollywood *is* New York; here the bankers, distributors, advertising agencies, Motion Picture Association of America, and the other media have their main offices. But let's take Macdonald's advice and go back for a few moments to Fort Lee and beyond.

flashback

By the end of the 19th century, science had contrived a number of inventions—some of them no more than toys—which, when combined, permitted the filming and projection of motion. The collaboration that marks today's movie production was also characteristic of motion-picture invention. As early as the 17th century a "magic lantern" could project single images upon a wall, and in 1834 a toy called the "zoetrope" presented a moving image to the child who spun its pasteboard drum and peeped through slots at moving sketches. About the same time, the Frenchmen Niépce and Daguerre and the Englishman Talbot were experimenting with the light-sensitive properties of silver halides, and by 1850 photographic negatives were made upon glass plates.

Though glass negatives were difficult to handle, Mathew Brady recorded the Civil War on film, and William Henry Jackson photographed the American West. Then, in 1872, ex-California Governor and horse-fancier Leland Stanford wagered that all four of a trotter's hooves were off the ground at one time during its stride. Stanford hired photographer Eadweard Muybridge to prove his case. Muybridge succeeded, and Stanford encouraged him to continue his photography of horses in motion. For seven years, with some time off to murder his wife's lover (he was acquitted), Muybridge experimented with cameras in series, their shutters tripped by strings snapped by running horses. In 1880 Muybridge attached his still pictures to the edge of a disk, from which could be projected a brief "moving picture."

Muybridge took his show to the East and to Europe. In Paris the scientist Étienne Marey, in the midst of experiments on motion, was inspired to take up the camera as a tool. His contribution was the invention of a circular, slotted shutter that permitted the use of a single camera. Within a few years he showed Thomas Edison his work with serial images on short strips of film.

In France, England, and America between 1885 and 1895 a number of inventors worked out problems of film, cameras, and projectors. Toward the end of the eighties, Edison encouraged his associate, William Kennedy Laurie Dickson, to build motion-picture devices. Dickson acquired a new, flexible film from George Eastman, and eventually fabricated the Kinetograph, a movie camera, and the Kinetoscope, a peep-show viewer that employed 40 feet of film. In France, the Lumière brothers patented an effective projector, and in December, 1895, showed a series of short films in the basement of the Grande Cafe. They charged one-franc admission and within a few months were grossing 7000 francs a week for such features as *Lunch Hour at the Lumière Factory.* In 1896 the Edison Vitascope projected ocean waves and prize fights between the acts of a variety show in Koster & Bial's Music Hall in New York. Vaudeville had clutched the asp.

The burgeoning cities provided eager audiences for films that made no great demands on purse or literacy. Movies were shown in vaudeville houses, penny arcades, storefronts, and eventually in more or less permanent Nickelodeons. Even so, there was not an endless audience for five-minute films of waterfalls, and soon news events, real and recreated, were presented. These too were mere episodes and not intentionally fictional. It remained for the imaginative Georges Méliès to explore trickery on film and to turn to storytelling at length. In 1897 Melies built a glassed-in studio near Paris. The glass admitted strong light and protected the set from rain. Méliès was a gifted storyteller and animator. Many of today's optical illusions had their origins with him.

About the turn of the century English directors experimented with closeups, cutting from one scene to another, and melodrama. In 1903 the English released *The Robbery of the Mail Coach,* and later that year Edwin S. Porter filmed *The Great Train Robbery* in the wilds of New Jersey. The audience was stunned when a bandit fired his pistol directly into the camera, and was not at all perplexed by intercutting. The American Western, and indeed the American movie, was born.

As the demand for films grew, studios sprouted in New Jersey, Flatbush, the Bronx, and on Manhattan rooftops. The largest filmmakers were the equipment manufacturers, who attempted to control production and distribution through a trust called the Motion Picture Patents Company and a subsidiary, the General Film Company. The trust had an exclusive contract with Eastman for film, and independents were forced to buy film, when possible, from Europe. The Patents Company also used goon squads to disrupt independent production and distribution. But independents such as William Fox, Carl Laemmle, Adolph Zukor, and the Warners staged a successful resistance through litigation and by making increasingly popular longer "features." The independents also discovered that in a place called Hollywood they would be a safe 3000 miles from the trust and a convenient few hours from the Mexican border. California also offered year-round good weather and a varied terrain.

So the trust, by default, emptied the greenhouses of Fort Lee, populated Hollywood, and gave rise to the feature film and star system. Laemmle, head of IMP, a leading independent, learned the value of publicity during the battle with the trust. He also perceived public affection for anonymous players like the Biograph Girl, whose services he acquired and whose name, Florence Lawrence, he shouted from his advertisements. Another inadvertent gift of the Patents Company was David Wark Griffith, who quit Biograph, a member of the trust, and moved to Hollywood in 1913. There he found the freedom to work on films large in length and scope. His *Birth of a Nation, Intolerance,* and *Broken Blossoms* were artistic and technical achievements of the first order, though variously flawed by bigotry, grandiloquence, and hokum.

Also boarding westbound trains in 1913 were Cecil B. DeMille, Jesse L. Lasky, and Samuel Goldfish (later Goldwyn), who were to insure the commercial success of the feature film. As the trust collapsed and taxation on studios grew more oppressive in the East, the exodus became a rout, and Hollywood was soon releasing what are now regarded as the classic films of the silent era—as well as a preponderance of rubbish.

In the 1920s Hollywood grew in opulence and ego, with stars commanding salaries (and sometimes percentages) that are still impressive. *Ben Hur*—the 1925 version—began with a budget of $750,000 and finished at nearly $4 million. MGM ultimately lost about $1 million on it despite a gross of over $9 million. Not that it mattered, because Hollywood, like the rest of the country, was riding the giddy boom of the twenties.

But not all the studios flourished. Warner Brothers, especially, felt a cooling of the audience to recurring cycles of westerns, romances, and melodramas. Some of the larger exhibitors were beginning to reach back into vaudeville for live attractions to supplement films, just as films once augmented variety programs. The Warners began to think seriously about talking pictures.

Sound with pictures was not new. Pit musicians, especially organists, accompanied silent films, and Méliès once had an opera tenor sing from behind the screen. Edison's early interest in film was tied to his wish to provide a visual element for his cylindrical records. The development of recorded sound was loosely parallel to that of film, and in 1923 the radio pioneer Lee De Forest exhibited a series of short talkies in New York. The next year he released a two-reel comedy in sound. Fox regularly distributed talking newsreels in 1927. Then late in 1927 Warner Bros. released the *Jazz Singer,* and Al Jolson put the silent film to death.

The timing, though inadvertent, was fortunate for the industry. All the studios adapted to sound before the stock market crash of October 1929, and many exhibitors had been able to finance sound equipment. As the movie historian Kenneth Macgowan points out, had the industry been a bit slower, sound might not have been widespread for another ten years.[8] It might also be noted that commercial television was feasible by the late 1930s, but was delayed by World War II. Perhaps without Jolson and Hitler, movies might have died with their mouths shut.

But Hollywood wasn't leaving everything to chance. It learned early the economic sense of monopoly. The first producers sold their films outright to exhibitors who, stuck with stale prints, exchanged them among themselves. Exchanges evolved into distributorships and the present practice of renting films evolved. About the time the Patents Company died, Paramount under Zukor devised "block booking"—the practice of requiring an exhibitor to contract in advance for a stated number of films and to contribute money (also in advance) to their production. The exhibitor took all or none. Smarting under this restraint, some leading theatre owners banded together as the First National Exhibitors Circuit and contracted for films—sans block booking—with independent producers. Partially thwarted, Paramount and the other major firms backed down a bit on booking and bought more theatres for themselves. First National, meantime, began to produce films. And in 1923 the Federal Trade Commission began sniffing monopoly.

In the early thirties, thanks to the novelty of sound and the power of monopoly and market-splitting, the movies seemed impervious to depression. Each of the five major companies—Fox, Paramount, Warners, Loew's, and RKO—made, distributed, and exhibited its own films. Where their theatres didn't compete directly, they rented films to each other. The Big Five, plus the smaller Columbia, Universal, and

United Artists, practically dominated the industry, from screenwriter to ticket-taker.

Quite understandably, Hollywood and Wall Street were mutually attracted. Financiers found what they thought was a depression-proof industry, and Hollywood sought more capital for further ventures into oligopoly. The struggle in the early thirties between RCA (which owned RKO) and American Telephone and Telegraph for dominance in motion-picture sound equipment further helped return the control of movies, though not the studios, to New York City.

In 1938 the Department of Justice brought antitrust action against the eight giants. The industry responded, as it had in 1922 to the threat of Federal censorship, with fervent promises of self-regulation. By 1940 a few of the companies entered into consent agreements with the government and divested themselves of their theatres. After another 10 years of waffling, Paramount and RKO agreed to get out of exhibition, and Loew's, Twentieth Century Fox, and Warners followed suit within a few years. This meant an end to exhibition controlled by the producer-distributors, and an end to block booking, which had never completely vanished. It also meant greater competition among producers, who now had more equal access to theatres. However, the consent agreements did not separate the studios from their foreign theatres or prevent them from collaborating with television networks. Nor have exhibitors failed to buy stock in producer-distributors.

If the major studios were prevented from vertical consolidation, they could still diversify, and this they did with a desperate vengeance. Some found oil on their back lots, most rented sound stages, all had real estate and film libraries to sell, and some veered into the record business, broadcasting, and electronics. Stanley Warner Theatres got into the girdle business. Studios merged with other firms as, in the late A. J. Liebling's words, the canary merges with the cat. Warner Bros., for example, after establishing its own record company and acquiring Atlantic and Elektra, in 1969 became a part of Kinney Services, Inc., a conglomerate founded on real estate, janitorial services, parking lots, and funeral parlors. Kinney also picked up National Periodical Publications, home of Superman and Batman, as well as *Coronet* and Paperback Library and the Independent News Company, which distributes 27 magazines, including *Playboy*.

flash forward

Whither the movies?

That depends on which coroner you consult. There have been many. Edison didn't bother to patent his Kinetoscope overseas, nor did he see a practical future for projected movies. In 1897 in Paris a fire

in a projection booth spread to a crowded auditorium, killing 180 social-
ites and frightening audiences around the world. In 1918 an influenza
epidemic and the absence of millions of young men cut sharply into
theatre revenues; and when the war ended, the producers had backlogs
of now-unwanted war films. After his first film, Charlie Chaplin announced, "I figure the cinema is little more than a fad. It's canned
drama. What audiences really want to see is flesh and blood on the
stage." The advent of sound killed the silent film and put hundreds of
actors and technicians out of work. In the late thirties exhibitors be-
moaned slumping receipts and resorted to double features, Screen-O,
and free dishes. In the forties the stars left for war and the government
pressed antitrust actions. In the late forties Communists were thought
to lurk behind every scenario and television began to kidnap the audience. By the sixties, the studios functioned mainly as branch banks for
independent producers. In 1970 United Artists was $177,368,000 in
debt, and Twentieth Century Fox was nearing a proxy fight. Producers
were filming abroad to escape high costs, and half of Hollywood's technicians were out of work. Only one film in six made money.

Yet the movies refuse to play dead.

In 1970 American distributors released 270 new films. This
figure is far below the post-war high of 425 in 1950, yet it was the
highest since 1958. Total admission receipts, too, were the highest since
1957 (though owing largely to sharp increases in ticket prices), and in
1969 more than 500 new theatres were opened, planned, or under
construction. This rate is expected to continue as theatres move to
shopping centers. The exhibitors are comfortable even if the distributors are not.

And, some would argue, movies are better than ever. Wide
critical acclaim has been awarded *Bonnie & Clyde, M*A*S*H, 2001: A
Space Odyssey, Catch-22, Easy Rider, The Last Picture Show,* and *Five
Easy Pieces,* to name only American films. (The U.S. ranks behind
Japan, India, and Italy, in that order, in film production, followed
closely by Taiwan, Korea, Turkey, and France.) Though films have
been accused of being a middle- to upper-class white youth recreation,
an eager black audience thronged to see *Sweetback* and *Shaft* and
their successors. Foreign receipts from American films are strong, and
in many cases the distributor expects half of his revenues from abroad.

Then too the "dying" industry managed to sire *Love Story* and
The Godfather, which are expected to gross $100 million and $150
million respectively by the time all receipts are in.

Many of the new films are neither artistic nor widely popular.
In quality they range from poor to rancid. Their titles are awful
enough: *Fanny Hill Meets Dr. Erotico, Mondo Freudo, Sex Family*

Robinson on the Farm. In 1972 Steve Krantz Productions released *Fritz the Cat,* the first X-rated animated film.

The industry has made more comebacks than Pauline of the Perils. Its latest lifeboat may be its youthful nemesis, television. Hollywood's major studios dominated the production field for the 1971–72 television season, and the demand for feature films on TV showed no signs of abating. But the big market on the horizon, more than a mirage, is subscription TV and video cassettes, both of which are expected to devour films at a ferocious rate. This is bad news for exhibitors, some of whom have displayed petitions in their lobbies to "preserve free TV." But pay television and cassettes could permit the studios, if they can hold out long enough, once again to control the movie process from story to exhibition. Which is all they ever wanted.

for further reading

Arnheim, Rudolf. *Film as Art.* Berkeley, Calif.: University of California Press, 1957.
Dunne, John Gregory. *The Studio.* New York: Bantam, 1970.
Howe, A. H. "A Banker Looks at the Picture Business," *The Journal of the Screen Producers' Guild,* December, 1965, pp. 9–16.
Jacobs, Lewis, ed. *The Movies as Medium.* New York: Farrar, Strauss & Giroux, 1970.
Jacobs, Lewis. *The Rise of the American Film.* New York: Teachers College Press, 1968.
Jarvie, I. C. *Movies and Society.* New York: Basic Books, 1970.
Jobes, Gertrude. *Motion Picture Empire.* Hamden, Conn.: Archon Books, 1966.
Kael, Pauline. *Kiss Kiss Bang Bang.* New York: Bantam, 1969.
Macgowan, Kenneth. *Behind the Screen.* New York: Dell, 1965.
Samuels, Charles Thomas, ed. *A Casebook on Film.* New York: Van Nostrand, 1970.
Schumach, Murray. *The Face on the Cutting Room Floor.* New York: William Morrow, 1964.

the news ethic

defining news to reach the masses

The purpose of a newspaper is to print the truth and make a profit, not necessarily in that order.
—Henry G. Gay, editor and publisher, *Mason County Journal,* Shelton, Washington

It is a too little recollected fact that today's news ethic—the system whereby news is defined—originated more nearly in the economics of the mid-1830s newspaper business than in the philosophies of great editors.

This system, which is really a set of conventions by which reporters and editors accept or reject content for the news columns of their papers, took about 70 years to develop fully, and has remained largely unchanged for another 70. Only within the past decade or two has there been questioning of these conventions from within the newspaper industry.

In their simplest form, the conventions reduce to about five:

1. *Timeliness*—to be considered "news," an event must have occurred recently.

2. *Proximity*—other qualities being equal, higher priority is given to the local event than to the similar event occurring in the next town, or state, or country.

3. *Prominence*—the divorce case of a U.S. Senator rates admission to the news columns well ahead of the marital problems of the corner druggist.

4. *Consequence*—the more people affected by an event, the bigger the news.

5. *Human Interest*—the universality of the emotional content of the story counts for a lot, even if the circumstances otherwise are inconsequential, old, and occur far away to obscure people.[1]

According to these conventions, then, a story—let alone a series of stories about living conditions in a black ghetto would stand little chance of reaching print. Though current, such a story would lack timeliness unless some event occurred, and if it did, it probably would have to be a crime of violence. The ghetto might be physically close, but its psychological distance would be very great for most readers. Moreover, events in the ghetto would have—under the conventional definition of news—little direct consequence for the average newspaper reader. Prominence would rarely be a factor. Human interest might occasionally be there, but for sustained emotion to exist, experiences must be commonly held, and for most readers the ghetto was as remote as the moon.

This definition of news came, in newspaper offices, to have almost the force of law. Perhaps the most succinct version of it anyone ever wrote was this: "News is anything timely that interests a number of persons, and the best news is that which has the greatest interest for the greatest number."[2] The basic criteria of judging newsworthiness thus had to do with time, and with interest on the part of masses of people. And the word "best" has to do strictly with characteristics that make the news a commodity attractive to the largest numbers possible. In this sense, newspapers are but prisoners of their human audiences, who always seem to gather in largest groups when great disasters present themselves.

But society has not always stressed time to the extent it does now, nor have there been masses of readers. The evolution of the newspaper from a small, limited circulation, very personal form of journalism into today's large, remote, something-for-everyone operation occurred as the result of two mutually nourishing trends in history: population growth and technological development. Simply put, they are people and paper.

monopolizing knowledge and keeping power

The newspaper, like most great institutions, depended for its initial growth upon a sizable audience whose members possessed similar interests and aspirations. Until there began to be a middle class, there was no real need for newspapers. For centuries, European aristocracy was small enough in numbers to keep itself informed about the doings of its membership. Having a fairly efficient system of couriers between royal houses, the governing elite needed no Rex Reed or Walter Scott to recount their comings and goings in terms suitably acerbic not to make the common folk too envious.

The great business powers of the pre- and early print eras had their own communication networks—newsletters they were called—which were very like the business letters available today at exorbitant prices to executives who want the feel of having the inside dope. Perhaps the most famous of these early intelligence reports are the Fugger News-Letters, commissioned by a great Austrian financial house, well aware that knowledge is power. Here's an example, dated November 12, 1580:

> On the report that four English ships have been confiscated in Spain the Queen of England has had four Spanish ships confiscated at Plymouth. It is believed that Spain is holding up the ships because of Captain Drake, who arrived in London a few weeks ago with a quantity of bullion. A year ago he attacked the ships on their way from New Spain, and the King of Spain demands that he be sentenced.[3]

Queen Elizabeth was not about to hang Sir Francis Drake, of course, nor was the gold returned to Spain. But the House of Fugger turned the Spanish misfortune to its own profit, since the King of Spain was the greatest debtor the financiers had, bankrupting himself twice in less than 20 years.

If the aristocracy was able, and the financial world went to the trouble to keep informed, the lower classes suffered two handicaps: they rarely could read, and they had little voice in affairs anyway. A monopoly of knowledge existed, occasioned in large part by the very scarcity of writing materials and written communication. Societies that for hundreds of years had been forced to rely upon animal skin parchment had neither need nor inclination to teach everyone to read and write. Paper-making was introduced by the East to the West around the eighth century, but it was hundreds of years before paper reached Europe, and even then it was not plentiful. The monopolists of knowledge—the government and the church—used it exclusively to record laws and religious documents. And great business used it to further itself.[4]

The two chief ingredients of the newspaper operation—paper and people—are inseparably linked. The first paper was made from rags, chiefly linen. These could only be obtained cheaply and in quantity in urban areas. Before there could be paper produced in large amounts, there had to be numbers of people, and before there could be large markets for the finished product, there had to be numbers of people who could read. It all happened slowly, over hundreds of years, though when the progression began, it eventually built tremendous pressure. In 1727, so scarce was paper and so great was the need, France forbade the export of all materials used in papermaking. Linen was so scarce in England in 1801 that a law was suggested which would forbid the burial of dead persons in any other cloth than wool, by which an estimated 250,000 pounds of linen would be saved annually. Every newspaper regularly appealed to its readers for old rags, offering to pay or trade for them. For four pounds of linen, announced a New Hampshire publisher in 1792, a reader might receive one copy of *Robinson Crusoe*. And a persistent witticism dealt with the worn out whore taking her linen underthings to sell to the papermill, where they would be turned into prayerbooks for young virgins.[5]

As late as 1800 the technology of printing was in essentially the same state it had been in for 300 years. Once rags were obtained, they had to be beaten to a pulp, which was then ladled into wire-cloth strainers to dry in sheet form. In this laborious way three men might produce a daily average of some 2000 sheets of paper 20 by 30 inches in dimensions. It was hardly mass production, and it helped keep the price of a newspaper so high that prospective buyers might well have asked, which shall it be, a copy of the paper or a pound of bacon? And the answer then as now was: if you have to ask, you can't afford it.[6]

In 1799, a Frenchman named N. L. Robert invented a machine that made paper on an endless web, thus allowing much faster production. But not until the 1840s was someone able to use wood pulp instead of rags for making paper. And wood pulp did not come to the United States until after the Civil War.

Other aspects of printing were equally slow. Type had to be imported to the colonies from England and Europe until about the time of the Revolution. Ink-making was time consuming, and dangerous, since it involved the boiling of varnish, which had a nasty habit of bubbling over and catching the whole place on fire. Presses were crude, and the whole process combined to keep the hourly press run at a little more than 100 sheets printed on both sides.

From the technological view, therefore, the key to printing as a truly mass medium of communication lay in paper. As long as it was relatively scarce, there was little need for improvements in other phases of technology. And as long as demand from the reading public might be fulfilled, there was no need for rapid and large-scale printing. But people, as today's great social problems only too well illustrate, have a way of increasing rapidly in numbers. In 1700, according to best estimates, the population of the British Isles was just under six million persons. By the time of the Revolution, there were seven and a half million, and by 1800 just over nine million. When the American Colonies gained their independence, fewer than four million souls were counted in the first census; yet by 1830 that number had grown to nearly 13 million. The people had to live in towns for newspapers really to take hold. If a town of 8000 is considered urban, then slightly more than 3 percent of the country's inhabitants were city dwellers in 1790. By 1830, the percentage had doubled as the population had tripled. And there were some good-sized towns—New York, Philadelphia, Boston, Baltimore. Even in those days before free public education, more people in one place meant more who could read, though perhaps not many more. Only about 5 percent of all the adults in New Jersey before 1830 were able to read. Admittedly low-grade urbanization, this rise in centralized readership was enough to permit the newspaper to assume most of the characteristics it has today.[7]

the modern newspaper emerges

If you picked up a newspaper and discovered that it had no banner headlines running across several columns, no photographs or other illustrations such as graphs and charts, no reports by foreign correspondents working for the news agencies, no interviews with famous persons, no reports on schools, churches or conventions, no weather reports, no columns by Ann Landers or Art Buchwald or William Buckley, no sports page, no financial section, no comics or cartoons—you would find a very thin newspaper.

Yet that is only a partial list of regular features which had not begun to appear in the newspaper of 1830. Few of us read all those features even today. But most of them are in every newspaper to greater or lesser degree, and the reason is simple: to supply items of interest to as many persons as possible. The men who used that technique to meet the convergence of more people and cheaper paper were the men who defined the shape and the content of the newspaper for the next 150 years. They were a New York printer-publisher named Ben Day and a 40-year-old failure named James Gordon Bennett.

In London, in 1832, the Society for the Diffusion of Useful Knowledge began publishing a weekly *Penny Magazine,* which actually sold for two cents. As it was a magazine, and not a newspaper, the publication escaped the high taxes that existed at that time on newspapers and that brought their price to 14 cents a copy. Within a year the *Penny Magazine* had a circulation of more than 200,000. The lesson was not lost on American printers, who got the idea of publishing cheap newspapers, since they were not taxed in the U.S. Almost immediately one-cent and two-cent papers sprouted in the population centers, New York, Philadelphia, Boston, and Baltimore. They quickly failed, however, because they offered little that was different from the usual newspaper fare of politics and long lists of merchandise for sale, and they could not hang on long enough to win readers from the established papers.[8]

Day, however, thought he saw an untapped reading public—one that was not particularly interested in moral uplift or politics but that would allow itself to be entertained. And if he attracted readers, advertisers would follow them.

So he attracted readers. He did it with a fresh, flippant style, and he stayed away from heavy politics. He hired one of his printers, George Wisner, on the proviso that Wisner get up at 4 A.M. and write up the activities of police court. Wisner did so, became the first police reporter in the U.S., and set a style of crime news reporting that exists to this day:

> William Luvoy got drunk because yesterday was so devilish warm. Drank 9 glasses of brandy and water and said he would be cursed if he wouldn't drink 9 more as quick as he could raise the money to buy it with. He would like to know what right the magistrate had to interfere with his private affairs. Fined $1—forgot his pocketbook, and was sent over to Bridewell.[9]

That kind of news treatment, so different in style and subject from the news covered by the six-cent papers, brought immediate results. In two months, Day's New York *Sun* had 2000 purchasers; in four months 5000. A year later, in the fall of 1834, Day claimed a circulation of 15,000, far surpassing any other paper in this country and, with perhaps two exceptions in London, in the world. And he bought the latest and most up-to-date presses available. The mass media had arrived.[10]

Day threw away the old prescription for newspaper content. The old formula had called for large doses of politics—which automatically excluded from the potential readership everyone of opposing convictions—and news about large events which was obtained rather unsystematically from "dispatches," meaning letters or other newspapers brought in by the mailman. But aside from the requirement that the content be exciting and breathlessly told, Day was not certain what should take the place of the old. For example, if the new criterion was maintenance of reader interest, did content have to be truthful? Not, Day answered, necessarily.

In the late summer of 1835, Day printed a series of articles copied from a "Supplement of the Edinburgh Journal of Science." The articles, taking their own good time over the next several days, began to reveal certain astronomical discoveries made in South Africa by the use of "an immense telescope on an entirely new principle." One of the research questions the telescope had "affirmatively settled" was whether the moon was inhabited, and if so, "by what orders of beings." The second installment concluded with "a glimpse of a strange amphibious creature of a spherical form, which rolled with great velocity across the pebbly beach."[11]

Competing papers, imagining themselves to be caught short, reprinted the articles in part or whole. Yale College sent a delegation down to New York to examine the supplement. But the main thing, in Day's mind, was that before the telescope suffered an injury that prevented further observations, the New York *Sun's* circulation had climbed to 19,000. And of almost equal importance, when author Richard Adams Locke got drunk with a *Journal of Commerce* reporter and confessed he had made up the whole story, the public did not seem to mind. The *Sun* sold out a pamphlet reprint, circulation continued to grow, and sometimes advertising occupied three-fourths of the paper's space.[12]

At that point, in 1837 with a circulation of 30,000, Day sold out, thus showing he had utterly failed to realize what he had stumbled onto. Failures of other penny papers impressed him, though his was truly different; he lost a libel suit; and he lost profits in a financial panic that year. Later, when it was clear to everyone that a revolution in mass communication was under way, he declared that selling out was the silliest thing he had ever done. Which shows that though a fool, he was not a complete fool.

the man who made "news"

While Day appears to have been a man of great intuition though limited vision, James Gordon Bennett comes down to us as a man whom destiny very carefully prepared for his role. What appeared to him as a series of failures up to the age of 40 take on, in retrospect, the glow of a set of assigned tasks, each one fitting him to make some innovation in the art of newspaper publishing a little later.[13]

To begin with, he emigrated from Scotland at age 25, thus bringing to his new country an adult viewpoint that helped him retain always an internationalist sense that things that happened abroad were important to this country. His first experiences in the U.S., at odd jobs, gave him a feel for the workers. His first newspaper job, for the Charleston *Courier,* involved translating from Spanish or French to English the latest news from Havana, which meant from South America and Spain. He went to New York and did hack work—writing to fit any point of view for anyone who would pay. Later he moved to Washington and did occasional pieces for the New York *Enquirer,* a pro-Jackson paper. He suggested that the editor might like a few light pieces, so he satirized the custom of handshaking and the methods of greeting of the various nations. After printing them the editor was amazed at the delight of many readers in such bright and lively accounts (though there were staid protests at the "froth" and "trash"). So in 1827 the editor made him the first full-time Washington correspondent. In addition to politics, Bennett wrote other stories, some about the growing social life of the city of 19,000. But when the paper was sold, and its support switched from Jackson to Clay, Bennett quit. Twice he tried to start his own paper and failed. A third time he attempted to set up in Philadelphia a partisan paper under the wing of some of Jackson's supporters. But they thought he would sell out to the opposition, as had others, so he had to fold that operation.

Finally, in New York, after Day would not take him on the *Sun,* Bennett began his fourth paper, in early May of 1835. The paper, he decided, would be independent of all political parties. It would entertain as well as enlighten. It would try to get accurately and quickly what people wanted to read. In his opening statement, he declared that he intended the paper for the great masses of the community: "the merchant, the mechanic, working people—the private family as well as the public hotel—the journeyman and his employer—the clerk and his principal." In short, James Gordon Bennett had found his middle class.

It took about a week for the *Herald* to catch on. Working from 5 A.M. until midnight, scrambling about to write news and editorials, read proof, sell ads when he could find buyers, Bennett watched most of his bankroll of $500 evaporate in the first few days. There were, after all, lots of other newspapers in New York, and it was difficult for the *Herald* to gain notice. Fortunately, Day's scorning of him when he had applied for work moved him to needle the *Sun.* On May 15, the *Sun* finally responded, and it was like a great light bursting through the clouds. Gleefully, Bennett joined battle, using the *Sun's* editorial columns to advertise his paper. Readers bought, and liked what they saw.

Promptly he attacked other papers to see what they would do. They humphed and harrahed, and fired back, naming names and handing out free advertising.

From then on, it was all fun and innovation. Bennett instituted what he called "the money article," based upon his daily visits to Wall Street. Whereas most other newspapers had been printing current prices, he added analysis and initiated the financial section (and won the readership of bankers, stockbrokers, and investors). He was not interested in police court, since the *Sun* had pioneered that lode, choosing instead to take up the more serious crimes and follow them to conclusion. When a young prostitute was found murdered in her chambers, he rushed to view the scene, and described the body as having the beauty of polished marble in death. Then he agitated for arrest of a suspect so loudly that police hastened to make an arrest and bring to trial a young man whose guilt, according to the other New York papers, which had been forced to follow Bennett's lead, was indisputable. Whereupon Bennett reversed himself and fought loudly for the young man's acquittal. By the time the trial opened, New York was in an uproar. "An immense multitude . . . collected in the avenues . . . round the city hall . . . rushed in and literally jammed every nook and corner" of the large courtroom, reported the New York *Transcript.* The young man was acquitted, amid charges by Bennett that police had falsified evidence and brutalized the accused.

But for Bennett, as for Day and the Moon Hoax, the important thing was that circulation had tripled.

Bennett refined the emphasis on getting the news ahead of one's competitors. This was a consequence of success of the penny papers, since more and more came into the field, and to stay ahead, Bennett needed to hustle. With Arunah Abell, publisher of the penny Baltimore *Sun,* and Daniel Craig of the Boston *Daily Mail,* he established something very like a press association. Craig would go north and meet the British ships when they made their first stop, in Nova Scotia. Then he would dispatch carrier pigeons with digests of the news, which would be relayed to New York and Baltimore. Bennett also sent out free copies of proofs of the *Herald* to newspapers in the hinterlands, thus giving them beats on their competitors. They would respond in kind with news from their areas. When the telegraph was invented, he made heavy use of it.

He expanded his coverage to sermons. Preachers disliked this at first, since they distrusted him, but because he insisted on accuracy, comprehensiveness—and prominent mention of their names—he soon won them over, along with their congregations. He decided names make news, so he covered conventions completely and he devoted columns to the doings of the socially prominent. They were aghast at first, then passive, and finally dependent on publicity.

By the time Bennett passed from the scene, he and his contemporaries had changed forever the face of journalism. He added system to what had been a rather catch-as-catch-can industry. If he did not begin it, he carried farther than any publisher the expansion of topics newspapers regularly treated. *The Man Who Made News* is the title of one biography of Bennett. And the title is apt. For all his devotion to the sensational (a "moral war" against the *Herald* by competitors and watch and ward societies forced him to give up certain techniques), he is remembered most as a journalistic innovator. And what that innovation meant more than anything else was that new ways were found to expand the audience. That was essentially the meaning of the great circulation war between William Randolph Hearst and Joseph Pulitzer 60 years later, and among the great New York dailies of the 1920s, the era of the so-called "jazz journalism."

technology rises to the occasion

And in the reach for ever larger readership, there began to be overlooked groups of people whose interests and preferences were not of the masses necessarily but whose importance was large. Thus, there were opportunities for newspapers who wished to seek the higher road, who wished to speak to more thoughtful audiences than the great mass papers could afford to address. Hence, Adolph Ochs was able to take a worn-out newspaper and build it into the mighty New York *Times.* ("When the *Daily News* prints it, it's sex," he would observe. "When *we* print it, it is sociology."[14])

And always technology kept pace, making newspapers more readable, making more of them, making it easier for more fishermen to go after the fish, making competition fiercer. But not, it should be added, making the process cheaper overall. Bennett started the *Herald* with $500. Bennett's son, largely an absentee owner, ran it into the ground and the paper was still sold after his death for $4 million. Following the Civil War, wood pulp came into general use as newsprint, and the price of paper declined from 8½ cents a pound in 1875 to 1½ cents in 1897. Yet the price soon increased—and with it the protests of politically powerful publishers—so that within a few years Theodore Roosevelt was launching a conservationist campaign with a cry that was sure to win support: "We are out of newsprint." Publishers were successful in the early 1900s in obtaining reduction, then abolition, of taxes on importation of pulp and newsprint from Canada.[15] They have been less successful since. Newsprint has climbed steadily in price until today its acquisition is the chief topic of discussion at every meeting of the American Newspaper Publishers Association. The acuteness of the current problem is well illustrated by the corporate structures of the largest and most successful contemporary newspapers. The New York Times Company for years saw most of its profits come from the news-print production companies it owned. The Chicago *Tribune* owns forests in Canada and paper mills, and the Times Mirror Company owns acres and acres of timberland and a $90 million paper mill in Oregon for its Los Angeles *Times.* Time Inc. is joint owner of a $31 million mill in Louisiana. Today's publishing conglomerate simply cannot afford to be without its very own source of supply.[16]

Likewise the growth of the printing press parallels both the increases in population and in newspaper circulation. First steam, then electricity, was applied to presses, and before the century was out presses were being grafted onto presses to make faster runs of large papers. From a system of printing sheet after sheet, the press was perfected to use an endless web of paper spinning out from giant rolls. By the last decade of the century presses were able to print 24,000 24-page papers in an hour. Naturally, methods of setting type more quickly became the life studies of numerous mechanics. Mark Twain invested nearly $200,000 in a typesetting machine; it would, he said, do everything but drink, swear, and go on strike. Unfortunately, it would not set type, and Twain spent the next several years feverishly writing himself out of debt. Finally a former watchmaker's apprentice from Germany, Ottmar Mergenthaler, devised a successful typesetting machine. Called the Linotype, it endured without major revision in principle for nearly 100 years, until doomed to obsolesence by electronics and photo-typesetting.

And the other inventions that made newspaper publishing faster and more elegant—stereotyping, engraving, the typewriter—followed one after the other in the last quarter of the last century, after the development of cheaper paper and after the realization that huge audiences might be congealed into one readership by applying a news definition that put the interests of the readers ahead of the interest of the publisher. And most of it went back to Day and to Bennett.

systemizing news gathering

The trends of expanding audiences and advancing technology created the need for faster and more efficient collection of copy. One way to do this was through use of the typewriter, but there were other, more subtle ways which had more influence upon the development of newspapers. One of these was the reporter's beat system. Strictly a matter of convenience, the beat system emphasized a geographical approach to writing news. The city hall reporter, for example, covered all news coming out of the offices there. Never mind that the story would have roots in a neighborhood, and would go on to touch people's lives long after the city had acted. The story was not news until it came to and was acted on by city hall. News thus was shaped by the demands of geography upon the newspaper staff. Competition was another factor influencing the development of the concept of news. In days when there were several newspapers in a city, every reporter was haunted by the fear that his opposition would get the story ahead of him. Such fear led reporters into errors based upon too hastily collected and too little digested information. A third consequence has come to be known as the daily news cycle, which tends to order all happenings according to the publishing requirements of the paper, which in turn were based chiefly upon transportation schedules of the trucks, trains, and children that carried the printed papers to the readers.

Tradition, once established, is very difficult to change; the tendency has been for the news tradition to be carried over into other media, such as broadcasting and news magazines. Any newspaper today carries almost as many examples of the daily news cycle, the beat system, and the competitive tradition as it carries news stories. But to illustrate all three of these in action, we choose an example from the two great agencies that provide most nonlocal news for newspapers—the wire services.

The Associated Press and United Press International, since they are disputing over a limited number of customers, are highly competitive. So much so, in fact, that their products—news from the four corners of the earth—are indistinguishable to all save the most expert professional newsmen. (As Bennett's competitors illustrated, and as today's television networks prove anew each season, competition breeds like, not unlike.)

On June 25, 1962, the Supreme Court of the United States handed down what has come to be known as the school prayer decision. That decision was immediately misconstrued on a large scale, and the misconstruction in large measure may be traced to the demands placed upon news gathering by the daily cycle. Of course, there was also the ever-present factor of people who were just too wrapped up in worlds of their own making to assimilate any truth contradicting their own.

Take a look at the first AP and UPI stories on the decision, hastily written in a fiercely competitive situation where success over the other fellow is measured in minutes.[17]

The "bulletin," or first notice of the decision, attempted to summarize the story in a few words. A few minutes later, after other competing news stories were given brief access to the "A wire" or main news channel of the wire services, it was the school prayer story's turn again. This time came a "first add," which presented additional information hastily drafted by the reporters covering the story. An hour and a half later, the "first lead," or first rewritten version of the original material, was sent out. Neither wire service gave details of the case until those later versions.

THE ASSOCIATED PRESS

11:54 a.m.—Bulletin
Washington, June 25 (AP)—The Supreme Court ruled today the offering of a 22-word daily prayer in New York State's public schools violates the U.S. Constitution.

12:02 p.m.—First add
Five parents with children in schools in New Hyde Park, N.Y., had questioned the practice as a violation of the principle of separation of church and state.

New York State's Board of Regents, the governing body of the public school system, recommended that this prayer be spoken in school opening exercises:

"Almighty God, we acknowledge our dependence upon Thee and we beg Thy blessings upon us, our parents, our teachers and our country."

Justice Black wrote the court majority opinion which declared:

"We think that by using its public school system to encourage recitation of the regent's prayer, the State of New York has adopted a practice wholly inconsistent with the establishment clause" of the U.S. Constitution.

The First Amendment to the Constitution commands that "Congress shall make no law respecting an establishment of religion."

Justice Stewart wrote a dissenting opinion which declared "the Court has misapplied a great constitutional principle."

Stewart added, "I cannot see how an 'official religion' is established by letting those who want to say a prayer say it. On the contrary, I think that to

UNITED PRESS INTERNATIONAL

11:58 a.m.—Bulletin
Washington, June 25 (UPI)—The Supreme Court ruled today that daily recital of an official state prayer in public schools, even though non-compulsory, offends the religious freedom guarantees in the Constitution.

11:58 a.m.—First add
The 6-1 decision came in a New York case but will affect many thousands of schools throughout the country.

12:10 p.m.—Second add
Justice Hugo L. Black wrote the court's decision. The dissenter was Justice Potter Stewart. Justices Felix Frankfurter and Byron R. White did not participate.

Black said "It has been argued that to apply the Constitution in such a way as to prohibit state laws respecting an establishment of religious services in public schools is to indicate a hostility toward religion or toward prayer."

"Nothing, of course, could be more wrong," he said.

But he added: "It is neither sacrilegious nor anti-religious to say that each separate government in this country should stay out of the business of writing or sanctioning official prayers and leave that purely religious function to the people themselves and to those the people choose to look to for religious guidance." . . .

12:29 p.m.—First lead
By Charlotte G. Moulton
Washington, June 25 (UPI)—The Supreme Court ruled today that the

daily recital of an official state prayer in public schools is unconstitutional because it violates the religious freedom guaranteed in the Bill of Rights . . .

1:18 p.m.—Second lead
By Charlotte G. Moulton
Washington, June 25 (UPI)—The Supreme Court ruled today that it is unconstitutional to have public school children recite official state prayers as a daily exercise . . .

deny the wish of these school children to join in reciting this prayer is to deny them the opportunity of sharing in the spiritual heritage of our nation."

Justice Douglas wrote an opinion concurring with the majority.

Justices White and Frankfurter took no part.

The Court's vote was thus 6-1.

1:39 p.m.—First lead
Washington, June 25 (AP)—The Supreme Court ruled 6-1 today that New York State sponsorship of a 22-word daily prayer for recitation in public schools violates the U.S. Constitution . . .

The reaction to this news was instantaneous, and the wire services picked up a lot of it, as did individual newspapers across the country. And following logically from the fact that the context of the decision had not been properly set, most of the comment was uninformed. Congressman George Andrews of Alabama asserted: "They put the Negroes in the schools and now they've taken God out of them." Dr. Billy Graham observed, "This is another step toward the secularization of the United States." Francis Cardinal Spellman was "shocked and frightened," while the general counsel of the American Jewish Congress was "highly gratified" by the decision. A great deal of editorial furor generated still more dismay, and in many quarters yet the first impression prevails, that the Court was outlawing all religious practices in schools. But the facts of the case were such that had they been included in initial news stories of the decision, many people who hotly denounced the decision probably would have supported it. For the situation was that state-employed teachers were given strong suggestion by the state to have their pupils recite in unison every day a state-written prayer. Under these circumstances, the decision was a victory *for* freedom of religion, not against it. Yet there remains to this day many a fundamentalist convinced that the Supreme Court is out to turn him into a Godless atheist. In failing to counter the swiftly moving misconceptions their own bulletins helped foster, the wire services thus fell victims to the negative aspects of the news ethic with its demand for speed and competition. And as late as fall of 1971, the U.S. House of Representatives was having to vote—when surely it had better things to do—on a constitutional amendment that would have "permitted prayer in schools."

The wire services should not be singled out for blame. They

simply behaved according to their competitive nature, just as Mr. Daniel Craig used to do when he scribbled a digest of the news from London, strapped it to the leg of a pigeon, and sent it south. Moreover, the beat system, designed to be efficient, performed so efficiently that the reporters assigned to the Court got their 16 decisions that day, but got them largely out of the blue, since the beat system tends to be set up more from geographical than topical considerations. The reporters covering the Court that day were not specialists in religious or education news who had followed the case since it was first filed. They were experts in the news ethic.

And lastly, as a result of the requirements of the daily news cycle, the story was dropped well before the erroneous impression of the early accounts could be thoroughly corrected.

We have more advanced technology, and we reach more people, but for too long our newspapers have been shackled by a concept of news that was originated to win audiences, not to keep them.

how are we to know truth?

Truth can be dissected in several ways, just as Disraeli was able to distinguish between "lies, damned lies, and statistics." First there is a distinction to be made on the basis of completeness—"truth, the whole truth, and nothing but the truth." Then there are different sources of truth: mystical revelation, rational consensus, or observable fact.

Revealed truth is the foundation of many of our religious beliefs. Rational or consensual truth is what we agree upon for the sake of convenience, policy, or common sense. For example, we accept as useful truth the idea that north lies in one direction and south in the opposite, and that days are divisible by hours. We have a policy consensus (with some dissent) that space exploration is worthwhile. Factual or objective truth, on the other hand, merely notes the appearance and disappearance of the sun at the horizons, and that astronauts leave earth by means of rocket-powered missiles.

It's human nature, and to some extent media nature, to mix these approaches to truth. However, in its strictest form, the news ethic demands that they be kept separate, and that news stories just stick to objective facts.

Thus, a major frustration with objective news is its apparent incompleteness. Facts tell the truth, but not always the whole truth. Though accurate, news stories often yield as many questions as answers.

Walter Lippmann wrote in 1922 that "news is not a mirror of social conditions, but the report of an aspect that has obtruded itself."

The bulk of the iceberg can go unreported, though its outcropping will be surveyed in detail. What can happen is illustrated by Ben H. Bagdikian:

> Under the strictest versions of the doctrine of objectivity, it would have been possible for the first-century reporter to describe accurately and at length the plight of lions being starved in the Roman Colosseum, together with official data on the decalcification of lion bones and other evidence of metabolic harm to animals, and if all the facts were accurate and properly attributed to the responsible officials, to meet the requirements of strict objectivity. But it would still omit the important fact that the lions were being starved in order to increase their appetites for human martyrs, whose deaths might never be reported.[18]

If objectivity is next to godliness, as many editors insist, then the camera should be nominated for sainthood. But instead we find J. Russell Wiggins, former editor of the Washington *Post* and ambassador to the United Nations, remarking that "It has been said that the camera does not lie. But the camera does lie. It is a notorious, compulsive, unashamed and mischievous liar."

Wiggins was wrong. News photographs are paragons of objectivity, accurate to a fault. Barring knavery in the darkroom, the photograph is a most literal truth-teller. The subject of a photograph can complain that lighting, camera angle, and cropping make him look dishonest and sinister. But precisely at that moment this is exactly how he appeared to the camera.

The fault is typical of strict objectivity; it is not in failing to tell the truth, but in stopping short of the whole truth. Pictures are accurate as far as they go; by themselves they don't go far. The limited truth entices the beholder to fill in the gaps, and here the lying begins. Is it the picture's lie or the viewer's? (Photos might even be accused of creating an information *deficit*—each requires a caption by way of explanation. And is a picture worth the proverbial 10,000 words? A wily old journalist, Herbert Jacobs, once calculated that the average newspaper picture, about 36 square inches in size, is "worth" 987 words —it displaces a news story of that length.)

A news photo is so narrowly truthful it invites the charge of chicanery. We distinguish here between photojournalism that provides the coherent clusters of pictures in magazines such as *Life*—these come closer to completeness in reporting—and the typical solitary-traveling newspaper photograph. Out of a long-smoldering event, which 1/250th of a second should the news photographer and his editor select? It's a tough enough problem for the word reporter, according to Wes Gallagher, general manager of the Associated Press:

Consider the problem of trying to write about the recent [1968] teachers' strike in New York which has involved all of the following: anti-Semitism by blacks, racial prejudice by whites, teachers concerned with their security, parents concerned with their children's education, a struggle for power between a powerful union and the board of education, another struggle among state education officials, the union, the city board and the local boards, charges of police brutality, counter charges of attacks on the police, a police slow-down during the teachers' strike, a power struggle by a Democratic city council against a Republican mayor and scores of local school confrontations.[19]

With luck and genius the news photographer can perform small and shining miracles. But he is always faced with Edward R. Murrow's question: "Most news is made up of what happens in men's minds, as reflected in what comes out of their mouths. And how do you put that in pictures?"

Most news photographers don't even try. Their editors want "impact." Even more than the pencil reporter, the photographer is encouraged to steer toward the largest flotsam in the stream of events.

As a consequence, the news photo is definitely disaster-prone —and rewarded for its bruises. In late 1968, Associated Press Newsfeatures circulated a selection of the 10 "greatest pictures" of the previous 30 years. Four of the 10 showed a person in the act of dying (Lee Harvey Oswald, a Buddhist monk, a woman falling from a burning hotel, and a Vietcong prisoner being shot in the head). Eight involved wars hot and cold, six contained men in uniform, and two depicted warships exploding and sinking.

Focusing as they did on crests of violence (the fairest game of all for a visual medium), the "greatest" pictures were mute on other aspects of three decades. They said nothing about Hitler, atomic energy, space exploration, biochemistry, ecumenicism, art, poverty, pollution, blacks, estranged youth, to name a few disparate topics. To be sure, other pictures, by the thousand, have treated these topics. The point is that greatness in pictorial reporting seems attached to bloody spectacle.

Prizes for word reporting tend to go in the same direction; in 1968 *Newsweek* observed, "Over the past ten years the Pulitzer judges have given half the prizes in the general-reporting category to stories about gun battles, floods and plane-crashes—the kind of surface news that was paramount in the '20s but largely irrelevant today. Stories about local graft and politicians consorting with gamblers are always strong candidates."

A recent anecdote holds that if a modern-day Moses descended from Mount Sinai, he'd be met by the lights and cameras of television crews. That night one of the items on the evening news would begin something like this: "In the Middle East today, Moses came down from Mount Sinai with Ten Commandments. The top three were . . ."

the "new" journalism—changing the news ethic

For those to whom the news ethic and its defects seemed not only sterile but misleading, the "new journalism" arrived on the scene in the late 1960s. Ranging in form from what Truman Capote described as the "nonfiction novel" to the outrageously wild put-on of the underground press, the new journalism within half a dozen years had heavily influenced reporting, and showed signs of bringing new life to traditional journalism.

The new journalism's severest critics—who were usually to be found dug in behind Fort Objectivity on the Plain of Facts—charged the new technique with being subjective and dangerous. A few said it was neither new nor journalism. In a way all these criticisms were correct, but only in the way that a match may be considered a deadly weapon. If used to start an apartment house fire, it can kill; if used to light a candle, it can illuminate the darkness.

Essentially, the new journalism brought to (or back to) traditional journalism the form and technique of the fiction writer. Thus, Gay Talese, in describing the operations of the New York *Times,* put himself inside the head of the editor, Clifton Daniel. Truman Capote did the same in recording the motivations of two murderers in Kansas. Suddenly the journalist as the off-to-one-side observer was gone, and the reporter-participant was in his place, filtering and telling the reader so outright. Tom Wolfe was adjusting his whole writing style, so that when he described a southern moonshiner, he didn't just let the man speak for himself, as traditional reporting would require. Wolfe adopted the language of the region for the entire article, much as the fiction writer adjusts his style to the style of the character being created: "working mash wouldn't wait for a man. It started coming to a head when it got ready to and a man had to be there to take it off, out there in the woods. . . ." It was not the rhythm of an eastern big-city journalist, which Wolfe was, but the folksy meandering of Ingle Hollow, North Carolina.

The public loved it. Capote's *In Cold Blood,* Talese's *The Kingdom and the Power,* and Wolfe's *The Kandy-Kolored Tangerine-Flake Streamline Baby* were best-sellers, reprinted many times, imitated, awarded, imitated, denounced, analyzed, imitated, and above all, imitated.

But danger clearly existed in the new form when it was carried to extreme. Some people saw the distinctions between *accuracy* and *truth* in a way that was unfavorable to accuracy. Ray Mungo, founder of the Liberation News Service, and an editor of an underground newspaper, could see accuracy in the casualty reports from Vietnam, but not a grain of truth. The truth he got from the Boston *Avatar's* article by Alexander Sorenson on torture in a Vietnamese village. Yet Sorenson did not exist, Mungo discovered, and the torture he described never in fact happened. It was still truth, argued Mungo, because it has happened in man's history and because the U.S. was responsible for it happening in Vietnam. Which goes back to what we said earlier about how we all rely not only upon ascertainable fact but upon revealed truth as well. Mungo's revealed truth may suit him but seem pessimistic to others. In ascertainable fact there is a meeting ground.

Yet unquestionably there is much that can only be felt, and can never be ascertained. This is where the new journalism draws its strength, and the writer must pull from within himself the threads of emotional reaction which create an impact on the reader. And the story may be no less true because the writer has tried to duplicate his feelings on paper.

Newspapers often have been credited with influencing magazines. *Time* editor Otto Friedrich, for example, in attempting to explain the success of magazines like *Time, Newsweek,* and *U.S. News & World Report,* gives a large share of the credit to an American (and Western) obsession for facts, as cultivated and harvested by the newspapers. Even spurious facts are used, Friedrich observed, in noting how one news magazine sought to convince its readers of a larger premise by presenting bushels of "facts." The writer needed—or thought he did—an estimate of the size of Russian forests. Away went his researcher to the U.S. Department of Agriculture, where she learned that an average acre of forest contained so many trees. Next to the Soviet government, where she discovered how many acres were officially listed as forest in the USSR. Quick multiplication and presto!: the number of trees in Russia.[20] But often overlooked is the extent to which magazines have influenced newspapers. And the new journalism is a good example.

So the news ethic continues subtly to change. If economics helped dictate its development, economics will influence its shift. In the 1930s, fearing that radio would kill newspaper street sales and "extra" editions put out when some great news event occurred, publishers tried to suppress radio news. They wheedled an agreement from the radio networks that only two news shows would be aired each day, and both were to be scheduled after completion of newspaper street sales in the morning and at night. That was a false step, of course. Radio's ability to gather and distribute news instantaneously was too great to be ignored. The agreement soon fell apart, newspaper street sales dwindled, and the "extra" died completely. Papers had to let radio do what it might do best, while they pursued lines of action best suited to print: lengthy coverage, details, interpretation, and analysis.

But perhaps the key observation about news is one that offers hope for the future of newspapers as well as the reading public. If editors and publishers can remember that news itself is not so much a commodity subject to precise definition as it is a way of looking at the world, they will continue to find their places in these changing times.

for further reading

Cater, Douglass. *The Fourth Branch of Government.* Boston: Houghton Mifflin, 1959.

Chafee, Zechariah. *Government and Mass Communications.* Chicago: University of Chicago Press, 1947.

Charnley, Mitchell V. *Reporting,* 2nd ed. New York: Holt, Rinehart and Winston, 1966.

Cohen, Bernard C. *The Press and Foreign Policy.* Princeton, N.J.: Princeton University Press, 1963.

Kendrick, Alexander. *Prime Time: The Life of Edward R. Murrow.* New York: Avon, 1969.

Lippmann, Walter. *Public Opinion.* New York: Harcourt, Brace & World, 1922.

Lyons, Louis M., ed. *Reporting the News.* Cambridge, Mass.: Harvard University Press, 1965.

MacNeil, Robert. *The People Machine.* New York: Harper & Row, 1968.

Nimmo, Dan D. *Newsgathering in Washington.* New York: Atherton Press, 1964.

Reston, James. *The Artillery of the Press.* New York: Harper & Row, 1967.

Rivers, William L. *The Adversaries.* Boston: Beacon Press, 1970.

Rothstein, Arthur. *Photojournalism: Pictures for Magazines and Newspapers.* New York: American Photographic Book Publishing Co., 1956.

Rourke, Francis E. *Secrecy & Publicity.* Baltimore: Johns Hopkins Press, 1961.

Small, William. *To Kill a Messenger.* New York: Hastings House, 1970.

the peculiarities of freedom

truth and falsehood grapple!
cast of thousands!

Free speech is the right to shout "theater" in a crowded fire.
—Abbie Hoffman

Abetted by technology, economics, and ingenuity, the fundamental need to communicate led society to devise mass communication. Many would agree with Dr. Frankenstein that it was a pretty good monster until it got free. But from the monster's point of view, freedom is everything.

In 1954, William Gaines, publisher of comic books, appeared before a special Senate subcommittee on juvenile delinquency. He was questioned by committee counsel and by the chairman, Senator Estes Kefauver. Here is part of the testimony:

Counsel: There would be no limit actually to what you put in the magazines?

Mr. Gaines: Only within the bounds of good taste.

Counsel: Your own good taste and salability?

Mr. Gaines: Yes.

Senator Kefauver: Here is your May 22 issue. This seems to be a man with a bloody ax holding a woman's head up which has been severed from her body. Do you think that is in good taste?

Mr. Gaines: Yes, sir; I do, for the cover of a horror comic. A cover in bad taste, for example, might be defined as holding the head a little higher so that the neck could be seen dripping blood from it and moving the body over a little further so that the neck of the body could be seen to be bloody.

Senator Kefauver: You have blood coming out of her mouth.

Mr. Gaines: A little.

The nonchalance of Gaines's testimony and the violence of his magazines owed largely to the same thing: a libertarian media system in which the mass communicator and his audience are generally free from restraint.

As time and the world go, libertarianism is a rare thing. Relatively few countries—most of them economically advanced—have a press that can be called free by our standards.[1] In only a bit less than half of the 500 years of its existence has the Anglo-American press been largely unrestrained.

It probably occurred to Gaines's listeners that free expression is not always good expression, and that communication can be harmful. Historically, this chilly thought has flitted through many minds, and when it occurs to persons of power, the result is usually an authoritarian media system in which the press is closely regulated by government. As historian Fred S. Siebert has observed, authoritarianism "is the theory which was almost automatically adopted by most countries when society and technology became sufficiently developed to produce what today we call 'mass media' of communication."[2]

The reasoning behind authoritarianism is straightforward: Those who have power are inclined to keep it; knowledge is power, and mass communication distributes knowledge. Or, alternatively, it is the duty of established authority to keep information away from persons who may misuse it or be corrupted by it. Little wonder that the Archbishop of Mainz was concerned that printers were translating the Bible from Latin into German; the job of "correct" interpretation belonged to the disciplined priests who upheld the Church, and not to the rabble.

Of course, the absolute monarch need not justify his actions. Power is enough. It's in the nature of *his* freedom to command and be heeded. For that matter, any absolutely free person does not have to rationalize his freedom; he can do as he pleases.

media theories: reality and philosophy

But as a practical matter there is no absolute freedom. Any despot of consequence must delegate powers to a bureaucracy and rely on allegiances. Similarly, no individual is free from physical needs and social ties. And where absolutes topple, philosophers prosper.

Philosophically, authoritarianism and libertarianism must deal with such questions as the nature of man, the relationship between man and society, and the nature of truth. If, for example, one views the man on the street as vulnerable to chicanery and falsehood, as dependent on society for self-realization and truth as possessed by a select few, then one is tempted to assign authoritarian powers to a wise elite that will decide the proper limits of mass communication.

But if man is regarded as rational enough to map his own destiny (with a little help, few strings attached, from society) and capable of figuring out the truth for himself, then he deserves a libertarian social system with great freedom to communicate.

Rich lodes of rhetoric are available to both the authoritarian and libertarian philosopher. For example, the authoritarian might be pleased with this:

> And as for regulating the press, let no man think to have the honor of advising ye [Parliament] better than yourselves have done . . . "that no book be printed unless the printer's and the author's name, or at least the printer's, be registered." Those which otherwise come forth, if they be found mischievous and libellous, the fire and the executioner will be the timeliest and the most effectual remedy that man's prevention can use.

To which the libertarian will surely retort:

> And though all the winds of doctrine were let loose to play upon the earth, so Truth be in the field, we do injuriously by licensing and prohibiting to misdoubt her strength. Let her and Falsehood grapple; who ever knew Truth put to the worse in a free and open encounter?

As it happens, both quotations come from the same source: John Milton's noble *Areopagitica,* a speech before Parliament in 1644. He was not being sly or hypocritical. He had in mind a certain brand of Protestant truth for which he wished unfettered printing. To him Roman Catholic pronouncements were not the truth but odious opinions, unworthy of circulation. In 1651 Milton became an official censor of newsbooks.

This should serve as a reminder that philosophers, like the rest of us, are affected by the real world. "The ideals of freedom, justice, representation, consent, law," Walter Lippmann has noted, "are of the earth, earthy." Milton wrote about freedom for practical reasons. Parliament was trying to suppress two treatises he had written in favor of divorce—a topic he found congenial because he wanted a divorce.

At any rate, Milton did not make a dent in the licensing laws, which remained in force until 1694 when the House of Commons permitted them to die, only slightly mourned, for reasons of expediency. In its later years, licensing was difficult to enforce—printers were numerous and restive—and the government was settling into a two-party system following the revolution of 1688. Each faction wished to preserve its partisan press and lacked the power to restrain that of the opposition. In killing the licensing act, Commons said nothing about the principle of freedom of the press.[3]

Through the 18th century, as it grew in practice if not in theory, press freedom owed a great deal to the weakening of the Crown and Church, to the rise in power of a commercial class (which included publishers), to the evolution of democracy, and to the questing nature of science. In short, centralized authority was crumbling, and smaller entities were picking up the pieces. It might be suggested that libertarianism is authoritarianism diluted and distributed—every man his own king, and each kingdom too weak to prevail over others.

The rhetoric of freedom, dormant since Milton, was to enjoy a revival. In the 18th-century Enlightenment, men felt themselves free to explore what they considered the "natural laws" implied by Newtonian physics and abducted by John Locke and Adam Smith to other fields. One great Truth was thought to lurk behind all of nature and society, and it was no one's personal property. Government, therefore, could not restrict the "natural" right to speak or print.

But authority did not shatter to atoms. Sizable factions remained: government, religion, and political and economic interests. Each enforced controls—threats, subsidies, and patronage, for example —upon its partisan press. The American colonial printer Isaiah Thomas was to remark, "One of my profession must be either of one party or the other (he cannot please both); he must therefore incur censure of the opposite party . . . though caressed and encouraged by others. . . ."[4]

But diversity of interests meant variety in journalism. In 1733 the new class of merchants in New York grew bitter under government restrictions. The only newspaper in town, the New York *Gazette,* was subsidized by the administration. The merchants therefore hired their own printer, John Peter Zenger, to publish their views, which were discomfiting to Governor William Cosby. In November 1734, Zenger was charged with sedition. According to the law of the time, it was a clear case against Zenger. The jury could only determine whether he had published the words; the judge would determine if the words constituted seditious libel, and he was hand-picked by the governor. Zenger's attorney, the elderly Andrew Hamilton of Philadelphia, admitted that his client was indeed the publisher, but he further argued that the jury —not the judge—should decide whether the words were seditious. His argument was eloquent and libertarian, and smacked a bit of Milton. The result was acquittal for Zenger—and no effect upon the law of sedition. As University of Michigan professor John D. Stevens has remarked of Zenger's victory, "It had about as much impact on American law as the Boston Tea Party had on American etiquette. Political impact, yes; legal impact, no."[5] The contending factions had fought to a standoff. Zenger was free, and though the law remained intact, no colonial court after 1735 attempted to prosecute for seditious libel.

The kind of freedom that results from stalemated power is not the most elegantly contrived, but it is real and can culminate in statements of principle.

Philosophers are typically Monday-morning quarterbacks, reconstructing the shambles of reality, full of this-is-why, should-have-been, and ought-to-be. Thus the Bill of Rights, guaranteeing personal and press freedom, was "more the chance product of political expediency on all sides than of principled commitment to personal liberties," as historian Leonard Levy has written.[6] Antifederalists saw the strong national government proposed by the Constitution as a threat to their interests. To head off another convention, which might undo their Constitution, the Federalists promised that a Bill of Rights would be added. Although many other Federalists were willing to renege on the promise, Virginia's James Madison insisted that Congress adopt a Bill of Rights and transmit it to the states for ratification.

Madison believed it fortunate that much of the opposition to the Constitution was concerned with civil liberties such as freedom of speech, press, and religion, and the right to trial by jury. To Madison, such civil liberties were not the most important consideration. He evidently felt that the stronger central government that the Constitution would provide was the essential ingredient for good government. Madison correctly guessed that a Bill of Rights protecting the liberties of citizens from central government would stop the clamor for a second constitutional convention. With a Bill of Rights, objections could be quelled, said Madison, without "endangering any part of the Constitution."

Thus we were bequeathed a Bill of Rights that begins, "Congress shall make no law respecting an establishment of religion, or prohibiting the free exercise thereof; or abridging the freedom of speech or of the press. . . ."

Despite the less-than-lofty origins of philosophical positions, they often provide a distillation of the better parts of reality. As historian Merrill Jensen has noted,

> The Bill of Rights was thus the product of eighteenth-century politics, but the ideals it expressed were centuries old then, and are ever-new today. However cynical the motives of the politicians, enough of the American people welcomed the Bill of Rights to make it an enduring part of the Constitution within two years of its submission to the states. And although the Bill of Rights is sometimes ignored or evaded, it remains an ideal for which people may strive in the twentieth century, as in the eighteenth.[7]

what does freedom mean?

No one has satisfactorily defined freedom. The first meaning that comes to mind is the riddance of restraint. Thus, "Congress shall make no law. . . ." Or, from Thomas Hobbes, "Liberty or freedom, signifieth (properly) the absence of opposition." So far, so good; freedom is a negative, hands-off idea. We are free when restraints are removed.

Or are we? It is in human nature to act, to do something. Philosopher William Hocking remarked that the "positive kernel of freedom lies in the ability to achieve the end." It's not enough, then, to be negatively free. "Tell an unprovisioned man lost in the desert," Hocking continued, "that he is free to eat, drink, bathe, read, pitch a tent . . . : no one is hindering him! . . . Unrestraint without equipment is not liberty for any end which demands equipment."[8]

Is it only power and equipment that set a person free? Again, no. Walter Lippmann, paraphrasing Montesquieu, adds: "We are free if we have the faculty of knowing what we *ought* to do and the will to do it." But if we do only what we ought, aren't we restrained? Mustn't there be freedom to do wrong? To act or not to act? Locke urged that liberty means "the power a man has to do or forbear doing any particular action."

Locke's mixed brand of freedom is especially attractive to the media. It means that a TV network could virtually ignore the hundreds of thousands who marched on Washington on November 15, 1969, to protest the war in Vietnam—and also could broadcast "Hunger in America" and "The Selling of the Pentagon." Media freedom also brings us *Hercules and the Masked Rider,* the Man From Glad, *The Love Machine,* and the Del Rio evangelist who urges us to send a dollar for "prayer handkerchiefs, individually blessed." Freedom also means the ability to publish the stolen Pentagon Papers, to remain silent on their source, to republish them in book form, and to make a profit.

Freedom to seek an audience means freedom to find the dollar: "Masscomm is preoccupied [with] making money," media critic W. H.

Ferry has asserted. "Masscomm's delight in the shoddy, the tasteless, the mind-dulling, the useless, is well-established. It is a direct consequence of masscomm's allegiance to organized rapacity," he continued.

As for the downtrodden, Ferry said, "Americans found out about poverty when two or three angry young men pulled back a blanket of ignorance and neglect and uncovered 40 million or so Americans living in degradation. The invisible poor discovered by Michael Harrington were invisible because masscomm didn't care. Masscomm was busy elsewhere, counting profits, celebrating the status quo, selling rubbish."[9]

But freedom—alas for polemic—is not that simple. Ferry neglects to mention that Harrington "pulled back the covers" by means of mass communication: a book called *The Other America.* Others, too, have tugged at the covers—in *Wealth and Power in America, Let Us Now Praise Famous Men, The Grapes of Wrath,* and the whole tradition of muckraking.

Freedom is a curious, mixed-up thing. It means that:
- Abbie Hoffman could write his *Steal This Book.*
- Thirty publishers could refuse to accept it.
- Hoffman could publish it through his own company—Pirate Editions, Inc.—and that Grove Press could distribute it.
- Many newsdealers and bookstores were free not to sell it; and that others accepted it.
- All the major newspapers in the country, with the exception of the San Francisco *Chronicle,* could refuse to advertise it.
- The New York *Times* Advertising Acceptability Department could tell Hoffman it does not accept advertising for books that advocate illegal acts.
- A review of the book in the New York *Times* could report that the New York *Times* would not accept the advertisement.
- No one had to buy or read the book.
- The book was able to become a best seller.

how much freedom?

Obviously freedom is imperfect. It is invariably limited by oneself, by others, and by sheer circumstance, as we noted in Chapter 2 regarding the gatekeeper and his environment. And although government control is milder today than when Henry VIII executed three persons for "erronious opinions," some regulation remains, even in libertarian nations.

Government can act both positively and negatively toward the press, and sometimes with a mixture of both, and it has done so from historic times to the present. The first acts of government were positive, after an initial period of indifference. In 1484, not long after William Caxton introduced printing to England, the Crown encouraged foreign printers to cross the Channel. But by 1523 a ceiling was put on the number of alien apprentices, and in 1534 importation of foreign books was halted altogether when domestic printers complained of being hurt by competition. Similarly, and much more recently, the Federal Communications Act of 1934, still in force, was designed "so as to make available . . . to all the people of the United States a rapid, efficient, Nation-wide, and world-wide wire and radio communication service. . . ." But the Act also limits majority ownership of a station to United States citizens.

Licensing, too, dates from Henry VIII, and was a source of Milton's gorgeous rage. Today, broadcast stations are licensed by the Federal Communications Commission. Print media are not licensed except for ordinary business permits. Some local censorship persists, especially over obscenity, and the Federal Trade Commission and equivalent state and local agencies attempt to suppress false and misleading advertising, and require labeling on food and drug packages, among other things. Libel remains as a restraint on free expression, though the threat of libel is diminishing, especially as regards public officials. (See Chapter 15.)

Not all regulation is repugnant to mass communicators. It was the broadcasters themselves, not government, who in the 1920s asked Secretary of Commerce Herbert Hoover to allocate channels. Licensing was not unattractive to the early English printers who enjoyed a monopoly and wanted to protect it, and recently the American Newspaper Publishers Association successfully supported the Newspaper Preservation Act, which legalizes monopolies in certain situations. The media treasure the law of copyright, a direct descendant of Elizabethan licensing, which is both a potent limitation on expression and a protection of it.

Although mass communicators argue in favor of freedom of expression, their behavior toward it, like the concept itself, is decidedly mixed. When Frank Stanton, president of CBS, was threatened with contempt of Congress, many media units (but not all) rose to his defense. When Mark Knops, publisher of an underground newspaper, *Kaleidoscope,* was found in contempt by a Wisconsin court and sent to jail, hardly any major media expressed concern. In the early 1930s, a scurrilous newspaper in Minneapolis, *The Saturday Press,* was suppressed under what was known as the Minnesota "gag law." Perceiving a threat in such laws to all newspapers, Colonel Robert McCormick of the Chicago *Tribune* financed an appeal to the Supreme Court. The decision went in favor of *The Saturday Press* and meant that the First

Amendment—which up to that time limited only the Federal government—applied to state laws as well. But in California in 1968, when a newsboy selling underground papers was chased away by local police, a suburban newspaper editorially applauded: "Credit goes to the persons who showed enough interest to contact the police department about [the] psychedelic newsboy. . . . We hope a way can be found to prevent a reappearance by this boy or some other hippie-type from making sales from our streets. The hippies we can do without." And despite freedom of the press, newspapers are closed by strikes and lockouts.

Even if governmental control is weak, self-restraint remains. The gatekeeper makes choices for both practical and ethical reasons. The New York *Times* withheld what it knew about the planned Cuban Bay of Pigs invasion, and the *Times* and the Washington *Post* knew and withheld the fact that the United States was conducting surveillance flights over the Soviet Union in 1960. In both cases disclosure might have averted disaster, but the editors were not clairvoyant.

The wisdom of foresight encouraged the media to engage in rigorous self-censorship during World War II—aided by official secrecy, of course. The American press eagerly accepted the guidelines set down by the Office of Censorship. If anything, the media engaged in excessive self-suppression. According to Theodore Koop, an executive of the censorship office, "So firmly had the idea of checking with a government authority been implanted in the minds of radio and newspapermen that it was difficult for them to reconvert to peacetime freedom. No Aesop is needed to draw the moral."[10] After the war, the director of censorship was awarded a special Pulitzer Prize for his work.

Freedom of expression ebbs and flows. In England and America, the long-term trend has been libertarian, but there are periodic revivals of secrecy and censorship. In his study of press freedom, Fred S. Siebert suggested why this might be so. He proposed that "the area of freedom contracts and enforcement of restraints increases as the stresses on the stability of the government and the structure of society increase."[11] He noted strong control of the English press during the insecure reigns of Henry VIII and Elizabeth, and a relaxation during the stable administration of Walpole. Then, reflecting on contemporary times, Siebert perceived strains arising during the early 1950s, when fear of Communism distressed this country's social system. Though he did not go into detail, he could have mentioned the widespread blacklisting and security investigations of the McCarthy era.

Against Siebert's proposition it might be argued that under stress people begin to squawk, and squawking constitutes expression. So if freedom to speak is measured by the amount of dissent and the diversity of expression during a given period, then when conflict arises we should find more free expression—up to a point, at least. Freedom during stress was noted by Dwight L. Teeter in his study of the colonial press. "The freedom which Philadelphia newspapers enjoyed from 1775 to 1783 appears to have been based largely upon factional divisions in Pennsylvania government and in Congress. These contending factions turned repeatedly to the newspapers to air their arguments, and statements deplored by one faction were heartily applauded by another."[12]

This does not necessarily invalidate Siebert's proposition. History lacks sufficient studies of performance under different kinds of conflict in order to make a firm conclusion. We suggest that in times and places of unity, expression is conformist, and social control impedes diversity of speech. As conflict arises and factions irritate each other, wider expression is stimulated and continues as long as the stress remains and no single faction dominates. But when stress on society becomes great enough—forms a critical mass, so to speak— freedom falters; one faction is victorious, or the factions perceive a common threat and unite to face it. If this theory is correct, it follows that during periods when people are shouting "repression," they are free; they speak out. When the shouting is *not* heard, freedom is either stifled or relinquished.

Thus, expression is not very free (as measured by amount and variety) during the great strains of a major war—or in a peaceful little community where everyone thinks alike. Something akin to this is argued by political scientist John P. Roche, who holds that "the diversity of opinion [in the United States] was a consequence not of tolerance and mutual respect ... but of the existence of many communities within the society each with its own canons of orthodoxy."[13] In a similar vein, John D. Stevens has proposed that "the more heterogeneous a society, the more freedom of expression it will tolerate."[14]

This suggests that freedom is born of stalemated conflict, not of consensus. Freedom begins with selfishness and the desire—and need—to express one's own views. It flourishes under conditions of grudging tolerance—when factions can not quite triumph—and ends when opinions are successfully coerced or accepted without thought.

The danger of a tyranny of the majority was clearly recognized by John Stuart Mill, who offered four practical reasons for upholding freedom of expression: First, an opinion that is silenced may turn out to be true. Second, a silenced opinion, though erroneous, may contain a grain of truth. Third, even if an opinion is wholly true it must be contested if it is to be rationally understood. And fourth, the truth must remain open to argument if it is not to lapse into dogma.

Therefore, the marketplace of ideas must remain open even in times of consensus. Thomas Jefferson acknowledged the ideal of the marketplace in 1787:

> The way to prevent . . . irregular interpositions of the people, is to give them full information of their affairs through the channel of the public papers, and to contrive that those papers should penetrate the whole mass of the people . . . and were it left to me to decide whether we should have a government without newspapers, or newspapers without government, I should not hesitate a moment to prefer the latter.

Jefferson also had some worries about the marketplace. He added, "But I should mean that every man should receive those papers, and be capable of reading them." These two conditions, accessibility of mass communication and a discerning audience, are central to a libertarian media system. As they weaken, so does the justification for press freedom.

The science of Newton and others was important in diluting the authority of church and state. It helped fashion the heady individualism of the Enlightenment. But science did not stop with Newton, nor with libertarianism, and the peculiar result has been to raise doubts about freedom of the press—negative freedom in particular.

the idea of responsibility

The belief in an orderly universe whose secrets were discoverable by rational individuals, so important to the Enlightenment, was drastically undermined in the 19th century. In 1859, when Mill published his essay *On Liberty,* Charles Darwin released *The Origin of Species.* Though to some people Darwin enhanced the idea of individualism, he revealed nature as changing and amoral; man was subject to ecological determination. Further doubts about man's rational control of his own destiny were raised by Marx and Freud, who perceived economic and psychological determinism. Newtonian physics, so vital a model for the Enlightenment, lost its mechanistic truth under Einstein. Moreover, as science advanced, it exceeded the grasp of the common man and became the domain of the specialist. The amateur could no longer provide himself the background, much less the equipment, to conduct advanced scientific experiments.

Technology continued apace. With a little brushing up, Gutenberg could have found work as a printer at the beginning of the 19th century. Within a few years, however, printing made quantum leaps forward from the lever-and-screw press that had served since the 15th century. By the end of the Civil War, printing had evolved rotary presses that used rolls of inexpensive wood-pulp paper. By 1889 the New York *Herald* had presses sufficient to yield 72,000 complete copies per hour. In Jefferson's time, 200 impressions an hour was rapid work.

Galloping technology did not mean that the nation was

suffused with thoughtful political debate. On the contrary, the steam presses of the 1830s meant that Benjamin Day and James Gordon Bennett could mass-produce entertaining content for a mass audience in growing cities (themselves the product of the industrial revolution). News—much of it titillating—was more salable than the partisan political content of the previous generation. The "penny press" of Day and Bennett demonstrated that political content was not especially vital to the mass audience. Soon the technology of the telegraph showed that it was not altogether desirable. The first press association or wire service was organized in New York in 1848, just four years after Samuel F. B. Morse strung his first intercity telegraph line. A wire service was able to bring big, bad news from a distance, forcing local coverage aside. It was expensive to use, and was therefore reserved for major news rather than political essays. The wire also meant uniformity of content among newspapers who shared the service. Wire reporting led to the inverted-pyramid (most important thing first) style of newswriting and taught it to home-town journalists. More significantly, wire reporting was objective. Because it served newspapers of varying political temperaments, the wire service wished to offend none; objective reporting—sticking to the facts—was a convenient solution.[15]

Objectivity has several attractions. As Ben H. Bagdikian points out, it arose at a crucial time in American journalism. Nineteenth-century publishers had grown wealthy from technology and were accustomed to viewing the world through industrialists' glasses. The standard of objectivity and the preeminence of news somewhat curbed the publisher's control over content. Objectivity also had, and still has, relevance to libertarian theory: give rational man the facts and he can make up his own mind. But Milton, Jefferson, and Mill had envisioned a marketplace filled with more than facts. They saw important truths arising from the clash of opinions.

Then, as science became the realm of experts, so did news gathering, publishing, and entertaining. Fewer ordinary people had access to print as contributors, much less as publishers, and when the media became massive, they also grew somewhat distant from their audiences. Mass communication was increasingly a one-way street.

Thus, the Enlightenment's view of journalism, man, and society suffered serious wounds at the hands of science and technology. Despite all of the industrial progress of the century, Americans emerged from it with doubts. Their ideal society had suffered a civil war, labor strife, and shameful political scandals. The universe was no longer orderly, and they themselves were caught in a potentially malignant determinism.

One response to such melancholy realizations, if some faith remains (and much did), is an attitude of reform. In the first 15 or so years of this century the spirit of progressivism wrought laws designed to protect the public, regulate industry, and cleanse politics. If man is a creature of his environment, the Progressives said, then let us provide him with a better environment. Segments of the press enthusiastically agreed, and engaged in muckraking attacks upon social evils, especially in big business and government.

Some of the criticism turned on the press itself. In 1911 journalist Will Irwin wrote a 15-part series for *Collier's* entitled "The American Newspaper: A Study of Journalism in Its Relation to the Public."[16] He found newspapers to be a powerful and not entirely wholesome force in society. At about the same time, several states passed laws against deceptive advertisements, and in 1912 a federal Newspaper Publicity Law, which was tied to postal regulations, required the label "advertisement" on any material published for money.

The spirit of reform gained a foothold in journalism. In 1923 the American Society of Newspaper Editors drafted a code that outlined good journalistic performance. Since then the ideas of reform and good conduct have been organized into a theory of social responsibility for the media. In the theory are touches of both authoritarianism and libertarianism. The idea of positive freedom—liberty for the sake of doing good—is firmly incorporated. This position reflects some doubts about the rationality of the audience and the richness of the marketplace of ideas. The freedom to be aimless, trivial, sensational—to be bad —is scorned under social responsibility, but not forbidden; after all, the theory is an outgrowth of libertarianism.

The notion of responsibility in mass communication also received impetus from widespread concern over propaganda in World War I, from "yellow journalism," and from concentration of media ownership in the hands of such publishers as William Randolph Hearst. At their peak in 1935, Hearst's 26 dailies had 13.6 percent of the total daily circulation in the United States and nearly one-fourth of the Sunday circulation. Since 1910, when 689 cities had competing dailies, the number of cities enjoying competition has declined steadily. Today, fewer than 40 United States cities have competing dailies.

The idea of responsibility coupled with freedom is not a new one. It existed under licensing, with much more emphasis on responsibility than freedom. In the last century Joseph Pulitzer set down the creed of his St. Louis *Post-Dispatch:* "It will serve no party but the people; be no organ of Republicanism, but the organ of truth; will follow no causes but its conclusions; will not support the Administration, but criticise it; will oppose all frauds and shams wherever and whatever they are; will advocate principles and ideas rather than prejudices and partisanship." Near the end of his career he urged that his newspapers remain "drastically independent," which is good negative libertarianism, and "never be afraid to attack wrong," which is the language of positive freedom and responsibility.

In 1947 many of the free-floating ideas of media responsibility were captured by the Commission on Freedom of the Press in a book called *A Free and Responsible Press*. The self-styled commission—really a private group of scholars and philosophers funded by Henry Luce of Time Inc. and by Encyclopaedia Britannica, Inc.—announced five duties of a responsible press:

> 1. The press must provide a truthful, comprehensive, and intelligent account of the day's events in a context which gives them meaning.
> 2. It must be a forum for the exchange of comment and criticism.
> 3. It must project a representative picture of the constituent groups in society.
> 4. It must present and clarify the goals and values of society.
> 5. It must offer full access to the day's intelligence.

Though this was substantially what many leading journalists had been saying for some time, the commission's report was badly received by the profession. What grated on journalistic ears was the commission's question as to "whether the performance of the press can any longer be left to the unregulated initiative of the few who manage it." A member of the commission, William Hocking, went so far as to suggest that the media might be improved, if need be, by a "touch of the state."

These were fighting words to a press steeped in libertarianism, and when the report was published most newspapers ignored it and some scoffed at the "impractical theorists" who populated the commission. The Chicago *Tribune,* which the commission had examined in particular, attacked the report in a news story and later in a book written by one of its reporters. Some newspapers implied editorially that the commission was a bit Communistic.

Whether because of the Commission on Freedom of the Press or in spite of it, the media have continued to adopt the theory (if not always the practice) of responsibility. The Associated Press Managing Editors (APME), no slouches when it comes to defending liberty of the press, in 1962 issued a brief set of guidelines called "Criteria of a Good Newspaper" which dealt with four major topics—integrity, accuracy, responsibility, and leadership—which echo the media requirements laid down by the Commission on the Freedom of the Press. Among the APME criteria:

> —[A good newspaper] reports fully and explains the meaning of local, national, and international events which are of major signifi-

cance in its own community. Its editorial comment provides an informed opinion on matters of vital concern to its readers.

—It shall provide a forum for the exchange of pertinent comment and criticism, especially if it is in conflict with the newspaper's editorial point of view.

—It shall maintain vigorous standards of honesty and fair play in the selection and editing of its content as well as in all relations with news sources and the public.

—A good newspaper should be guided in the publication of all material by a concern for truth, the hallmark of freedom, by a concern for human decency and human betterment, and by a respect for the accepted standards of its own community.

—It shall select, edit, and display news on the basis of its significance and its genuine usefulness to the public.

There have been misgivings about theories of responsibility. Bernard Kilgore, who guided the *Wall Street Journal* to a position of excellence after World War II, argued that "whenever you start nibbling away at freedom of the press, it's hard to know when to stop. . . . We've got to have a free press, whether it's responsible or not." Having acquired a good deal of freedom, the media are not disposed to give it up.

For example, responsibility theory calls for interpretative reporting—or, as the Commission on the Freedom of the Press remarked, "It is no longer enough to report *the fact* truthfully. It is now necessary to report *the truth about the fact.*"[17] Interpretation is resisted by journalists baptized in the doctrine of objectivity. They see interpretation as a sort of creeping opinionation in news columns. But interpretation can stop short of *advocacy;* it is a reasoned analysis based on facts —an "objective appraisal," in the words of Lester Markel, former Sunday editor of the New York *Times.* Objectivity and interpretation are mutually reinforcing: one informs and the other amplifies.

Another requirement of responsibility is fairness, a balance of views within a medium. This requirement would have struck the early libertarians with surprise and skepticism and the authoritarians as an absurdity. The libertarian marketplace was to be an arena where competing biases could grapple in the sunshine. But the industrialization of mass communication made it expensive, if not impossible, for the individual to bring his goods to the major markets. The concept of fairness attempts to rectify this constriction. It has succeeded to a surprising extent; good newsmen habitually seek out contrasting views, and editorial pages are regularly adorned with politically differing columnists. The balance is never perfect, and the contenders are sometimes only a few split-hairs apart in their opinions. This is scandalous to militants, but it represents a long march forward from the days of Hearstian monologues.

Responsibility's dangerous perch on the brink of authoritarianism is revealed in the question, "Responsible to whom?", asked by journalism scholar John Merrill.[18] He argues that the theory of responsibility ultimately means government control because no other agency is capable of enforcing responsibility.

But the answer is that mass communicators are to be responsible to themselves and to their perceptions of the audience's information needs. Social responsibility is libertarianism with a conscience, many consciences.

This is something distinctly different from correct performance laid down and enforced by an authoritarian government. It is also quite different from the surly independence voiced by an editor of two generations ago: "A newspaper is a private enterprise owing nothing whatever to the public, which grants it no franchise. It is therefore affected with no public interest. It is emphatically the property of the owner, who is selling a manufactured product at his own risk."[19]

Responsibility is much closer to what Humphrey Bogart once said: "I owe my audience nothing but a good performance." Bogart was not beholden to his audience. He did not truckle. But he chose for himself the constraint of doing the best he could.

for further reading

Barrett, Marvin, ed. *Survey of Broadcast Journalism, 1969–1970.* New York: Grosset & Dunlap, 1970. Also see subsequent editions.

Commission on the Freedom of the Press. *A Free and Responsible Press.* Chicago: University of Chicago Press, 1947.

Gerald, J. Edward. *The Social Responsibility of the Press.* Minneapolis, Minn.: University of Minnesota Press, 1963.

Geyelin, Philip L., and Douglass Cater. *American Media: Adequate or Not?* Washington, D.C.: American Enterprise Institute for Public Policy Research, 1970.

Hughes, Frank. *Prejudice and the Press.* New York: Devin-Adair, 1950.

Lippmann, Walter. *Public Opinion.* New York: Harcourt, Brace & World, 1922.

Mill, John Stuart. *On Liberty.* New York: Appleton-Century-Crofts, 1947.

Nelson, Harold L., ed. *Freedom of the Press from Hamilton to the Warren Court.* Indianapolis, Ind.: Bobbs-Merrill, 1967.

Reston, James. *The Artillery of the Press.* New York: Harper & Row, 1967.

Rivers, William L., and Wilbur Schramm. *Responsibility in Mass Communication,* rev. ed. New York: Harper & Row, 1970.

Siebert, Fred S. *Freedom of the Press in England, 1476–1776.* Urbana, Ill.: University of Illinois Press, 1956.

The Uncertain Mirror. Report of the Special [Canadian] Senate Committee on Mass Media. Vol. 1. Ottawa: Queen's Printer, 1970.

Wolff, Robert Paul, Barrington Moore, Jr., and Herbert Marcuse. *A Critique of Pure Tolerance.* Boston: Beacon Press, 1965.

part
2

the
media
and the
environment

what the media
do to us, maybe

the famous suicide song and other hits

The Press (that *villanous* Engine) ... hath done more mischief to the
Discipline of our Church, than all the Doctrine can make amends for. ...
Two or three brawny Fellows in a Corner, with meer Ink and Elbow-grease,
do more harm than an *Hundred* Systematical *Divines* with their Sweaty
Preaching. ... *O Printing!* how has thou disturbed the Peace of Mankind,
that Lead, when moulded into Bullets, is not so mortal as when founded
into Letters!
—Letter to the Boston *Evening Post,* March 31, 1741

So far we have dealt mainly with the effects of the social environment
upon the mass media. Now we turn to the effects of the media upon
society. This division of emphasis is convenient but not entirely realistic, because the media and society continually interact, constantly respond. To concentrate one's vision in one direction is to risk being
trampled from the other.

In some other chapters we concentrate specifically upon the
functions of information and entertainment and cite the particular
characteristics of each. Here, as we examine communication effects, we

draw examples from both—an unhappy wedding, we suspect, in eyes of professional journalists, who do not care to have their important function entangled with the silliness and banality of popular entertainment. We sympathize with this view, and agree that the media consumer's highest respect and closest attention should go to news and information and to the best in art: be concerned about the FBI, not "The FBI." Yet we find that the media themselves mingle information and entertainment. Movies such as *Z* are filmed in a documentary style; TV dramas strive for "authenticity," and, as we shall see in a moment, entertainment sometimes derives from brute fact. Newspapers have their comic strips, and some newscasters—too many—engage in "happy talk" between news items. The audience, we think, can and should distinguish between fact and fun. But we also recognize that if a person is deeply moved by a mass-communicated message, it may matter little to him whether it arrived as information or entertainment. Then, too, some effects attributed to the media have nothing to do with content. The message, Marshall McLuhan asserts, is not the message.

Many of the things society has done to (or for) the media are in answer to the effects of mass communication, good and ill, real and imagined. The theories of authoritarianism, libertarianism, and social responsibility all assume that mass communication has effects. Evidence seems to support the idea. In late 1966, when NBC announced that it would show a film entitled *The Doomsday Flight,* the Air Line Pilots Association urged the network to keep the program off the air because it described the placement of a bomb on a passenger plane. The bomb was to be triggered by a barometric device when the aircraft descended to less than 5000 feet. The pilots feared that the program would cause irrational persons to imitate the film and sabotage a plane.

NBC ignored the request and ran the film as scheduled on December 13. Even while the movie was still on the air a bomb threat was phoned to one airline. Within a week, eight hoax calls were received by various U.S. airlines—equally the number received during the entire preceding month.

Later *The Doomsday Flight* went into syndication and was reshown by stations in the United States and around the world. In August 1970, an Anchorage, Alaska, station showed the film, and shortly afterward Western Airlines paid $25,000 to an extortionist who said a barometric bomb was on one of its planes. In 1971 similar threats were made after showings in Florida and Australia.

At this point *Doomsday Flight* author Rod Serling, who said he got the idea for his teleplay from an actual case, announced that he wished he'd never been born. He was, of course, safe from retroactive contraception, and prints of the film were in the hands of about 500 television stations. The Federal Aviation Administration requested all 500 not to show it. A month later 20 stations said they would comply. Presumably the other 480 were still making up their minds. Meanwhile, the film was shown in Canada and a week later a Montreal-to-London flight was threatened by a barometric bomb.

To the airline pilots, the effect of the film was a foregone conclusion. The network and individual stations were not so sure, and still aren't. Scholars, too, differ on media effects; there is no unified theory regarding media influence, but a good place to start is with the idea that the media are profoundly effective.

X big effects, certain effects

Conventional wisdom holds that if you spit in the Pacific at Santa Cruz, the shoreline of Japan is raised. If this is so, then the cascade of mass communication upon the American psyche must, by all odds, have major effects. For example, psychologist Alberta Siegel, in a report to the National Commission on the Causes and Prevention of Violence, noted that by the age of 16, the average American child has spent as many hours watching television as he has spent in school. Many of these hours are filled with violence—84 killings in 85½ hours of prime evening and Saturday morning time, according to a census taken by the *Christian Science Monitor* in 1968. Dr. Siegel observed:

> The evidence that we do have indicates that films and television are profoundly educative for their viewers, teaching them that the world is a violent and untrustworthy place, and demonstrating for them a variety of violent techniques for coping with this hostile environment. Whether this message is beamed as fact or fiction, it is accepted by young children. They incorporate in their own behavior patterns all the sequences of adult behavior they observe on television.[1]

Charles H. Keating, Jr., a member of the Commission on Obscenity and a founder of the Citizens for Decent Literature, reasoned:

> If man is affected by his environment, by circumstances of his life, by reading, by instruction, by anything, he is then certainly affected by pornography. The mere nature of pornography makes it impossible for pornography to effect good. Therefore, it must necessarily effect evil. Sexual immorality, more than any other causative factor, historically speaking, is the root cause of the demise of all great peoples.[2]

Squatting in his filthy garret, sunk in shabby thoughts (or so we envision him), the pornographer should be flattered that he is able to destroy whole nations.

On the other hand, the legitimate mass communicator is pleased to know he can help *build* nations: "An adequate flow of information, and in particular an appropriate use of the mass media [can] make a substantial contribution to national and economic and social development," says Wilbur Schramm, a leading scholar of media in developing nations.[3]

Yet there is a cloud inside of that silver lining. While acknowledging major effects by the media, Professor Herbert I. Schiller warns that weak societies "are beginning to be menaced with extinction by the expansion of modern electronic communications, television in particular, emanating from a few power centers in the industrialized world." He fears the dissemination of "cultural mush" and believes that "cultural patterns, once established, are endlessly persistent. . . . In modern mass communications hard and inflexible laws, economic and technological, operate. If these are not taken into account *in the beginning,* and at least partially overcome, courses of development automatically unfold that soon become unquestioned 'natural' patterns."[4]

Among the alleged purveyors of cultural mush, advertising agents and network executives are frequently wounded by critics such as Schiller. For many years advertising has been accused of debasing taste and of inspiring unwarranted consumption—truly grand if not wholesome effects. Badly buffetted by social criticism, the creators of mass culture were understandably delighted by the timely arrival of Marshall McLuhan, the extraordinarily popular media theorist and a leading proponent of Big Effects. "The historians and archaeologists will one day discover that the ads of our times are the richest and most faithful daily reflections that any society ever made of its entire range of activities," McLuhan said. To him, television had done what artists had been struggling to do "ever since Cezanne abandoned perspective illusion in favor of structure in painting. . . . TV is the Bauhaus program of design and living, or the Montessori educational strategy, given total technological extension and commercial sponsorship."[5]

These were gilded words to Madison Avenue. Though McLuhan has had some reservations about the content of advertising, it really did not matter because, after all, the medium is the message.

To a person who believes that society is shaped in large part by its technology, the widgets a machine produces are much less important than the way society reorganizes around the machine. Thus, the significance of the automobile is not its ability to transport people but the existence of smog, drive-in theatres, and Middle East oil crises. Similarly, the meaning of the invention of steam power is the labor union, the slum, and the factory.

Before McLuhan, technological determinism had been applied

to the study of mass communication by Robert E. Park, a sociologist, and his student, Harold A. Innis, a Canadian economic historian. To Innis the major social consequence of the invention of writing was the conquest of time and space. In an oral society, rules and traditions are necessarily closely shared, and space is amorphous and bounded by the limitations of earshot and collective mysticism. Literature, being spoken, is participatory and history is imaginative because it is not fixed by records. Writing changed this profoundly. With writing, society could set geographic boundaries and maintain them through a dispersed bureaucracy. With written symbols as an aid to memory, complicated systems of logic could be developed, and inherited wisdom could be objectively tested. Writing permitted political unity and the development of law. It also fostered monopolies of knowledge and power—which were painful to Innis, an antimonopolist.

In Innis' perception, written communication disclosed a pantheon of effects:

> The use of clay favoured a dominant role for the temples with an emphasis on priesthood and religion. Libraries were built up in Babylon and Nineveh to strengthen the power of monarchy. Papyrus favoured the development of political organization in Egypt. Papyrus and a simplified form of writing in the alphabet supported the growth of democratic organization, literature, and philosophy in Greece. Following Alexander empires returned with centres at Alexandria and elsewhere and libraries continued as sources of strength to monarchies. Rome extended the political organization of Greece in its emphasis on law and eventually on empire. . . . Improvement of scripts and wider dissemination of knowledge enabled the Jews to survive by emphasis on the scriptures and the book. In turn Christianity exploited the advantages of parchment and the codex in the Bible. With access to paper the Mohammedans at Baghdad and later in Spain and Sicily provided a medium for the transmission of Greek science to the Western world. Greek science and paper with encouragement of writing in the vernacular provided the wedge between the temporal and spiritual power and destroyed the Holy Roman Empire.[6]

All of this even before Gutenberg. As for printing, Innis wrote, "The effect of the discovery of printing was evident in the savage religious wars of the sixteenth and seventeenth centuries." Or, as McLuhan was later to say in a jazzier fashion, "The hotting-up of the medium of writing to repeatable intensity led to nationalism and the religious wars of the sixteenth century."

McLuhan leaped well beyond Innis—and into hot air, according to some of his critics—by contending that media affect individual and social psychology by imbalancing the senses. He asserted that anything that extends the senses is a medium—the caveman's ax, the book, electrical circuits. Each extension changes the balance among the five senses and creates new outlooks and attitudes, and, eventually, a new psychological environment. Print, for example, involves one sense—vision—at the expense of the ear. Printing is logical and linear in form, and ultimately results in logical, linear life styles that are a far cry from the deeply involved simultaneity of life in a preliterate tribe where, according to McLuhan, the ear was dominant.

Thus, "Gutenberg technology had produced a new kind of visual, national entity in the sixteenth century that was gradually meshed with industrial production and expansion," McLuhan wrote. The atomistic alphabet led to the atomistic individual, and to detribalization.

But then, according to McLuhan, along came the mighty medium of electricity, and "telegraph and radio neutralized nationalism [and] evoked archaic tribal ghosts of the most vigorous brand." What radio and television are doing, he said, is to retribalize mankind. Electronic media provide an instant interconnection between social atoms, forming a global village. What's more, television is psychologically involving; its low definition requires more participation in order to receive images. And the images themselves are mosaic—even tactile—in quality. TV is so involving an extension of our senses that we wear it like hair.[7] The electronic media are thus exonerated from sin; instead of sapping us with the "Beverly Hillbillies," they are coming to our rescue, righting our psychic wrongs, as "the human family becomes one tribe again."

Even if this were all true, it would be scary. McLuhan implies that the reconciliation of mankind is futile as a conscious human effort and must occur as a by-product of machinery.

That much of McLuhanism is untrue is argued by Jonathan Miller in a closely reasoned and, yes, linear/logical book. Miller challenges McLuhan on sensual balance, the importance of content, the properties of speech and print, and the nature of television—which is just about everything.

Yet, as Miller points out, "For all the maddening slogans, paradoxes, and puns; for all the gross breaches of intellectual etiquette —or perhaps even because of them all—McLuhan has forced us to attend to the various media through which we gain our knowledge of the world."[8]

McLuhan, as medium, has had an effect.

There are many who argue that media have no great effects, and that conditions must be very favorable before anything attributable to mass communication can occur. The conditions are numerous, they say, and effects are not definite and direct.

sometime effects

In 1933 Hungarian composer Reszo Seress wrote a poignant love song called "Szomoru Vasarnap," or, in English, "Gloomy Sunday." It had some remarkable effects, and let us permit *Time* magazine, vintage 1936, to tell the story:

> *Gloomy Sunday* droned along in comparative obscurity until last month. Then it began to make news aplenty. Budapest police, investigating the suicide of a shoemaker named Joseph Keller, found that Keller had left a note in which he quoted lyrics from Composer Seress' [song]. Further inquiry revealed that the lugubrious ballad had persuaded 17 other impressionable Magyars to take their lives. Two shot their brains out while hearing a gypsy band play the piece, others killed themselves listening to recorded versions, several leaped into the Danube clutching the sheet music. The Budapest police banned *Gloomy Sunday*.

Another effect of "Gloomy Sunday" was a race among American music publishers to be the first to provide the public with what was hawked as THE FAMOUS HUNGARIAN SUICIDE SONG. But as *Time* reported, with something of a pout, nothing much happened. "As played by Hal Kemp and his usually lively band, Brunswick's *Gloomy Sunday* wallows dismally along in E flat minor." No American deaths were discerned.

Similarly, not everyone—hardly *anyone*—who watched *The Doomsday Flight* called an airline to say a bomb was aboard. Then there is the case of Franklin D. Roosevelt, Harry S Truman, and John F. Kennedy. All were editorially opposed by a majority of American newspapers, and all were elected just the same. Consider too the 1966 California gubernatorial campaign between Edmund G. Brown and Ronald Reagan. Brown's TV commercials were biting and witty—minor masterpieces. In surprising contrast, Reagan's were dull, flatfooted, and featured the "talking head" approach of 1950 television. Still, Reagan won.

Obviously something is fishy about theories that attribute awesome and invariable power to the press, and a large kettle of fish was indeed uncovered by a 1940 study of voting behavior. The study disclosed that voters managed to expose themselves to what they wanted to hear in the way of political arguments, and that personal conversations were much more important in changing their minds than were the outpourings of the media.[9]

For many years—thanks to fears of wartime propaganda, "scientific" advertising, and the sociological notion that urban people lack strong personal ties—it had been assumed that mass communication directly affects the heterogeneous, detached public: give the audience a stimulus and it will largely respond. But this and other election studies made it increasingly apparent that people still talked to each other, had personal biases, and paid attention to what they found agreeable.

The 1940 study suggested that media influence, if it occurred at all, came by way of personal interaction in a two-step or multi-step flow, and was shaped to the contours of individual and group norms and values: "Ideas often flow from radio and print to opinion leaders and from these to the less active sections of the populations."

Personal biases are apparent in an individual's tendency to select what he wants from media content and to ignore the disagreeable. A study of a 1958 senatorial election found that Republicans were about twice as likely as were Democrats to have watched a Republican-sponsored telecast.

What's more, individuals appear capable not only of selective attention but of being choosy about how they interpret what they perceived, how much they remember, and what they do about it.

Thus, says Joseph Klapper:

> 1. Mass communication *ordinarily* does not serve as a necessary and sufficient cause of audience effects, but rather functions among and through a nexus of mediating factors and influences.
> 2. The mediating factors are such that they typically render mass communication a contributory agent, but not the sole cause in a process of reinforcing the existing condition. . . .[10]

Klapper's "mediating factors" include selective exposure, selective perception, selective retention, interpersonal dissemination, personal influence and leadership, and the very nature of the media.

Therefore, media effectiveness is a sometime thing, depending on a great many intervening factors. As Bernard Berelson wrote, "Some kinds of communication on some kinds of issues, brought to the attention of some kinds of people under some kinds of conditions, have some kinds of effects."[11]

And so mass communication drops in status from an engine of persuasion to a back-seat driver.

no effects? negative effects?

The balkiness of the audience led to greater research on what happens between the stimulus of communication and the response (if any) by the receiver. Considerable study has been devoted to the believability, order of presentation, and one- or two-sidedness of messages; to the prestige and credibility of the source; to the personality, knowledge-ability, roles, and psychological process of the receiver; and to his groups and their norms, values, and cohesiveness.

Increasingly, all of these things were taken into account before effects could be attributed to mass communication. Against a huge array of social and psychological influences, the stimulus of impersonal mass media grows a trifle pale, and in these terms it is not surprising to find the Commission on Obscenity and Pornography saying, despite Commissioner Charles Keating's views to the contrary, "Exposure to erotic stimuli appears to have little or no effect on already established attitudinal commitments regarding either sexuality or sexual morality," and that "empirical research ... has found no evidence to date that exposure to explicit sexual materials plays a significant role in the causation of delinquency or criminal behavior among youth or adults."[12]

One of the leading studies of television and children has observed:

> In a sense the term "effect" is misleading because it suggests that television "does something" to children. The connotation is that television is the actor; the children are acted upon. Children are thus made to seem relatively inert; television relatively active.
>   Nothing can be further from the fact.
>   It is the children who are most active in this relationship. It is they who use television, rather than television that uses them. ...
>   As between two favorite images of the situation—the image of children as helpless victims to be attacked by television, and the image of television as a great and shiny cafeteria from which children select what they want at the moment—the latter is the more nearly accurate. ...
>   Something in their lives makes them reach out for a particular experience on television. This experience then enters into their lives, and has to make its way amidst the stored experience, the codified values, the social relationships, and the immediately urgent needs that are already a part of those lives. As a result, something happens to the original experience. Something is discarded, something is stored away, perhaps some overt behavior occurs. This is the "effect of television."[13]

What had happened among scholars was a fundamental shifting of the locus of effect from the media to the audience, with the result that the media were at least partly exonerated. The shift of emphasis skidded much too far, according to sociologist William R. Catton, Jr.:

> It became necessary to recognize significant variations in the desires and inclinations of audience members, in the way they received media stimuli, and in their socially shaped opportunities to respond. The upshot of all these complications was that it began to seem as if

what the media do to us, maybe   *131*

the answer to the question, "What effects do mass media produce" had to be, "It all depends . . .", and it was only a short step from that to a feeling that the media really don't *produce* effects at all. The contingent nature of mass media impact made it seem that the effects ought to be attributed to the intervening variables instead of (rather than in conjunction with) to the mass media stimuli.[14]

But few if any scholars went so far as to exonerate the media completely; at most they implied that "bad" media influences will have tough sledding against individual and group norms, and "good" influences will be chosen by the audience from the "great and shiny cafeteria." Still, problems remain with this more moderate position. Among other things, the menu is limited. For example, in a study of live television coverage of the return of a war hero, Lang and Lang found that television's squinty vision focused only on the spectacular aspects.[15]

And then there is the matter of side effects, some of which are rather monumental, like the slag heaps adjacent to gold mines.

some side effects

"Since TV," McLuhan said, "children average about six and a half inches from the printed page. Our children are striving to carry over to the printed page the all-involving sensory mandate of the TV image." The ruination of vision was one of the early sins attributed to television, and more recently rock music has been charged with damage to hearing, if not to morals. Television has also been accused of irradiating the audience and bending the spines of children and of keeping them up too late. Laws have been passed against having TV sets in automobiles, and the Houston police department has asked for a ban on wearing stereo headphones in cars. Newspapers have impeded family conversation at the breakfast table, and divorces have resulted.

These are all effects of some kind, unintended by mass communicators and unanticipated by society. Even if one is skeptical of McLuhan's assertion that the media have reorganized man's senses, there is no denying that TV has rearranged American parlors and that drive-in theatres have affected mating customs. And there's more.

Reinforcement. Many writers have noted that the media tend to reinforce existing values and attitudes. This is understandable. Communication of necessity begins with what is familiar and builds from there. A mass communicator is especially aware of common denominators in his huge audience and he seizes upon sure-fire themes and repeats them endlessly in his entertainment.

Given the choice, an audience will naturally select what is

understandable in terms of past experience and agreeable in relation to his values. The purveyor of mass entertainment, a very practical person, sees little reason to exceed those experiences and values unless some avant-garde communicator has demonstrated a change in the audience or has uncovered a new (and large) audience.

By the time any social organism is sufficiently large and cohesive to engage in mass communication, it has a natural interest in its own survival, and its leaders wish to preserve their status. Hence, any mass communication sponsored by the social group will contain content that is conservative of group values. Hot rod and surfing magazines urge their members to promote safety and avoid breaking the laws of the larger society. Even groups that reject the larger society have media whose messages reinforce their special views and criticize deviation.

From the perspective of the group, the reinforcement function of its media is usually important and wholesome. Reinforcement keeps old members in line and socializes new ones. At its best, socialization is an introduction to, and a reaffirmation of, what is good for people. Any mass medium that is closely attuned to its group and that seeks to maintain its own popularity will reinforce group values.

But what if change is needed? From a more critical perspective, reinforcement inspires mindless conformity to the status quo. In this view the media are peddlers of stereotypes and drivers of bandwagons. Lazarsfeld and Merton assert that "since our commercially sponsored mass media promote a largely unthinking allegiance to our social structure, they cannot be relied upon to work for changes, even minor changes, in that structure."[16]

Is reinforcement an "effect" or not? By definition reinforcement means no change; therefore, it might be argued that reinforcement, which mass media perform so naturally, is not an effect. Catton rejects this argument as mere definitional wrestling: "If existing opinions are reinforced by mass media when they would otherwise have been changed by other factors, the mass media have produced an effect; pointing out the conservative nature of this effect cannot argue it out of existence."[17]

✕ *Narcosis.* From April 22 to April 29, 1967, writer Charles Sopkin locked himself into his New York apartment and continuously viewed six television sets for "seven glorious days, seven fun-filled nights," just to see what it was like. A result of this heroic experiment was that "on some days, for certain periods, the drone of the sets left me in a semi-comatose state, just sitting there unblinking."[18]

It is not a goal of mass communication to stupefy the audience —at least not during the advertisements—yet long before Sopkin's adventure, critics alleged that mass entertainment encouraged escape from reality. Charles Siepmann wrote in 1948 that "There is an indolence in each of us which is resistant both to growth and change. As radio indulges us in this respect it retards rather than advances our growth. . . . It can make of this potential instrument a drug rather than a stimulant."[19]

But what's wrong with escape? After all, some kinds of content provide a route *into* important realities beyond our immediate horizons. And escape *from* everyday problems—respite—can be refreshing. Then, too, psychiatrist Eugene David Glynn notes what at first glance is a certain therapeutic value in TV: at a hospital for schizophrenic adolescent girls, the inmates "want nothing so much as to be allowed endless hours of television. Without it they are soon noisy, unruly and frequently destructive." But there are some unwholesome implications. He adds: "These, then, are traits television can so easily satisfy in adults, or foster in children: traits of passivity, receptiveness, being fed, taking in and absorbing what is offered. Activity, self-reliance, and aggression are notably absent."[20] The mixed virtues of escapism are apparent in the last sentence. One may be alarmed at a loss of self-reliance and activity but pleased that aggression is blocked.

Lazarsfeld and Merton perceive in mass communication a "narcotizing dysfunction" that distracts the audience from real problems and prevents doing something about them. They note that:

> Scattered studies have shown that an increasing proportion of the time of Americans is devoted to the products of the mass media. . . . Yet, it is suggested, this vast supply of communications may elicit only a superficial concern with the problems of society, and this superficiality often cloaks mass apathy.
> Exposure to this flood of information may serve to narcotize rather than to energize the average reader or listener. As an increasing meed of time is devoted to reading and listening, a decreasing share is available for organized action. . . . The interested and informed citizen can congratulate himself on his lofty state of interest and information and neglect to see that he has abstained from decision and action. . . . He comes to mistake *knowing* about problems of the day for *doing* something about them.[21]

This view is alarming because it refers not to entertainment —which is designed for respite—but to informational content, which of all communication should rouse us to action. If narcosis occurs, a basic function of mass communication mentioned in Chapter 3—correlation of components of society for a *response* to the environment—is short-circuited.

However, the idea of a narcotizing dysfunction, first proposed in 1948, seems woefully outdated in view of contemporary mass demonstrations and other means of direct protest. In the spring of 1970 the mass-communicated news of the invasion of Cambodia and the shootings at Kent State sparked demonstrations throughout the country. Yet, curiously, the relative quiescence of campuses during the following year was attributed (by some, at least) to a surfeit of big, bad news.

Catharsis. Closely related to escape and narcosis is the idea that mass entertainment—violent entertainment in particular— drains away the viewer's own aggressiveness. Although this theory likens television to a storm sewer, the industry has been pleased to use it as a defense against charges that TV violence inspires real violence.

Psychologist Seymour Feshbach has found support for the hypothesis that when certain conditions are met, exposure to aggressive fantasy leads to a lowering of aggressive drive. In an early study he assigned college men to different experimental conditions. After the group was arbitrarily insulted and criticized by the experimenter, the men were then divided into smaller groups and were shown either an aggressive film of a brutal prize fight or a fairly dull "control" film. Afterward the students were asked to give their opinions of the experimenter who had insulted them. The results indicated that those who had seen the aggressive film felt less punitive toward the experimenter than were those who had seen the control film. The difference was attributed to catharsis induced by the violent film. In a later experiment he exposed more than 500 students at West Coast boys' schools to six weeks' viewing of either aggressive or nonaggressive TV diets. Measures of their personalities and attitudes were taken before and after the experience, and their behavior was observed throughout. Feshbach concluded that "witnessing aggressive TV programs serves to reduce or control the acting out of aggressive tendencies rather than to facilitate or stimulate aggression."[22]

Other experiments have yielded contrary results. Leonard Berkowitz conducted an experiment in which students (like Feshbach's) were initially either insulted or not insulted by a confederate. But in this study the confederate was introduced either as a boxer or as a speech student. Then the students were assigned to see either a violent boxing film or a neutral, nonviolent film. Afterward all subjects had the opportunity to give electrical shocks (under the guise of a separate experiment) to the insulting confederate. The largest number of shocks were given to the "boxer" by those who had seen the boxing film. Apparently the "boxer" cue heightened the likelihood of aggressive response.

In related experiments one group of young children watched a short film that showed violence or aggressive behavior and another group viewed a nonviolent film (or no film at all). The two groups were then observed, immediately afterward, for signs of violence. Several of these studies have found children imitating filmed aggression, especially if the aggressor has been shown to receive a reward. The implications for TV are alarming. Cowboy heroes, for example, are often rewarded for their violent solutions to problems.

The National Commission on the Causes and Prevention of Violence concluded that the weight of evidence goes against the catharsis theory. The elaborate studies sponsored by the Surgeon General's Scientific Advisory Committee on Television and Social Behavior also discounted the validity of catharsis theory in connection with televised violence. The committee concluded, on the contrary, that there is "a preliminary and tentative indication of a causal relation between viewing violence on television and aggressive behavior."[23]

Incidental learning.   When Clark Gable took off his shirt in a 1934 movie, *It Happened One Night,* American women were reputedly shocked, but their consternation was nothing compared with that of the men's underwear manufacturers. Gable was not wearing an undershirt, and, according to legend, he thereby "taught" American men how to cut down on their wardrobe expenses. On the other hand, the shoe industry is said to have profited after Cary Grant displayed a red-lined slipper in *Indiscreet.*

Buckminster Fuller has remarked that the present generation is the first to have been reared by three parents—the usual two, plus TV. Whether or not education is offered by commercial television and other media, learning is taken from them. And this is what worries a good many people who note the amount of time children spend with television and comic books and who note what those media contain.

Not all incidental learning is "bad." Parents try (and often fail) to be good examples at all times because children naturally imitate familiar models, whether or not that model is behaving purposefully. Mister Rogers, the host of a popular children's program on public television, seems to be quite aware of incidental learning. When he makes his entrance before the camera, he removes his coat—but he doesn't toss it over a chair; he carefully hangs it in a closet, as good children should.

At least one study has found that upon entering school, children raised on television have picked up a one-year advantage in vocabulary over children whose city has yet to acquire television. The advantage, however, disappears by the sixth grade.

The entertainment media offer much more than vocabulary. A content analysis of prime-time television by Professor George Gerbner and his associates revealed that about 80 percent of programs contained at least one episode of violence. The violent acts were usually inflicted at close range by a weapon, about half of them on strangers, and in most cases upon opponents who could not or did not resist. Gerbner summarizes the picture of violence offered by television:

> Most violence was individual, selfish, and often directed against strangers and victims who did not resist. Violence stuns, maims, and kills with little visible pain. A count of casualties may find an average of five per play injured or dead. Those who inflict violence may be "good guys" or "bad guys," but they are not as likely to reach a happy ending as non-violent types. All major characters, especially males in the prime of life, have a better than even chance to commit violence, at least one chance in ten to kill, and still reach a happy ending nearly fifty per cent of the time. Foreigners and non-whites are more violent than white Americans, but pay more dearly for their actions. Television drama projects America as a violent country, a world of many violent strangers, with a mostly violent past and a totally violent future.[24]

But are such fictional portrayals really learned and accepted as reality? Yes, says Professor Alberta Siegel: "Everything that social scientists know about human learning and remembering tells us that this carnage is being observed and remembered by the audience." She does not, however, go so far as to say the learners will be doers, although others suggest as much.

Forbes, a businessmen's magazine, wrote that "One of the reasons that narcotics consumption is rising so rapidly, particularly among the young, may be the help it gets from the mass media. Case in point: Columbia Pictures' 1969 box-office smash 'Easy Rider,' which projects Peter Fonda and Dennis Hopper as culture heroes." (No student of mass communication can fail to develop a sense of irony. In an accompanying article, *Forbes* discussed the economics of the heroin traffic: "It's a real growth industry, expanding in the U.S. at 10% or more yearly ... Profitable? Incredibly so. Ten kilos (roughly 22 pounds) of the raw material costs $350. Processed and packaged, it can bring in anywhere from $280,000 to $500,000 with profits of perhaps 15% to 1000% for everyone along the line." As *Forbes* said, the narcotics business may be getting some boosts from the media.)

Incidental learning takes place at all ages, but there is reason to believe it is especially effective among the young. As Schramm, Lyle, and Parker point out, "a child is more likely to pay attention to and store up some fact or behavior if is is *new* to him." To children, almost everything is new. (There are some built-in safeguards; communication must begin with something that is at least a bit familiar.) They add, "There is another reason why television should be an especially effective agent of incidental learning while the child is still young. This is because at that time it seems so *real.*"[25] Later, they note, a child develops the "adult discount"—the ability to say "it's only a story." Thus, children learn skepticism and consumer skills.

But even this kind of learning has a nasty little side effect of its own. Some recent research has shown that as early as the second grade children indicate a "concrete distrust" of commercials and by the sixth grade they have a "global distrust" of all commercials. There may be a "trend toward cynicism around the second to the fourth grade," the study reported. Critic Joseph Morgenstern is appalled: "We want our kids to grow into something more than wily purchasers who've learned from bitter experience that life is one big con, that everything ties into everything else out of mutual greed, not mutual need."

Reflex effects. Not all incidental learning is on the part of the audience. Mass communicators are inveterate reviewers of each other's work. Reporters assiduously read competition newspapers and listen to newscasts. In the meantime, broadcast newsmen are avid readers. Copycatting is a familiar phenomenon, and not necessarily an intentional one. We noted in the previous chapter that local newsmen apparently learned the norm of objectivity and the inverted-pyramid structure from the wire services. The press associations pay attention to each other, and sometimes talk like twins. The following stories were transmitted almost simultaneously:

MILWAUKEE (UPI)—The nation's political eyes today watched 15 northern and eastern Wisconsin counties, where residents of the 7th Congressional District were electing a new member to the House of Representatives. . . .

MILWAUKEE (AP)—The nation's political eye, trying to focus on the 1970 congressional elections, borrowed a lens from Wisconsin's north woods today where voters in the 7th Congressional District were naming a successor to Melvin R. Laird. . . .

On a much broader scale we find vogues passing among the media like quicksilver: near-simultaneous discoveries of "the national mood"; a sudden passion for ecology; a spate of beach-blanket-bingo movies; a plum-pudding of holiday football bowl games; a clutch of cute witches in TV comedy.

The vogues sometimes self-destruct. In 1952 four cowboy series rode the video range, and their number gradually increased to nine by 1957 and became "adult" in orientation. Collectively their ratings jumped 25 percent, and by 1961 there were 29. As a result, their ratings were diluted—not even the most avid fan could watch them all—and in 1962 the number of westerns dropped by half, and the following year fell by half again. TV had oversupplied itself.

The effects of new media upon the old (and vice versa) have been widely noted. Television absorbed many characteristics (and characters) of radio, film, and family magazines. TV learned from itself that because it *can* show interesting events, it *must* show them. After TV, newspapers began running more and bigger pictures, and baseball coverage became more interpretative because the fans had seen the game on the tube. In the early 1960s the faltering *Saturday Evening Post* was redesigned, a la television, for "visual excitement." Executives of the *Post* considered buying some "Bonanza" TV scripts and converting them into short stories. Earlier, television had transformed a *Post* cartoon series, "Hazel," into a comedy show. Newspapers covered the dashing performances of such lawyers as F. Lee Bailey, news magazines spotted a trend in trial lawyers, and television entertainment gave birth to "Judd for the Defense."

what does it all mean?

We find the field of media effects in some disarray and overlaid with a patchy fog. Entertainment media are believed to provide a healthy respite for the audience, and yet they also encourage escapism. The news media arouse anxieties, but perhaps also induce a kind of narcosis. Mass communication is both cathartic and stimulating, and probably more the latter. Reinforcement of social norms is valuable, but beware of blind conformity.

The National Commission on the Causes and Prevention of Violence perceives harm in media violence. The Commission on Obscenity and Pornography sees little damage in explicit sexual materials.

Communication scholars have gotten away from the idea of an atomistic *gesellschaft* society that is directly persuasible, and call attention to the strong interventions of social ties. But sociologist William Catton proposes that "the trend in modern society apparently has been toward the weakening of the actual influence of these intervening social variables. Society has been moving closer to being the way we once thought it was [that is, atomistic] while we have been abandoning that once inappropriate image of it."[26]

Down in the trenches the psychologists, sociologists, philosophers, mass communicators, and ordinary viewers, listeners, and readers are debating. And above the din soars Marshall McLuhan with a telescope in his ear.

for further reading

Baker, Robert K., and Sandra J. Ball, eds. *Mass Media and Violence, A Report to the National Commission on the Causes and Prevention of Violence.* Washington, D.C.: U.S. Government Printing Office, 1969.

Innis, Harold A. *The Bias of Communication.* Toronto: University of Toronto Press, 1951.

Klapper, Joseph. *The Effects of Mass Communication.* Glencoe, Ill.: The Free
 Press, 1960.
McLuhan, Marshall. *Understanding Media.* New York: Signet, 1964.
Miller, Jonathan. *Marshall McLuhan.* New York: Viking, 1971.
Report of the Commission on Obscenity and Pornography. New York: Bantam
 Books, 1970.
Schiller, Herbert I. *Mass Communications and American Empire.* New York:
 Augustus M. Kelley, 1969.
Schramm, Wilbur, Jack Lyle, and Edwin B. Parker. *Television in the Lives of
 Our Children.* Stanford, Calif.: Stanford University Press, 1961.
Schramm, Wilbur, and Donald F. Roberts. *Process and Effects of Mass Commu-
 nication,* 2nd ed. Urbana, Ill.: University of Illinois Press, 1971.
Steiner, Gary A. *The People Look at Television.* New York: Knopf, 1963.
Surgeon General's Scientific Advisory Committee on Television and Social
 Behavior. *Television and Social Behavior: The Impact of Televised
 Violence,* and *Reports and Papers,* 5 vols. Washington, D.C.: U.S.
 Government Printing Office, 1972.

pop culture

the 24-hour brainwash

pop´u•lar, adj. 1. Of or pertaining to the common people.
cul´ture, n. 4. The enlightenment and refinement of taste acquired by
intellectual and aesthetic training.
—*Webster's New Collegiate Dictionary*

Of course you can stop handling the stuff, but it won't stop handling you.
Or has someone discovered a way not to hear Muzak, not to see billboards,
not to be touched by propaganda?
—Bernard Rosenberg, in *Mass Culture Revisited*

Take me to your leader. Togetherness. Police action. Forty lashes with
a wet noodle. Squaresville, man. You're so dumb, you think manual
labor is president of Mexico. You think Sherlock Holmes is a housing
project. Well, I'll be a dirty bird. See you later, alligator. Pogo. Norman
Rockwell. Point of order. Davy, Davy Crockett (second incarnation).
Red Buttons. Old soldiers never die, they just fa-a-a-de away.

      Do these cultural artifacts seem a little strange? Surely they
denote the time period from which they are drawn as clearly as a neon
sign. But the 1950s are not peculiar in that sense. Nearly every decade

has its markers, which flavor it not only for those who live through it but for all who come after. It's the cultural wash, sweeping over us and influencing us in subtle ways, pushing us here, keeping us out there.

University faculties may be the most consciously intellectual groups assembled in society. Tell them their profession long ago adopted Hollywood techniques and they would be shocked. But ask any one of them if his university uses the "star system" and he will know exactly what you mean. Throughout the 1960s, the term was "white backlash," but early in 1972 it became "the Archie Bunker vote," named for a TV character who did not exist a year before. James Reston, Jack Anderson, and William Buckley to the contrary, the most influential editorialists in the nation may be a pair of fiftyish twins from Sioux City, Abigail van Buren and Ann Landers, who deal daily with half a dozen letters and in the process give personal advice to millions of readers.

What is this popular culture that touches our lives so pervasively? Critic Dwight Macdonald has argued that for about a century (and it has been the mass media century) Western culture has been divided in two. One part he calls "high culture," by which he means the traditional kind we read about in books on art, music, drama, poetry, and study in literature classes. The other is mass or popular culture.[1]

Distinguishing between high culture and mass culture is a little like trying to decide who or what has "soul." Everything depends upon who you are and where you begin. For some, high culture is blessedly elitist; for others it is snobbishly so.

But there is one aspect of mass culture that all agree on. Mass culture, popular culture, *kitsch* (a German term used mostly by those who look down their noses at pop culture), or however you want to label it, is machined and programmed in large amounts. Baled like hay (or like stacks of Rod McKuen albums), widely distributed (as with *Love Story,* the book with the largest paperback first printing in history—4,350,000 copies—which went not just to bookstores and drug stores, but to discount houses and just about every five and dime in the country), and calculatedly homogenous (as with Johnny Cash, poor white but also enough Indian to be oppressed minority with touches of jailbird, drug user, drunk, you-name-the-problem-I've-had-it).

Sure, it's entertaining, but is it art? Frankly, we're going to cop out on that one. For us, the test of art is simple: does it last? And there is simply no way to tell now.

What survives tends to show something basically true about the human condition, so that it communicates with us over even centuries of distance. Pop culture must be saying something, too, for we all listen to it at length. But much of what it says is the opposite of true: hokum designed to fix the attention without engaging the mind.

why isn't pop art good art?

It *may* be, and you are free to decide for yourself. Charles Dickens was, according to the critics of his time, Mr. Kitsch himself as he serialized many of his major works in newspapers and magazines. Today he is recognized as perhaps the greatest of English novelists. He is certainly the most popular, as he was then, and his stories have a depth those of the other kitsch-vendors did not. A willingness to treat the tough questions of life honestly seems to be one characteristic that separates art likely to survive from art that won't. Most entertainment does address life, but much of it evades anything more than the cheap answer. Partly this is because truth tends to be unpalatable to most of us. Partly it is due to the seemingly self-contradictory fact that truth in literature requires substantial imagination on the part of the artist, something generally in short supply.

But partly, too, there is in the mass media an emphasis on haste. While the tough questions may be asked, the answers rarely get pursued. To illustrate, let us take a scenario from one of those doctor-nurses-relevant shows. (Bet you it'll seem like something you saw last week but you can't name the series. If you get curious, check the footnote at the back of the book.) The episode begins when a call girl is hospitalized with a heart attack:

> Drama develops when the young woman, previously regarded as a model, acknowledges that she is a prostitute. Bedside solicitude vanishes at once. The student nurses, bundles of wholesomeness until now, are full of prurient curiosity. A young resident who had obviously been smitten by the young "model" is now grimly moralistic. But liberal good will—TV's staple commodity—takes over. The student nurses settle back into straight-faced professionalism. The head nurse—a Wise Elder—castigates the resident for his priggishness. Full of remorse, the resident rushes off to apologize to the call girl who has already checked out of the hospital. And now we come to TV's dilemma: Does the call girl elicit the same mental hygiene dispensation as the juvenile delinquent, the junkies, the mentally sick, the divorced, and the suicidal? Or is she too threatening to middle class stability for that? Can vice be rewarded with kindness? Has TV gone hipster on us? In the end, the script utilizes the oldest dodge in *kitsch.* The young physician intercepts the call girl as she is leaving her handsomely furnished East Side bagnio. (She has just been discharged as a bad health risk: What if she should have another heart attack while in the company of an important client?) As the young resident murmurs his Hippocratic apologies, she is stricken with another heart attack and dies in his arms. Before she does, each has learned something: she, that the world is not a jungle; he, that it is. In any event, the day is saved for tolerance, but nobody has to face up to life with Clarissa.[2]

The first observation that may be made of this story is that while there is a flirting with reality, the ultimate decision is to equivocate, to let the Big Sleep intervene to solve the problem. Some basic facts about the nature of human beings might have been developed had the doctor and the call girl been allowed to proceed with their relationship. But some of those basic facts might well be disturbing to the viewers—hence the posing and immediate begging of the questions in the TV version. Hard answers are not good answers for TV. Or for life either, perhaps. After David Susskind's interview show on educational television featured a group of prostitutes, an Iowa legislator threatened to withhold appropriations for the state's educational TV network. Such programs are pornographic, he asserted, and said Iowa wanted no such content on its educational television.[3]

But cheap answers bring escape. Critics of television who point out that the Saturday morning cartoon shows pose violence as an acceptable solution to problems often overlook the fact that the audience seems to desire quick answers in all its network drama. No one knows for certain whether this is a result of our American character with its impatience or a result of long-time habituation to mass media entertainment. As an audience, however, we respond best to the neat solution, the problem stated succinctly and wrapped up within 58½ minutes, including commercials and station breaks. Thus, David Rintels, a television writer, has observed that "television brings you a detective in a wheel chair and that is a success so next they bring you an insurance investigator who is blind and that is a success with a result that now ABC is trying to put together a new show about—I wouldn't kid about this—a sheriff in the Old West with a stiff trigger finger."[4] Unreality is acceptable in the mass entertainment world, but reality may not be.

Another point needs to be made: while individual examples of mass culture, pop culture, or *kitsch* do not seem to last, *kitsch* as an art form does. Do you tire of an interminable series of family situation comedies? Better learn to live with them. "The Partridge Family" started out in the fall of 1970 as just another program trying to survive the year on network TV. By December the show's first recording, "I Think I Love You," was on its way to selling 3.5 million copies. In two months alone, royalties from "Partridge Family" bubble gum amounted to $59,000. The only thing very different about the show is that it combined a story line with music. Aside from that fairly minimal feature, the show sat astride the main channel of family sitcoms such as "My Three Sons," "Family Affair," "To Rome With Love," ad nauseam. The long-time head of marketing at Screen Gems, which produced the show, knew the program would be a success as soon as he read the pilot script. "I've been at this business so long I can smell it," he said.[5]

Before the family shows on television, there were family shows on radio. The longest running show in American broadcasting history was a family show—Carleton Morse's "One Man's Family," which lasted 27 years (April 29, 1932 to May 8, 1959) through some 134 "books," a record we hope will never be equaled.

Let us try one more synopsis:

> A valiant and respected soldier of a different race has eloped with his chief's daughter. Brought to trial for it, he defends himself and persuades his judge to find in his favor. The soldier is promoted to command against an invading force, and off he goes, leaving his wife in the charge of a faithful lieutenant. The lieutenant is treacherous, having seen a rival advanced over his head to the position he long coveted. Hatching a plot for revenge, the lieutenant convinces his superior that his bride has been unfaithful with the rival. The soldier smothers his bride, but soon learns her innocence, and takes his own life in remorse. The troublemaker, found out, is scheduled for the worst punishment ingenuity may devise.

Does this sound familiar too? Something out of the *kitsched* Indian culture of our own Wild West? Perhaps from the many television shows devoted to "the organization"? Or a story from the warrior-code days of the Samurai? Perhaps even from some high culture, maybe Shakespeare? Shakespeare did use the story, for his *Othello,* but other writers have used it, too. The first known telling of it was Giraldo Cinthio's *Il Moro de Venezia,* published in 1565, 40 years before Shakespeare decided to use the plot. And who reads Cinthio today? It seems fair to say that it is not the story that is art, but the artful telling of it, even though the plot survives, too.

Then how can we tell what is likely to survive as art, and what is not? How can we tell, in other words, what has enough truth in it to be worth our serious attention? Art is elusive, we admit, and usually the observer has to become a critic in order to get anything out of what he sees. But if you ask yourself three or four questions, you can reach a pretty close approximation of a play's survival chances, and you can have a lot of fun watc'   g bad television as well as good:

1. What i.   .   lationship between what the program describes and the actuality?

2. What does the drama *say* about life?

3. What kinds of attitudes are implicit *in* it?

4. How does it illuminate the life-style or character of the society in which it is set?

a test case

The story to movie to book example of *Love Story,* a recent example of great popular cultural success, came under the flinty-eyed scrutiny of sociologist Herbert J. Gans, who put to it the questions listed above. He found some interesting answers. *Love Story,* as you may know, concerns Jennifer, a Radcliffe music major of humble Italian-American origins, and Oliver, a Harvard hockey star who is also quite wealthy and of a famous family. They meet, fall in love, marry in spite of his father's objections, sacrifice her career to his law school education, and start out in pursuit of happiness with the highest salary of any member of his law class. Jenny dies shortly of leukemia. In the book, Oliver reconciles with his father; in the movie, the reconciliation is uncertain.

Question One: Story versus actuality. Upward mobility is an aspiration we all have, Gans acknowledged. But what he took to be the primary message, that there need be no conflict between love and success, stands contrary not only to 2500 years of Western literature, but also to the life experience of many people, according to divorce court records. And, taking a shot at the improbability of Italian Jenny and WASP Ollie ever meeting, much less mating, in real life, he observed that of the 1200 names in Radcliffe's student directory, only about a dozen were Italian. But perhaps what makes the story so attractive to the many millions who find it so is just the romantic improbability of it all. Which makes it pop culture, not art.[6]

Question Two: What statements about life? Gans listed some statements the film seems to make. Older moviegoers are told that some young people still subscribe to the eternal verities: money, love and marriage, ambition, college education even at a sacrifice, and respect for one's elders if not for one's parents. The rich are shown that wealth is good and that their sons will amass more. The poor are shown that a working class girl can still win an American prince. Young women are shown that they can reject their parents, and young men that if they find the right girl, they can cut themselves off from their families. Gans asked himself, is this the way it is? Not particularly, he replied, else why all the fuss these days?

Question Three: What implicit attitudes? Here *Love Story* is more accurate, Gans found, though not obviously so. For one thing, Jenny gloms onto her rich kid by putting him down constantly. This feeds his self-hate and at the same time fosters her desire for his dependency. What the audience widely takes for romantic foreplay is really, upon closer examination, slightly sadistic on her part and somewhat masochistic on his:

"Jen . . . what would you say if I told you . . ."
I hesitated. She waited.
"I think . . . I'm in love with you."
There was a pause. Then she answered very softly.
"I would say . . . you were full of shit."
She hung up.
I wasn't unhappy. Or surprised.[7]

But perhaps *Love Story* is art. It permits analysis on several different levels, as all great art does, even though the story is quite straightforward on the surface. Without doubt subsequent generations will be interested in *Love Story* for what it can tell them of the aspirations of a people who were at the time engaged in a brutal war abroad and often violent upheavals at home. Is Jenny the American girl of the 1960s? Is she what we wish the American girl was? It's safe to say we don't really know. Only history will tell. And probably, as has been said, history will tell lies, as it always does.

the comics as art

One thing is clear: Erich Segal did not set out to write art in *Love Story,* and Paramount Pictures did not set out to create art on film. Further, movies were not created to bring art to the masses. Hollywood was born not of art, but money. It wasn't art that attracted the men who developed the large Hollywood studios—Carl Laemmle, a bookkeeper; Adolph Zukor, a one-time floor sweeper; Samuel Goldfish, later Goldwyn, a glove salesman; William Fox, a cloth sponger; Nick and Joe Schenk, druggists; Marcus Loew, a furrier; Lewis Selznick, a jewelry salesman; and Louis B. Mayer, a junk dealer.

Nevertheless, a good deal of art came out of Hollywood, as it emerges sometimes from the crassest financial schemes. What is crasser than figuring ways to shuck nickels and dimes from little kids during a massive depression? That is when the comic books began as a serious form of mass communication. Introduced by Famous Funnies in 1934, comic books were soon selling millions of copies a month. Superman, Green Lantern, Captain Marvel, Batman and Robin, Plastic Man, even Donald Duck and Mickey Mouse became sellers totaling more than 600 million copies yearly. And today copies of those early comic books bring premium prices at the used-book stores. *Someone* thinks they are valuable.

Furthermore, the comic strips have those who seriously advocate them as art. Imagine a comic strip with only three characters—a cat who loves a mouse with unrequited passion, a mouse whose sole object in life is to hit the cat with a brick, and a police dog who is in love with the cat and whose aim in life is to protect it from the bricks and put the mouse behind bars. Not too many possibilities in this triangle, you say. But George Herriman, working a strip a day from 1916 until his death in 1944, drew such an infinite variety of twists on this situation that the strip, "Krazy Kat," is deemed by some the greatest comic strip of all time, and has been the subject of books and articles.

Newsweek, in doing a cover story on Charles Schulz, creator of "Peanuts," went to pains to point out that not only did the strip and its spinoffs gross $150 million in 1971, it did so in some very artful and artistic ways. (Though perhaps any financial success impels some people to see art beneath the surface.) Jules Feiffer, himself a comics artist of stature, has analyzed Superman at length, and found him to be a secret masochist and third member of a rather weird love triangle which includes Lois Lane and Clark Kent.[8] Superman and all the comics are junk, concluded Feiffer, but therein lies their artistic value. Junk can get away with doing or saying anything, like the drunk at the wedding. It can say things that need to be said to people (mostly kids, but not always) who for reasons of their own need to have them said. Schulz was eulogized thus by Stanford theologian Dr. Robert McAfee Brown: "We learn new truths about children and, even more important, about ourselves. We see ourselves mirrored in his characters." *Newsweek* reported that Brown had a forceful reminder of that in a Schulz original framed on the wall of his study. A-student Linus, blanket-addicted as ever, sermonizes in the last panel: "Hoping and praying should never be confused with studying."[9]

Art or nonart, "Peanuts" is culture for the masses. It runs in 1340 daily newspapers, reaches 60 million readers, and appears in 19 languages.

enter the counterculture

Perhaps, however, the true measure of mass culture's influence on our lives is not told by testimony of persons who might have better things to do, or circulation figures or dollar amounts. Perhaps a better measure is the extent to which the counterculture must choose mass culture instruments to express itself.

During the early and mid-1960s, when underground papers were sprouting like hemp in Kansas, almost untended, they were not immediately recognized as mirror images of mass culture media. Within a few years, however, they had shaken out not only a successful formula, but a system of star performers who themselves appeared to be alter-egos of mass media fixtures:

• Dr. Hippocrates, for the *Berkeley Barb* and later the Los Angeles *Free Press,* treated questions on the same topics but from a different orientation than his straight counterparts, Playboy Advisor and Dear Abby.

> Question: Is masturbation physically harmful if I do it once a day? Answer: There is a story about a little boy who was found masturbating and told that he would go blind unless he stopped. "Well," he pleaded, "can I do it until I need glasses?" . . .

Dr. Hip soon found himself syndicated in a dozen and a half underground papers, and by 1969 even the San Francisco *Chronicle* was running his column on Sunday.[10]

• Ron Cobb, who seemed to combine the one-shot-kills styles of Bill Mauldin and Herblock into heavy cartoons showing America at the brink of destruction, became *the* editorial cartoonist of the underground.

• Underground Press Service and Liberation News Service, the AP and UPI of the counterculture, provided the content from outside the local community, written and illustrated in proper middle-of-the-underground-road style.

• Classified ads for bargain-hunting swingers, astrology guides for the astrally afflicted, and yes, even comic strips, proved to be effective reader lures.

And naturally enough, the counterculture donned khaki as its adherents entered the military or were recruited from it. By the time there were some 500 civilian underground papers (not counting perhaps thousands of high school publications that also fit the counterculture definition), there were also nearly 100 antiwar GI papers, talking about the Vietnam war (nearly 18 percent of the time) but mainly stressing such noncivilian topics as GI rights (50 percent of the time).[11]

The Revolution even went to some pains to go electronic, although Federal Communications Commission control of frequency allocation made this more difficult than for print media. One way of airing an underground radio station was found by KLFR in Berkeley, California, an unlicensed station that would go on the air for about 45 minutes daily using the same frequencies assigned to taxi cab companies. The audience obviously could not be large. If you weren't a taxi driver, you had to have a walkie-talkie or shortwave radio to listen in. KMPX-FM, a San Francisco station that did have a license, tried an underground, free-form style beginning in 1967. Other stations tried it, too, notably WNEW in New York. "We accept Modess ads so we can do a documentary on George Jackson," one station manager declared, trying to explain the need to be both commercially and counterculturally oriented.[12] Typical content included announcements of lost dogs, free clinics, appeals for student demonstration bail money, and (perhaps most important) music that was definitely not top-40. In addressing their audiences, the underground radio stations were not unlike rural 250-watters in South Dakota. But KMPX found it could not make it financially, and switched back to above-ground programming. Fewer than 300 listeners phoned to protest.[13]

Television was still another matter. The best the underground could manage was to use the videotape recorder and make its own programs. No way yet to turn this into a truly mass medium, but then one of the objectives of the underground was also to fracture the "culture for the masses" concept. Cable TV offers the hope that home-grown TV programs may be aired over a public-access channel, but for the counterculture at the moment, it is the doing it that's important. To encourage this, Michael Shamberg and Raindance Corporation published a manual of do-it-yourself TV called *Guerrilla Television.* Some of the fun things they suggested doing (once you have come up with $1500 to $10,000 for your own videotape recorder) include taping "housewives shopping at those sterile shopping centers. Ask them if they really like it. Play back on the spot." Also recommended was taping President Nixon's speeches and adding canned laughter.[14] For a counterculture to exist, a mass culture must first exist.

mass culture takes over

As the 1970s began, however, the counterculture showed definite signs of decline. The reasons are many, ranging from decreased U.S. participation in the Vietnam war, which had done so much to stimulate protest, to a weariness with the counterculture life-style. Possibly Establishment harrassment had also taken its toll. But unquestionably, too, there was the fact that, willingly or not, the counterculture had influenced mass culture very heavily. And the most obvious characteristics and objectives of the counterculture had been embraced by mass culture. Long hair, boots, and Levis. The bra-less look. Students on school boards. Even comic books have become anti-Establishment: the Green Lantern has taken on the population explosion, and Lois Lane has become a women's liberationist.

And it has always been thus—at least, ever since we have been a mass society, with mass culture and mass communication. Any popular development soon brings media attention, which further stimulates interest. As skiing has developed from the fairly obscure and elitist winter sport it once was to the mass activity it is today, media attention has also increased. Likewise, during the 1870s and '80s, as the bicycle emerged from a plaything of London regency dandies to popularity, it was accompanied by magazines devoted to cycling. By 1895 there were more than 30 such periodicals and nearly every city of any size had a cycling paper. Beginning in 1894, more than a quarter of a million bikes were sold in the U.S. each year, so that by 1900, according to one estimate, there were 12 million in the U.S. Such numbers meant power, and the League of American Wheelmen, with more than 100,000 members, sought to influence legislatures to spend money for better roads.[15] But not even cycle magazines could talk about roads, pneumatic tires, and races all the time, so they branched out. Some discovered a social consciousness in cycling, some that the sport had moral (or immoral) implications. *Harper's Bazaar* and *Vogue* put out bicycle fashions every spring. Women found in the wheel a means of their liberation—"To men, rich and poor, the bicycle is an unmixed blessing; but to women it is deliverance, revolution, salvation," wrote Mrs. Reginald de Koven in *Cosmopolitan* in 1895.[16] Some saw, as some always do, the new fad as simply a way to get to hell faster—one magazine reported that 30 percent of the "fallen women" who came to the Women's Rescue League of Boston had been "bicycle riders at one time."[17] The *Journal of United States Artillery* and the *Army and Navy Journal* devoted articles to the bicycle as a military weapon. Travel magazines carried articles on long trips by bike.

Everything was looking rosy for the bicycle-publishing world until one thing happened. And even when it did, the *Cycle Age and Trade Review* knew what to do. In 1901, it merged into *Motor Age.*

magazines—the national press

Such stories of how magazines struggle for survival by adapting themselves to a changing society strongly suggest that popular culture is a product of interchange between the people and the media. Perhaps the interchange is most clearly illustrated by the magazine industry. In a 1968 study of how people in Oklahoma receive news of the rest of the world, FCC commissioners Nicholas Johnson and Kenneth Cox described nonnewspaper and nonbroadcasting input that reached Oklahoma City, a metropolis of nearly 400,000. Magazines concerned with public affairs included *Time,* with 7569 subscribers in Oklahoma County, *Newsweek* with 4120, and *U.S. News & World Report* with 3826. *Look* had 20,752 and *Life* 15,395 subscribers. *Harper's* reached 1478 Oklahoma City households, while *The New Republic* went to 670 subscribers in the entire state.[18]

These figures show the limited access of magazines to the people and contain a concealed hint of the industry's real importance. The limited access indicates the difficult financial situation of the industry. Yet the fact that magazines provide additional channels from the rest of the world must be stressed, too. For magazines in a real sense form the only national press that we have. As a class, they are not beholden to the daily news cycle, to the top 100 companies that advertise on television, or even to the millions of us who constitute the mass audience. They tend to rely instead upon some highly specialized audiences which are assembled from all over the country, so that the magazine industry offers a sort of grid overlay on the communications network that is quite different from the patterns of newspapers or broadcasting.

Some 750 general circulation magazines (the largest 50 range from *Reader's Digest,* with a circulation of about 18 million, to *Successful Farming,* with a million subscribers) provide merely the top of the iceberg of the industry. The bulk of magazines are house organs and corporate publications. How many of these there are no one knows, but estimates run as high as 8000. The group ranges from *Action,* published by AC Spark Plugs for its employes, to *Zip News,* put out by the Zip Feed Mills of Sioux Falls, South Dakota. Included in the list is *Ford Times,* with a circulation of nearly one million. But there are also thousands of magazines belonging to special interest groups—religious organizations, professions, hobbyists, dental patients, and, among countless others, sadomasochists. A survey in 1970 by Los Angeles defense attorney Franklin Laven estimated that 24 million copies of "adults only" magazines are published each year.[19] Laven estimated that some 2000 separate titles of such magazines are published in the United States.

Despite the fact that magazines number in the thousands, the industry remains in trouble, as it has been from the start. "The expectation of Failure is connected with the very name Magazine," Noah Webster wrote almost 200 years ago, in mourning his *American Magazine.* Today's magazines face at least three major problems distinct from the competition for reader's time other media have always presented. One of these is the rising cost of mailing. By 1976 magazines may have to find an additional $130 million just to pay for postal increases. Probably that means raising circulation and advertising rates. But advertising has already been declining, at least in the general-circulation periodicals, since larger numbers of potential buyers can be reached by television than by magazine. In addition to rising costs and declining advertising, magazines face a circulation crisis. The big magazines, anyway, have found that the greater the circulation, the more expensive the magazine is to produce. If subscriptions sell for as little as 10 cents a copy, and costs average 40 cents a copy, then the more subscribers the more the cost. The hope for the industry thus becomes the special-interest magazine.

Whatever happens, the magazine as a species will continue to scramble successfully for its existence. In doing so it will remain an important current in the cultural wash, just as it has always been. In 1789, *Christian's Scholar's and Farmer's Magazine* was carrying instalments of 38 series on rhetoric, farming, theology, oratory, manners, painting, music, Greek history, and many others. Clearly, Christians, scholars, and farmers were gluttons for information then, as they are today.

for further reading

Becker, Stephen. *Comic Art in America.* New York: Simon & Schuster, 1959.
Glessing, Robert J. *The Underground Press in America.* Bloomington, Ind.: Indiana University Press, 1970.
Goodstone, Tony, ed. *The Pulps: Fifty Years of American Pop Culture.* New York: Chelsea House, 1970.
Hammel, William M. *The Popular Arts in America: A Reader.* New York: Harcourt Brace Jovanovich, 1972.
Johnson, Michael L. *The New Journalism: The Underground Press, the Artists of Nonfiction, and Changes in the Established Media.* Lawrence, Kans.: University of Kansas Press, 1971.
Mott, Frank Luther. *History of American Magazines.* 5 Vols. Cambridge, Mass.: Harvard University Press, 1939–1968.
Peterson, Theodore. *Magazines in the Twentieth Century.* Urbana, Ill.: University of Illinois Press, 1964.
Rosenberg, Bernard, and David Manning White, eds. *Mass Culture: The Popular Arts in America.* Glencoe, Ill.: The Free Press, 1957.
———. *Mass Culture Revisited.* New York: Van Nostrand Reinhold, 1971.
Shamberg, Michael, and Raindance Corporation. *Guerrilla Television.* New York: Holt, Rinehart and Winston, 1971.
Voelker, Francis and Ludmilla, eds. *Mass Media: Forces in Our Society.* New York: Harcourt Brace Jovanovich, 1972.

advertising

it loves us, but is it our friend?

Our business is to try our damnedest to make people want what we're
selling.
—Leo Greenland, president, Smith/Greenland Advertising Co., New York

Certainly it marks a profound social change that this new institution for
shaping human standards should be directed, not, as are the school and the
church, to the inculcation of beliefs or attitudes that are held to be of social
value, but rather to the stimulation . . . of materialistic drives and
emulative anxieties. . . .
—David Potter, in *People of Plenty*

Who was Bob Hope's announcer during the comedian's years on the
radio? What was the consolation prize on the TV program "The $64,000
Question"? Who sang "Come-on-a-My-House"? These are some of the
questions posed during a Trivia contest held at Columbia University.
Teams from Yale, Princeton, Penn, Barnard battled it out in the finals.
When the winner was finally picked, he was awarded a trophy while
a chorus sang the "Mr. Trivia" song—"There he goes, think of all the
crap he knows." You have to get your basic training from the time you

are six until perhaps 12 or 13, the champion opined, crediting his success to "my garbage-filled mind."

It's no accident that he got the garbage almost exclusively from the mass media. There's a reason, and it has to do with what has become one of the basic functions—perhaps *the* basic function—of the mass media.

Put on your classical economist's hat for a minute. What is the *product* of television? Is it entertainment, news, distraction? If so, then who pays for the product? The audience benefits, and therefore should pay, right? But do we? Well, maybe indirectly, through a slight increase in the price of goods advertised on television and which we buy. But we don't pay directly, and if we don't buy the goods, we don't pay at all. Furthermore, even if we *do* pay, we don't make the purchase in a clean, cash-on-delivery method. Nor do we order the entertainment or distraction. We don't pay the actors, the director, or anybody we ever see. There's a lot of talk about what the audience will or will not buy, will or will not accept on television, but how many of us ever really have the chance even to express our opinions to the network, or the magazine editor? Almost never, unless we use our letterhead and our postage to do it. When you get right down to it, we're not purchasing much of anything. We subscribe to the paper, but if we complain about rates going up, the publisher will tell us our subscription pays for only about 40 percent of the cost of producing our copy. And what about those free-circulation papers that are just tossed on the doorstep at night? Who pays for them? Advertisers, of course.

The money, the big money, when it changes hands, goes from the advertiser through the advertising agency to the proprietor of the medium. But what does the advertiser get for his money? If you've watched much prime-time television lately, you know there's rarely one sponsor for any given show. Various companies take commercial slots in a particular program. Nor are these advertisers really "buying time," although that's the term they use. If they were, there would be great competition for the cheapest time possible, but there isn't. And soon all time would cost about the same. It doesn't, of course. "Prime" time costs more than afternoon time, and the Super Bowl time costs most. Why? Obvious, again. That's when the largest number of persons watch.

we the product

Now, what is the product of television? What is manufactured, bought, and sold? It's not entertainment: it's us, the audience. The networks are really in the business of manufacturing audiences, which are then advertised and sold to advertisers who wish to reach large numbers of people at relatively little cost.* This simple truth explains why networks seem determined to return again and again to the scene of former successes in a kind of deification of cliches. For cliches work at this level of art, at least for the purposes to which they are put. If "Gunsmoke" draws an audience of 20 million viewers, and if a commercial minute on the program sells for $40,000, the advertiser who buys that minute will reach that huge audience for a cost of $2 per thousand persons. This is a fantastically cheap cost, and if "Gunsmoke" is what it takes to get us all together, then "Gunsmoke" it will be.

Moreover, the responsibility for content undergoes a subtle shift. No longer is the network, or the publisher, or the record company executive responsible for the garbage. Neither is the advertiser. The person who bears ultimate responsibility is the viewer-reader-buyer. It becomes *his* good taste or poor taste, likes and dislikes, program preferences, which determine what bait is employed to attract him in the largest numbers.

So, it is all our fault. To put it another way, we get the kind of media we deserve. Or to put it more positively, the media seek to serve our wants, because in doing so they assemble the largest audiences and earn the highest revenues.

promise her anything, but give her . . .

But we cannot let advertising off that easy. It is a major industry in the United States, with close to $20 billion a year spent on advertising in newspapers, on radio and television, billboards, direct mail, and many other forms of communication. The 600 largest advertising agencies account for more than half that amount, as they plan campaigns, select media in which to advertise their clients' products, and earn their keep by taking some 15 percent of the total ad charges made by the media. The largest agency, J. Walter Thompson Co., has 7200 employes spread among its more than 50 offices in 29 countries.[1] Any industry this large has an influence on its society, but when one so large is intimately associated with the mass media of communication, its potential for influencing the public is greatly increased.

The origins of the system whereby advertising is placed by agencies that themselves do not actually manufacture the article being sold are hazy. They have roots, however, in the developing mass media, and in the need for media specialists who study just what kinds of people attend to what kinds of publications. Also important, as the

---

*It's not necessary to talk with a radio or television time salesman to obtain confirmation of this fact. Pick up a copy of *Broadcasting,* the chief trade journal of the industry. Look at the advertisements, and decide for yourself what the product of broadcasting is.

major corollary, was how to find just the kind of promise the reading public would swallow.

In the 1890s, for example, the Woodbury Dermatological Institute was offering to remove "permanently" and "without pain" (two important promises) the following: pimples, dandruff, freckles, moles, warts, eczema, red nose, blackheads, birthmarks, oily skin, and superfluous hair. Who among us would not like to believe? And who can? Yet when Mr. Woodbury decided to let the young J. Walter Thompson Co. handle its account, he just the same as filed his claim on the Mother Lode. Who reads the *Ladies Home Journal,* asked J. Walter Thompson. Ladies, he replied, who have yearnings beyond the removal of warts and superfluous hair, or else they wouldn't be reading the kind of thing printed in *Ladies Home Journal.* Woodbury soap, for "The Skin You Love to Touch," hit the right promise—sex appeal. Also, that was one promise the consumer would not care to make a fuss about its not being kept. Woodbury was thus off to millions in profits, and so was J. Walter Thompson.

Seventy-five years later, makers of toilet soaps are spending $30 million on television advertising alone, and Thompson is handling accounts spending $764 million on advertising throughout the world.

And it all has to do with Seller stalking Buyer (and vice versa).

Consider these two ads from the personal column of the *New York Review of Books:*[2]

Witch-woman, intelligent, attractive, long-legged (5'11"), old-fashioned, highly romantic, but crazy with literary musical and philosophical penchants, age 25, seeks mature, sincere, witty, not necessarily Rock Hudsonish, hopefully professorial man of varied intellectual interests, age 30 to 60. Located Midwest—will travel.

Extraordinary man, early 40s, Anglo-American background, wide interests, eclectic tastes, largess of humor, seeks extraordinary woman in San Francisco area who has gotten past image and identification and should like to explore fully the emotional, intellectual, physical, sexual, and spiritual nature of being—while delighting in the moment. Not interested in money, matrimony, or a monogamous relationship.

Whether or not Witch-woman and Extraordinary Man were made for each other, their ads do illustrate the basic function of advertising, which is to bring seller and buyer together. That, of course, is well and good, even essential. The problem arises in the techniques used to accomplish that bringing together. Back in the 1700s, when Samuel Johnson was helping to sell off the unprofitable Anchor Brewery, he made the key observation about advertising as an industry: "We are not here to sell boilers and vats, but the potentiality of growing rich beyond the dreams of avarice." Samuel Johnson *knew.* "Promise, large promise, is the soul of an advertisement."

selling rocks that aren't stones

If the operational word in advertising has been "promise," the words "promise and deliver" sum up the whole thrust of consumerism and government regulation of advertising in the 20th century. Does the soup ad appear to offer a broth filled to the brim with chunks of meat and vegetables? Then, says the law, better deliver meat and vegetables and not the dozen marbles stirred in by the photographer just before he snapped his shutter. Indeed, for most of the long life of advertising, the philosophy of the craft has been make great promises and let the buyer beware.

Four hundred years ago a chunk of a certain kind of rock was thought to have curative powers. Seller told Buyer, "This is a Bezor stone." Buyer bought, discovered his rock was not a stone, and sued Seller. Court said Buyer could collect only if Seller had said, "I *warrant* this to be a Bezor stone." Simply *saying* so was mere puffery, quite legal, for the honorable purpose of selling the rock.[3]

It was a fine point, wasted on most buyers, but it did sum up the law regulating advertising. Since then, a gradual erosion of advertiser freedom to say anything has set in, until today advertisers hardly know what to say, and the whole concept of puffing, or making exaggerated and unprovable claims, is being questioned.

Advertising offers promises not only to the consumer, but to the advertiser as well. Power lawnmowers, to give but one example, were expensive to produce and buy. Advertising cured all that, and stimulated business for toe surgeons as well. If the neighborhood on Sunday morning now sounds like the Red Baron's home aerodrome, the fault (we are told) is the consumer's, not the manufacturer's. Advertising simply performed its chief economic contribution—promoting a dynamic, expanding economy.[4]

By helping to increase demand, advertising helps lower the unit price of an article. And make no mistake about it, advertising does seek to stimulate demand. The Association of National Advertisers in 1963 listed 52 separate tasks performed by advertising. The stimulation of consumption was clearly behind every task listed. Task number four, according to the list, is to remind people to buy. Task 26 is to remind people who are already users to buy again. Task 37 is to explain where to buy. Task 19 is to hold present customers against the inroads of competition, while task 20 (can you guess?) is to convert competitive users to the advertiser's brand.[5]

just because they
are there

Thus it is clear that if the basic contribution of advertising is to keep the wheels of commerce oiled and turning, that aim alone provides the industry with its chief ethical basis. Judged by the ethical standards of traditional religion, or even the more humanistic conscience of the social responsibility theory discussed in Chapter 7, advertising may at times appear amoral, lacking in the kind of morality that puts contemporary value judgments on its actions. Not *immoral,* simply without morality. Or, to put the whole thing bluntly, you can reduce advertising's system of values to eight words: as long as it's there, let's sell it.

But if promises could not be made, there would be no need for an advertising industry, since there would be no scurrying about to find just that promise which means more to the consumer than the opposition's promise means. If a standard of truth were required, all products could be listed in large handbooks, along with price and any other distinguishing characteristics. The consumer would consult his handbook and then make his decisions largely as he makes them today—impulsively. Witch-woman would be required to list the fact that she weighs 165 and Extraordinary Man to admit that "early 40s" really meant mid-50s. Fortunately for those who place matrimonial ads, that area of life is one in which the old rule of advertising, let the buyer beware, still holds. But it would be a duller world. Examine the bare-bones bluntness of this ad from the same column:

> Jewish husband wanted. Slightly published Midwestern woman, 32, wants to stop writing and become homemaker.

Set up a truth standard and those words meet it. Head on. If we were prospective Buyers, our common sense would tell us Seller is an honest person. There is a good buy. But still, wouldn't we owe it to ourselves to check out Witch-woman? After all, you never know.

So we mustn't get the notion that advertising is really manipulating us all that much. We want to be convinced to do this or that, perhaps to do what we know is not good for us. If someone comes along with a persuasive message that helps tip the scales, and that we can blame later when things don't turn out just as we hoped they would, so much the better. The most effective advertisers have always known that they aren't selling us anything; they are mostly finding ways to let us sell ourselves.

the curious case of indian henbane

Perhaps the outstanding example of how we the public have gone along with attempts to sell us something that has no use whatsoever beyond the image we feel the product gives us and which has, in fact, harmful effects, is the case of Indian henbane. The term was given by the English, who found the American Indians using the herb for a variety of remedial purposes, including curing infection, toothache, and reducing fevers. One of the things it did best, according to the Indians, was soothe coughs and catarrh, or inflammation of the air passages of throat and head. All of which helps explain why the life span of the average Red Man was so short, since Indian henbane, or tobacco, is one of the least healthy of man's vices.

By the mid-1920s, the combination of commerce and man's willingness to be exploited had brought the tobacco industry a long way. But there was one segment of the population (not counting children) that was not yet part of the smoking public: women. There was a mild sexual revolution underway, brought on in part by the moral looseness engendered by World War I and the advent of the closed automobile. Cigaret smoking was a good way to announce one's liberation to the world, and quite a few women were doing so already by the time Chesterfield ran its famous ad of a man and woman sitting on a moonlit river bank. The man was lighting up, the girl coaxing, "Blow some my way."

The systematic development of the new market took its chief impetus from the American Tobacco Company, and its enterprising young advertising head, George Washington Hill. In turn, Hill received his impetus from Albert Lasker, a leading developer of the mass advertising that we know today. Lasker, so the story goes, became angry when his wife was refused permission to smoke in a Chicago restaurant. He pointed out to Hill, who doubtless did not need such instruction, the fact that most of womanhood represented new territory for the cigaret companies in general and American Tobacco in particular.

There can be little question that, for reasons deeply buried in woman's psyche, she wanted to smoke cigarets in public. The desire was there, and what Lasker and Hill had to do (indeed, about all they or any advertiser could do) was find reasons why smoking was acceptable. The first reason they advanced was that outstanding women smoked. They proved this by running testimonials by practically all the women in the Metropolitan Opera Company. Such ads sought to establish two things: prominent women smoked, and they did so at no harm to their voices. The ads did not make an effective promise, since not too many women wanted to be opera singers. But it was not long before Hill found a slogan that did. Here he tells it in his own words:

> I was riding out to my home, and I got to 110th Street and Fifth Avenue; I was sitting in the car and I looked at the corner and there was a great big stout lady chewing gum. And there was a taxicab . . . coming the other way. . . . I looked, and there was a young lady sitting in the taxicab with a long cigarette holder in her mouth, and she had a very good figure. . . . right then and there it hit me; there was the lady that was stout and chewing, and there was the young girl that was slim and smoking a cigarette. "Reach for a Lucky Instead of a Sweet." There it was, right in front of you.[6]

The promise was clearly there, and the idea was so good Albert Lasker later took credit for it, or at least half-credit. Promising a slender figure in return for smoking won more converts than the opera singers could ever hope to. "There's real health in Lucky Strikes," sang the ads now. How to get that health? By smoking Luckies instead of eating those between-meal sweets. "For years this has been no secret to those who keep fit and trim. . . . They know that Lucky Strikes are the favorite cigarette of many prominent athletes who must keep in good shape. They respect the opinions of 20,679 physicians who maintain that Luckies are less irritating to the throat than other cigarettes."

getting rich on the "right" promise

Such advertising brought American Tobacco earnings of from around $12 million in 1926 to $40 million in 1930. There were objections, of course, from moralists to candy-makers. But the tobacco company paid little real attention to their complaints, and there was no requirement to prove the truth of the slogans used. By the late 1960s, American was spending $45 million on television advertising alone. Only in one significant respect did the promise change over the years. At the start, it was made primarily to nonsmokers. Later, after the revolution had been engineered, the promise was to smokers of other brands. "Smoke the Smoke the Experts Smoke," "LS/MFT—Lucky Strike Means Fine Tobacco." The final compliment to the sales value of a slogan—marketing a cigaret designed especially for women—was paid by Philip Morris with Virginia Slims, perhaps the biggest success of any of the five dozen new brands introduced within the past few years. "You've come a long way, baby," women were told, "and now you even have your own cigarette."

But now women have more. The Cigar Institute of America, the public relations front office for the cigar industry, is planning (surely you've noticed) to expand the nation's total of 15 million cigar smokers. One large segment of the campaign is being devoted to women. In 1970, there were, according to the Cigar Institute, some 200,000 women cigar smokers in the country. Small as that figure is, it was double the number a decade previously. Among the female smokers of cigars, reported the Institute, are a number of prominent women, including Marlene Dietrich, Mia Farrow, Mrs. Sargent Shriver, Mrs. Abe Fortas, and Gloria Vanderbilt. And, if they were a bit beyond the younger generation's level of identification, there was also 23-year-old Patty Keating, who "about four months ago took a drag from her boy friend's cigar and liked it." Furthermore, no nonsense about smoking only at home for her. "Cigars are chic," she said. "I smoke on the street. I smoke in restaurants. I guess the only place I wouldn't light a cigar is in church."[7]

Yes, you've come a long way, baby. But you haven't learned very much. Or, in the words of the dedication in the front of American Tobacco Company's golden anniversary commemorative volume, " . . . we are proud to dedicate 'Sold American!' to the American public. Their good taste has made it all possible."[8]

Or has it? A more likely reason has been the skillful exploitation of the self-criticisms and doubts felt by a public largely unaware that it is being subtly urged to buy and use a product, not for some inherent utility it possesses, but because its use fosters an improved self-image. In doing this, advertising sometimes outsmarts itself and its critics.

During the last days of cigaret advertising on television, when the industry could see that Congress was moving toward a complete ban (which did go into effect in January 1971), an interesting stopgap measure was advanced. Much of the criticism of cigaret commercials centered around the youth pitch of the commercials. The reason for this, of course, was that smoking in and of itself performs little if any service to the smoker. Advertising therefore seeks to arouse happy ideas in our minds, and tries to get us to transfer those happy thoughts to the product. And what's a happier idea to a 40-year-old man than the suggestion he's not, as his wife and friends have been telling him, over the hill? But if you have frisky young things cavorting in the greenery, aren't you also holding them up as peer models for teen-agers? That's the way the argument went, anyway, and to stave off doom, the advertising-tobacco forces yielded to pressure and began to feature only models who were obviously over age 25.

So the industry outsmarted itself by fishing for the youth crowd, and hooking the critics. To head off still further criticism, the advertisers retained the older models in subsequent print media ads. But wait. Motivational research shows that one of the main reasons young people smoke is to appear *older.* And a year after the cigaret commercials left television, cigaret consumption had increased by 12 billion to a total of 536 billion, the largest increase of recent years. As the executive director of the Pittsburgh Tuberculosis League told a New York *Times* reporter, "It looks like more young people are beginning to smoke than older people are quitting."[9]

It was not long before the antismoking forces within government began to suggest that perhaps a mistake had been made in banning cigaret commercials from the air. When cigaret commercials sank from sight, so did anticigaret commercials, which were required under the FCC's fairness doctrine. While tobacco companies learned to their delight that they could survive without television, the foes of smoking learned they could not.

feeling the public pulse— carefully

The point here is that the media always are heavily influenced by their environment. Torn between two loyalties—to his audience and to his profit motive—the proprietor of the newspaper, magazine, or broadcasting station often finds those loyalties conflicting. He tries to resolve the conflicts, usually in a very conservative way, and usually finds himself marching along at the rear of the parade. To avoid "lewd advertising," the Los Angeles *Times* in 1965 announced a screen code for entertainment advertising. The assistant advertising manager, Marvin M. Reimer, announced the new rules in a letter to 300 ad agencies, movie distributors, and nightclub managers. He explained the *Times'* decision this way:

> It is not our intention to be either picayunish or prudish in our evaluation, but we are convinced that moral and social values have not decayed as frequently as portrayed, and we trust that together we can find a better standard of values in the area of good taste.[10]

Subjects to be avoided included burlesque, bust measurements, compromising positions, couples in bed, double meaning, excessive cleavage, violence or sadism, horizontal embrace, nude figures or silhouettes, nymphomania, perversion, promotional use of the word "sin," short bikinis, and half a dozen others. Words to be avoided included girlie, homosexual, immorality, lesbian, lust, naked, nudies, nudist camp, nymph, party girls, pervert, prostitute, rape, seduce, sex, strippers, and third sex, to name but a few. The Los Angeles *Times* thus was banning in advance ads for most of the top box-office attractions of the late 1960s.

Seven years later, in 1972, a glance at the *Times* movie ads showed the newspaper in retreat. The two-column ad for *Sweet Sisters* declared that the movie featured "Hardcore pornography as it's never been shown before!" *Easy Virtue* was billed as the "diary of a teen-age prostitute." A three-column ad for *The Deviates* announced it was "the first complete feature film on sexual deviation." To make things perfectly clear, the ad also carried a definition: "de•vi•ates—persons who depart noticeably from the norms of social behavior." *All About Sex* was advertised as "quite possibly the only film in existence that can make even the 'DIRTIEST OLD MAN' BLUSH!"[11]

What caused this turnabout in the space of a few short years? It was not the unfettered greed of the publishers of the Los Angeles *Times:* the Times Mirror Company is one of the wealthiest of the media conglomerates, with assets of some $200 million. It could get along very well without the revenue—steady though it is—from ads for pornographic movies. What had happened was that society's values had undergone a change that not only permitted such films to be shown legally but made lining up outside the box office more socially acceptable as well. So the *Times* changed too.

There is nothing new in this. During the mid-1800s, for instance, publishers, in their natural wish to conserve—and not offend —their audiences, refused to allow large type to be used in advertisements. Their reasons had to do with considerations of taste. The advertisers never saw the logic of that position, and to defeat the ban, used scores of small letters to build a single large one. Thus, a rather effective multi-column display ad might be constructed entirely from small type, despite objections of publishers. In the 1920s, a lively debate developed over the question of whether it was advisable to allow commercial messages to be broadcast over the new medium of radio. Broadcasters were certain that radio somehow had a holier mission than to allow the salesman to come into the sanctity of the home, when little children were gathered about the dinner table and might be corrupted by crude commerce. But no other form of support for radio was forthcoming, and the rest is history.

and then going ahead

One of the more final blows to the myth of the home as sacrosanct came in the late 1960s, when *Mademoiselle, Harper's Bazaar, Cosmopolitan,* and other publications accepted full-page advertisements for a certain new product. A nude model stared out from under a headline that advised: "Relax. And Enjoy the Revolution." The revolution in question was the sexual one, and the product advertised was Cupid's Quiver, a liquid feminine douche offered in two floral scents (orange blossom and jasmine), and two flavor scents (raspberry and champagne). Naturally, the advertising agency that handled the account, Marsteller, Inc., had conducted extensive pre-tests of the product to discover its acceptability. Most members of the test panel bought the idea, Marsteller reported, though some recommended eliminating the heavy, sweet flavors, like peach rum.

So much for problems of taste.

But in the way great advertising innovations have of opening new vistas (and incidentally working as social catalysts), the new feminine hygiene products brought the kind of technical problems ad agencies love to solve. Question: Could such product advertising go on radio and television? Answer: Does the sun set in the West? Answer to answer: Yes, but slowly.

Traveling under the euphemistic name of "personal product ads," the various feminine hygiene commercials encountered scant objections from the broadcast audience. Partly this was due to apathy, partly to acquiescence, and partly to lack of clear channels through which to respond. The National Association of Broadcasters, the industry trade organization, did not in its list of advertising standards prohibit such advertising. What was required was an "especial emphasis" on ethics and the canons of good taste. "Such advertising as is accepted," said the association in hinting that the coast might not be entirely clear, "must be presented in a restrained and obviously inoffensive manner."[12] But the absolute ban on such advertising had been off for radio since 1965, and was lifted for television in January 1969. The pioneers in breaking this new ground, in addition to the makers of Cupid's Quiver, were Alberto-Culver with its FDS and Intec Laboratories with Feminique.

Once the door was shown to be open, and competition began to be apparent, the problems facing advertisers got tougher. The search was on for just the right promise. By late 1970, the Television Code Review Board was complaining of hard-sell techniques. Specifically, the Board was concerned about direct comparative claims, such as "X is the best one around." Keep it generalized, begged the board. "Very effective," "lasts and lasts," and so on. And avoid showing men in the commercial.[13] In other words, make the promise sufficiently vague to allow different segments of the audience to interpret it, or discount it, as they wish.

No such constraints applied to print media, however, where product competition might be quite keen. A *Ladies Home Journal* ad for Demure, a deodorant douche concentrate, showed a young man and a young woman looking into the camera. Fully dressed, even to the high collar of her long-sleeved blouse, but looking pretty smug about something, she appeared to be leaning with arms crossed against her fellow model. "Love," instructed the copy, "but keep it lovely. You've found your man, and you intend to keep him. Hint. Demure helps. It's the liquid douche concentrate created by a gynecologist to keep you fresh and clean and desirable. No fake cover-up." But what there might be in some of those products, it turned out, was enough chemical to cause serious skin reaction on some women. Thus, the advertising industry and its clients, through research, had solved the problems of how to market a new product, how to advertise it, how to overcome any guilt feelings women might have in buying it, but in doing so had produced yet another item of questionable value to the welfare of the consumers, who bought it by the carload. (In 1969, $48 million was spent advertising depilatories and deodorants on television alone.)

All of this suggests that the consumer is a passive little bundle of hidden fears and unrecognized desires, just waiting for someone to come along and present an excuse to drink, smoke, go get a tub of fried chicken instead of cooking supper, or to buy the "New! Improved!" model of X, when the only thing "New! Improved!" about it is the label. And all the time willing to undergo a bombardment of new tastelessness without complaining.

If that is depressing, consider what Leo Greenland, the president of Smith/Greenland Co. (a middle-sized advertising agency doing $17 million in billings annually), told a conference of his peers. "The most disgraceful statistic in our business," he said, "is the one that says 85% to 90% of all advertising is ineffective, ignored, not remembered and acted on. Our business *is* to manipulate people, to stir human yearnings, to use human motivation to sell goods. It is not only our business but everyone's business."[14]

When we read something like that, we don't know whether to cheer for people being skeptical enough to resist some of such efforts, or to weep because concepts like peace, brotherhood, and goodwill do not seem to be consumer goods.

for further reading

Cone, Fairfax. *With All Its Faults.* Boston: Little, Brown, 1969.
Della Femina, Jerry. *From Those Wonderful Folks Who Gave You Pearl Harbor: Front-Line Dispatches From the Advertising War.* Edited by Charles Sopkin. New York: Simon and Schuster, 1970.
Mayer, Martin. *Madison Avenue, U.S.A.* New York: Harper & Row, 1958.
McGinniss, Joe. *The Selling of the President, 1968.* New York: Trident Press, 1969.
Ogilvy, David. *Confessions of an Advertising Man.* New York: Atheneum, 1963.
Packard, Vance. *The Hidden Persuaders.* New York: David McKay, 1957.
Sandage, Charles, and Vernon Fryburger. *Advertising Theory and Practice,* 7th ed. Homewood, Ill.: Irwin, 1967.
Simon, Morton J. *The Law of Advertising and Marketing.* New York: W. W. Norton, 1956.

Turner, E. S. *The Shocking History of Advertising.* London: Michael Joseph, 1952.

Wood, James Playsted. *The Story of Advertising.* New York: Ronald Press, 1958.

relating with the public

speak loudly and don't call it a big stick

Never has anyone ruled on this earth by basing his rule on anything other than the rule of public opinion.
—José Ortega y Gasset

An organization of radical instructors at a Midwestern university announced in a newsletter that "the mass media is [*sic*] at the heart of the imperialist mythmaking and propaganda machine, operating both domestically and internationally. . . . We must plan movement strategies against the media." But after identifying the villain, the article concluded on a peculiarly Establishmentarian note: "We must discuss movement policies regarding our public relations with the media."[1]

Everyone knows that politicians, industrial titans, and big-time fund-raisers conduct public relations campaigns. Yet so do PTAs, the Black Panthers, trailer parks, and the National Association of Artificial Breeders. Public relations is a natural extension of the fundamental need to communicate.

The term itself (often abbreviated "PR") describes both a means and an end. The desired effect is a favorable attitude on the part of various publics—customers, political constituents, club members, employes, and many others. The means to this end are also various. Advertising, publicity, promotion, and personal influence are all part of the PR practitioner's armory. Any or all may be used to create and preserve a good opinion toward the individual or organization that foots the bill.

Ideally, public relations is not just a matter of saying good things, but of doing good as well. Though much of PR is just a slather of frosting on stale cake, the best is a disclosure of an active social conscience.

why public relations?

When favorable opinion makes a difference, public relations becomes a necessity. As a consequence, what we now call PR has a long but spasmodic history. Almost 4500 years ago, the citizens of the Sumerian city-state of Lagash were so irritated by heavy taxes (on cattle, fish, wool, onions, divorce, burial) that they overthrew the Ur-Nanshe dynasty and installed a new ruler named Urukagina. Though Urukagina acquired considerable power, he remembered how he got it, and he wisely reduced taxes—the first such reduction in recorded history.

Most authoritarian rulers conduct PR with a whip or a sword. They couldn't care less about public opinion. "Let them eat cake," Marie Antoinette is supposed to have said. Before long she contributed her head to the guillotine. But her contemporary, Catherine II of Russia, remarked, "I praise loudly; I blame softly." Catherine's reign was 34 years, and she is remembered as "the Great."

Modern public relations—the term wasn't much used until this century—had its origins in the development of mass communication, democracy, social conflict, and industrialization. Mass communication permitted persuaders to reach large audiences rapidly. Democracy made public opinion a power to be courted and feared. Conflict among elements of a democracy is most handily conducted and resolved through communication. Industrialization created many new publics and put some distance between them; it also gave birth to specialized functions in management, one of which is public information.

The modern public relations man has a remarkably mixed

ancestry. Certainly he can link himself to all the great evangelists, particularly those who have flourished since the invention of printing, from Martin Luther and John Calvin to Billy Graham and Oral Roberts, whose crusades are monuments to publicity as well as piety. One result of the Reformation, incidentally, was the establishment by Pope Urban VIII in 1623 of the College for the Propagation of the Faith, from which we get the term "propaganda."

One prominent root of the PR family tree stretches back to the American Revolution, to Madison, Jefferson, Hamilton, and especially Tom Paine and Sam Adams. Conflict always inspires great exhortation, and the Colonial newspapers were a prime outlet for revolutionary passions.

"These are the times that try men's souls," wrote Tom Paine in the dark winter of 1776. "The Summer Soldier and the sunshine Patriot will, in this crisis, shrink from the service of their country; but he that stands it now, deserves the love and thanks of man and woman. Tyranny, like Hell, is not easily conquered; yet we have this consolation with us, that the harder the conflict the more glorious the triumph." No one in the Pentagon has ever put it better. The day before the battle of Trenton, Washington read Paine to his troops, and his words were given much credit for the victory.

Publicity lost some dignity after the War for Independence, when the parties of Hamilton and Jefferson stooped to vilification. "Should the Infidel Jefferson be elected to the Presidency, the seal of death is that moment set on our holy religion . . . ," said a Federalist newspaper. Jefferson's press responded in kind.

Some new and strange creatures nested in the family tree during the early 19th century when the press, freed by technology from tight constraints on space, found room and audience for the trivial, the freakish, and the selfish. James Gordon Bennett, the great innovator of popular journalism, published some self-promotion on the eve of his marriage:

> I cannot stop in my career. I must fulfill that awful destiny which the Almighty Father has written against my name in broad letters of light against the wall of heaven. I must give the world a pattern of happy wedded life, with all the charities that spring from a nuptial love.[2]

By little coincidence P. T. Barnum hove into view in 1835, the same year Bennett founded the New York *Herald*. Barnum noisily unveiled a hag named Joice Heth, alleged to be 116 years old and formerly the childhood nurse of George Washington. She grossed $1500 a week for Barnum. When her authenticity was doubted, Barnum himself joined the attack, charging that she was merely an automaton made of rubber, whalebone, and springs operated by a ventriloquist, and this made her all the more valuable. After she died (at about 80, doctors guessed), Barnum exposed the entire fraud, buried her sumptuously in his family plot, and cheerfully pleaded that he himself had been duped.[3] About the same time, Andrew Jackson's political opponents confected a legend for their candidate, the doltish Davy Crockett. The Crockett myth had no impact on voters, but it was later to strike Walt Disney quite forcibly.

By the end of the century, politicians had to rely heavily on paid advertising, whistle-stopping, and campaign pamphlets. News had become the prime commodity of the leading dailies, and the press flaunted its independence.

The modern public relations man came to birth early in the 20th century with the unintentional midwifery of the muckrakers— crusading journalists of Progressivism who sought to reveal the excesses of industrial czars. Muckraking induced reforms, but it also inspired the hiring of publicity advisers such as Ivy Ledbetter Lee, who eventually became a spokesman for the coal industry, the Pennsylvania Railroad, and the Rockefellers.

Lee's great insight, shared by another pioneer, Theodore N. Vail of American Telephone & Telegraph, was that there is more to public relations than keeping the public hoodwinked or ignorant: the public could, and should, be informed.

Even in the early stages of PR, the news media were suspicious of handouts from publicists, though not always for the right reason. In 1908 the American Newspaper Publishers Association opened a campaign against "free publicity"—because it might mean a reduction in advertising revenues.[4]

Some moralistic criticism was heard, too, including the argument that newspapers should cover news for themselves to insure impartiality. But then, as now, the news media realized (without often admitting it) that the PR man has reportorial value. He provides stories, and, what's more, they're free.

Under the news ethic, which we sketched in an earlier chapter, the press was, and still is, peculiarly vulnerable to publicity. Editors adopted the attitude "if it happens, we'll print it," and publicists grew adept at making things happen.

At the same time, the doctrine of objectivity created a vacuum for public relations to fill. Bare-bones news stories tell the reader what happened, but may neglect to say why it happened. For example, news coverage of the savage coal strike at Ludlow, Colorado, in 1913–14 concentrated on eruptions of violence between miners, company guards, and the state militia. Little was said of the underlying political, economic, and social issues—except in press releases from the combatants. Within a few weeks of the notorious "Ludlow Massacre" of April 1914, Ivy Lee was hired by the Rockefellers to defend the policies of their Colorado Fuel and Iron Company. Like the coal operators, the United Mine Workers also released statements of their position and their views of the causes of the strike. Local newspapers and the wire services reproduced those statements at length, and from them a reader could glean the central issues.[5]

During World War I, public relations became a tool of national mobilization. Headed by George Creel and staffed by two men who would become giants of PR, Carl Byoir and Edward L. Bernays, the Committee on Public Information successfully persuaded the public to buy Liberty Bonds and the press to adhere to a code of self-censorship. Creel also distributed President Woodrow Wilson's rhetoric to foreign countries, both enemy and ally.

The Committee on Public Information proved the value of public relations and showed that it could be conducted on a grand scale. Bernays recognized this quite clearly when he entitled his 1923 book *Crystallizing Public Opinion.* (In it he coined the term "public relations counsel.")

As a result of World War I propaganda, considerable scholarly and popular interest focused on public opinion and its molding. Newspapers grew more skeptical of PR and more aware of their own need to interpret—as Walter Lippmann pointed out in his *Public Opinion,* published a year before Bernays' opus. A further stimulus both to PR and to interpretative reporting was the Great Depression, whose causes and cures demanded copious explanation.

Again during World War II public relations aided mobilization, and efforts were centered in the Office of War Information. After the war, the OWI transmuted into the United States Information Agency, which now conducts American foreign propaganda. Domestic governmental publicity is widely dispersed. In the private sector, the early lessons learned by fund-raisers and industrialists have been repeated and refined during the postwar years.

Today PR is a big business itself. In the United States and Canada, the total annual expenditure is perhaps $1 billion annually (not counting government, which spends nearly $500 million). *PR Reporters,* a trade newsletter, estimates that 66,000 are employed in U.S. and Canadian PR firms and corporate PR departments. If government information officers, small firms, part-timers, press agents, and clerical helpers are counted, the figure may be close to 100,000.[6] And this does not include the thousands of amateur publicists who serve clubs and societies.

the corporate conscience

During the process of canonization, the candidate for saint-hood is represented by a "postulator of the cause," who furnishes the Church with evidence of the candidate's worthiness. But it is not a one-sided procedure. A "promoter of the faith"—a *promoter,* mind you —is appointed to attack the evidence in order to test its soundness. Over the years these *promotores fidei* have been nicknamed "devil's advocates."

One of the better justifications for PR is its potential for devil's advocacy—for questioning corporate policy on the public's behalf. This occurs most readily if PR is built into the management process and not merely tacked on, and if the corporation follows what PR authors Cutlip and Center propose as the four steps toward a sound PR program: fact-finding, planning, action, and evaluation.[7]

So if the president of a manufacturing firm wishes to climb aboard the ecology bandwagon, his PR director will survey the public's opinion regarding the company and pollution—and, just as important, he will take a critical look at the company's conservation practices. If they are lax, the ethical PR man will say so, and see to it that they are improved. He knows that a campaign of words unsupported by deeds is merely a wisp of dime-store perfume.

Some companies, such as Cummins Engine of Columbus, Indiana, have long records of good works as well as fine words. Practical PR, as well as the ability to make french fries, is taught to McDonald hamburger franchisees—for example, if their area is stricken by a natural disaster, they are instructed to provide free hamburgers and coffee to rescue workers.

During the social upheavals of the 1960s, many companies developed a social conscience, while others had one thrust upon them, and still more manufactured one on a mimeograph machine. By 1972 there were over 200 corporate "public affairs directors" in the nation, compared to only a handful a few years earlier, according to a *Wall Street Journal* survey. Some of these were little more than recycled publicists who had little to do with policy, but several wrought important changes in company practices.[8]

Even mere words can sometimes have a salutary effect on corporate morality; executives, like celebrities, occasionally begin to believe their own publicity and try to live up to it. Some large companies have come to agree with A. R. Marusi, president and chairman of Borden, Inc., who told the National Association of Manufacturers' urban affairs committee that "the fulfillment of valid, rational human needs in a viable, economic way is becoming as much a concern as profit."

A professor of corporate law, Phillip L. Blumberg, has remarked that some of this talk is merely "felicitous rhetoric," but he adds, "The vital significance of such statements is that the objective of service to the society, which such business spokesmen are applying to business, inevitably will become the objective which the public generally will first accept as an appropriate role for business, subsequently come to expect, and ultimately to demand."[9]

Or, as the early practitioner Arthur Page constantly reminded AT&T, "You must remember that your promises are hostages to your performance."

In many ways, public relations has also served as a national conscience. In a brief but illuminating booklet, Roger E. Celler cites more than 60 organizations "dedicated to changing the private sector of America." Among them are Common Cause, Operation Breadbasket, Public Interest Research Group, and the Sierra Club. They and their leaders—including Ralph Nader, the Rev. Jesse Jackson, Paul Erlich, and John Gardner—know the value of public relations coupled with action.[10]

The sturdiest obstacles to "ideal" public relations are economics and human nature. The plain fact is that managers are hired to make money for owners, and that a conscience can cost money. In the long run, it is money well spent, but many stockholders and managers fix their vision on the short run. Then, too, an abrupt change in corporate policy amounts to a public confession of past misbehavior—or so it seems to many executives. The natural temptation is to play up the good, and to let it go at that.

up with the good

Appearing before a convention of the National Lawyers Guild, radical lawyer William Kunstler told his listeners, "You have an obligation to your client to work the mass media for all it's worth. We should talk to the press, and our clients should talk to the press. If you, as a lawyer, are afraid, let your client do the talking—but see that the press is told everything favorable."

This is not startling advice. A typical publicist's first thoughts are of trumpeting what is good about his client or his products or policies. Any politician—and government in general—leaps to a mimeograph machine when anything faintly favorable is ready to be said. A Congressman may denounce someone else's legislation as straight from the pork barrel, but he will present his own as the fruits of statesmanship. Industry behaves similarly. The American Mining Congress is more pleased to boast of its contribution of 50 Christmas trees to the annual Pageant of Peace in Washington than it is to discuss strip mining. After the Atlantic-Richfield Company dumped old car bodies into the ocean, it proudly announced that the sunken carcasses had become shelters for fish.

Chiropractors are forbidden by law to prescribe medicine, and they have adjusted their publicity accordingly: "Chiropractic does not employ force, coercion, drugs, medications or heroic measures. The chiropractor is not content with the mere masking of symptoms or the simple treatment of effects. He seeks the cause of the malfunction, disease, or ailment."[12]

In seeing the sunny side, the publicist does not necessarily lie. He merely recognizes some fine distinctions between the truth, the whole truth, and nothing but the truth. He seizes the most striking and attractive truths. So when P. T. Barnum advertised that his sideshow featured "a horse with its head where its tail ought to be," the rubes who thronged to view the freak found the literal truth: a horse hitched backwards to a buggy.

If the truth fails to glitter, it can be glazed with euphemisms. Military circles have given us "preemptive strike," "protective reaction" and "interdiction" in lieu of bloodier terms. From the New Left we heard of "armed love."

A few years ago the American Railway Magazine Editors Association became worried about their public image and proposed a few changes in traditional railroad language:

—"Dead man control" should become "safety control."
—"Gang" should be called "crew," lest the public be reminded of chain gangs.
—"Hot boxes" ought to be described as "overheated axle bearings."
—"Wreck train" should be changed to "emergency work train," and "wreckmaster" should become "derrick foreman."

The railroad editors urged these changes, they said, because "without clarity of expression, all else suffers."

Shrewd publicists tell their stories in the right place at the right time. In the 1968 presidential election campaign, Richard Nixon's "ethnic specialist" proposed these placements for two TV commercials:

Great Nation: This is fine for national use, but viz. local emphasis, it strikes me as best suited to the South and heartland. They will like the great nation self-help, fields of waving wheat stuff and general thrust of Protestant ethic image.

Order: Entirely suitable for national use, emphasis on cities which have had riots (Cal., Ill., Ohio, Mich., Pa., N.J.) . . . and in the South to reinforce RN's hard-line image.[13]

Jeffrey O'Connell, a law professor and critic, compared the automotive industry's statements on safety to its advertising. He concluded that "at the same time the car maker is disseminating ... safe driving materials, he is publishing advertisements urging youngsters to hit everything—or everyone—in sight!"[14] O'Connell found, among many others, these examples from General Motors:

From a safe-driving publication:	*From a magazine advertisement:*
... We can identify [an immature driver] ... without even looking—just by hearing the way he drives. A reckless or discourteous driver can be a quiet one, but usually isn't. He tends to make harsh, distinctive noises that reveal his dangerous presence as the rattles, growls, hisses, and buzzes of other menaces.	... Hulking under the 2 + 2's hood is our whacking great 4 BBL 421. Horsepower—338. Torque—459 lb.-ft. Blam! ... For stab-and-steer men, there is a new 3-speed automatic you can lock in any gear. Turbo Hydra-Matic ... Just straighten right leg, wind tight, move lever. Repeat. Make small noises in your throat. Atta boy tiger! ... [The 2 + 2 is] just a friendly little ... saber-toothed pussy cat. ... One of these at fast idle sounds like feeding time at the zoo.

hide and seek

To some observers, PR is an elaborate game of hide and seek —of concealing the bad and shouting the good. The players are the media and the publicists, and the prize is influence. No need to say who are the pawns. It's not that simple, of course, but there are some elements of gamesmanship.

Government agencies—especially those having at least a fleeting connection with security—are strongly tempted to hush unfavorable information "in the national interest." Similarly, corporate management avoids contributing to its own demise through confessions of misjudgment.

At times everyone is disposed to secretiveness. In 1970 a building at the University of Wisconsin was blown up by explosives made of nitrate fertilizer. Two months later 400 pounds of nitrate was stolen from a farm store in Monroe, Wisconsin, on the eve of Monroe's biennial "Cheese Festival," a promotional event that attracts thousands. City officials managed to say nothing about the theft until after the festival.

Usually the PR man is uneasy with secrecy because he likes to communicate and because he is aware of the newsman's appetite for exposé. He would prefer to point the newsman's nose in another direction. When actor Ronald Reagan prepared to run for governor of California in 1965, his public relations adviser, Spencer-Roberts &

Associates, was annoyed to find several embarrassing passages in Reagan's autobiography, *Where's the Rest of Me?* Rather than attract attention by trying to withdraw the book, Spencer-Roberts ingeniously took the opposite course. It bought thousands of copies and pressed them upon newsmen with the admonition to quote generously. The result was that the media largely ignored the book.[15]

Many years ago Cecil B. DeMille demonstrated how to make a silk purse from a sow's ear. In his 1915 film, *The Warrens of Virginia,* DeMille experimented with indirect lighting, and the results were murky. In New York, Sam Goldwyn previewed the film and wired DeMille that he couldn't possibly sell a movie in which "you couldn't even see the characters' faces half the time." DeMille pondered for a moment and wired back that he had used "Rembrandt lighting." Goldwyn was so delighted that he promptly raised the rental fee on the film.

Another face-lifting was disclosed in 1971 when Texas meat packers attacked a truth-in-labeling provision of the Federal Meat Inspection Act. The Texans had been making hot dogs containing "chevon"—a perfectly good term, they argued, for goat meat.

Though it may be sheerest gossamer, image makes a difference, and a publicist will go to elaborate lengths to mold an image. When the natural gas industry learned from a public-opinion survey that its image was stodgy and Victorian, the American Gas Association hired a team of publicists to inject some dash. They built a rocket-powered automobile fueled by liquified natural gas, and called it "The Blue Flame Special." They hired clean-cut Gary Gabelich—"perfect from a public relations standpoint"—to drive it across the Bonneville salt flats. To the relief of the publicists, the Blue Flame set a new land-speed record without blowing up, Gabelich was modestly heroic, and the media covered the event in exquisite detail.[16]

Historian Daniel Boorstin identifies this sort of thing as a "pseudo-event"—a happening that is planned, planted, or incited for the sake of being reported. He regards interviews, news "leaks," press conferences, news releases, and celebrities as leading examples. "Pseudo-events from their very nature tend to be more interesting and more attractive than spontaneous events," Boorstin says, and here's why: pseudo-events are more dramatic than real events, easier to disseminate and to make vivid, are repeatable at will, heavily promoted, convenient to witness and to talk about, and they add the bonus of spawning other pseudo-events.[17]

From the publicist's point of view, the trick is not to be stumped by the banality of the subject. Instead of thinking about natural gas as something that goes through a pipe to a hot-water heater, he sees it powering a rocket car past TV cameras.

Take the case of the Benrus Corporation, manufacturer of

watches, which hired the PR firm of Robert S. Taplinger Associates to boost its fame. *Public Relations News* enthusiastically tells what happened (all the italics are theirs):

An annual Benrus Citation Awards Program for the "Best Time of the Year" was planned. "Unique and superlative" time-based *achievements by 24 individuals* in entertainment, science, broadcasting, government, sports, etc., would be honored. The awards would mark fast-*time,* first-*time,* and shortest-*time* accomplishments and endurance or sustained efforts in terms of *time.*

Climax of the program would be *a gala awards presentation* reception in NYC, with widely known celebrities attending. The date of that event would be timed to coincide with *an important convention of jewelers* whose attendees would be invited to the reception.

The program, which has been operating for the past two years, follows essentially the following format: Distinguished and unquestioned authority is given the program by the members of the *Editorial Board of the World Almanac* who serve as judges. They have ready information about record-making events and people and happenings involving *time* all over the world. (Also, Taplinger keeps an eye out for interesting applications of the *time* idea in connection with entertainment and other widely publicized personalities.)

Nominations for awards are sought *from special-interest mediamen.* (For example, sports editors and sports writers are mailed postpaid cards on which they may submit nominations for specific "best *time"* categories.)

Continuing publicity is cultivated. . . . Two months in advance of the reception (usually held in mid-January), *tailored releases* are sent to selected media. These name several personalities "under consideration for awards" (e.g., a release about women nominees goes to women's page editors and it cites the *time*-related achievements of each). . . . *Special releases* also go *to media identified with each nominee and his or her field of endeavor.* . . . *A general release* in early December announces the "search" by the World Almanac for the 24 people who have made the most outstanding *time*-based achievements during the year. . . . Information about the several *persons who will make the presentations* is released piecemeal. . . . There are *stories about nominations* "put forward so far" . . . And *the locale* for the presentation's is separately announced.

Just before the reception, releases name *the actual winners.* These have included such achievers as *Joan Crawford* (for reigning longest *time* as a film star), *Lee Trevino* (for setting three types of pro golf records in the same year), *Lowell Thomas* (for his "longest-*time* contributions" to journalism and to international broadcasting), *Chi Cheng* (for setting world records in the women's 100-yard dash and 200-meter and 100-meter hurdles), and *David Merrick* (for the musical "Hello, Dolly!" then the longest *time* on Broadway).

Formal two-fold, deckle-edge *invitations* to the reception are *jointly extended by [Benrus] and the World Almanac editors* to media representatives, VIP's, and some 600 Benrus retailers and potential retailers. The invitation carries the names of the distinguished awards presenters (for 1971, there were *Bob Considine, Jack Demp-*

sey, Alan King, Yvette Mimieux, George Plimpton, and Jack Valenti)
and states that "other celebrities from the fields of sports, entertainment, business, government, and the arts will be our guests." The
reception time (5:00 P.M. to 7:30 P.M.) and the time of the presentations
(6:00 P.M.) are given.

At the reception, *a slide presentation* shows the winners in action.
Each is presented with a gold Benrus "Citation" chronometer, a
commemorative plaque, and a personalized copy of a special edition
of the World Almanac.

After the reception, *interviews* with the award winners are arranged and radio announcers *tape interviews* for immediate or future use. Media pick-up has been varied and extensive. . . . Each year
there is good *TV-radio* coverage, both local and network. For example, one of the 1971 winners appeared on the *David Frost Show*. He
was *Mitch Michaud,* who had climbed the top elevations in all 50
states in one year, and was identified as a Benrus award winner. . . .
The *wires* have carried the reception story. . . . *Syndicated columnists*
(e.g., *Leonard Lyons* and *Earl Wilson*) have described the event. . . .
Hundreds of other items have appeared in *major papers* (e.g., Time).
. . . Typical of the valuable media comment that ensued was a report
in the *New Haven* (Conn.) *Register* that the reception was "loaded
down with celebrities that crossed the lines of sports, show business,
science, and journalism."

What's the value of this hocus-pocus? Does it inform and edify
the audience? Not really, but doubtless many viewers and readers were
at least mildly entertained. Award winners and "distinguished presenters" received publicity for themselves, as did *World Almanac.* The
news and entertainment media acquired space- and time-filling material at little cost to themselves. As for Benrus, its president, Victor
Kiam II, remarked that the "best-time" program was a "considerable
assist" in boosting sales by 145 percent. He rated the costs as "amazingly low in relation to results."[18]

biting the handout that feeds

The author of *Madison Avenue, U.S.A.,* Martin Mayer, has
attributed a certain sneakiness to PR and, by comparison, some rectitude to advertising:

Advertising, whatever its faults, is a relatively open business; its
messages appear in paid space or on bought time, and everybody can
recognize it as special pleading. Public relations works behind the
scenes; occasionally the hand of the p.r. man can be seen shifting
some bulky fact out of sight, but usually the public relations practitioner stands at the other end of a long rope which winds around
several pulleys before it reaches the object of his invisible tugging.[19]

True enough, there are ropes and strings being pulled. A

young publicist for Paramount Pictures was mystified when an executive gave him $60 in cash and sent him to certain New York bookstores to buy an armful of Mario Puzo's novel, *The Godfather.* Other employes did the same. The publicist later discovered these bookstores were sampled by the New York *Times* when it compiled its weekly best-seller list, and that Paramount, which owned screen rights to *The Godfather,* was ensuring its fame.[20]

Newsmen resent playing puppet to PR men, whom they call "flacks." A handbook prepared by the Associated Press Managing Editors has this to say:

> A flack is a person who makes all or part of his income by obtaining space in newspapers without cost to himself or his client. Usually a professional. . . . The flack is the modern equivalent of the cavalier highwayman of old who looted the king's coach. The elegant manners of the earlier gallants obscured the basic fact, they got the gold. Today it is the courtly P.R. gent who waylays your male or female editor.[21]

Correspondent John Chancellor of NBC News detected the shadowy hand of a ghostwriter aboard an Apollo spacecraft when astronaut Alan Shepard remarked, "We're reminded as we look at the shimmering crescent that is earth that we still have fighting there. We are reminded that some men who have gone to Vietnam have not returned, and that some are still being held there as prisoners of war. It is our wish tonight that we can in some way contribute through our space program to better understanding and peace throughout the world."

Chancellor observed that "one is tempted to say: Hey, wait a minute! Those are noble sentiments, but what is the Vietnam war and the prisoner issue doing out in space? . . . Can it be that some bureaucrat in Washington decided that the astronauts should be used as an advertising medium for a propaganda policy?"[22]

The newsman's attitude toward the PR man is an odd mixture of contempt for his craftiness and puffery, disgust with his special pleading, envy for his pay and perquisites, and unblushing acceptance of his wares. While there is much to condemn in public relations, a large share of the criticism of it is equally an indictment of the media.

Though Chancellor decries PR, he himself served as director of the Voice of America from 1965 through 1967. His network's "Today" show accepted funds from Japan to broadcast from that nation. NBC's "Andy Williams Show" accepted $60,000 from the city of San Diego to originate a broadcast there (which city officials later refused to pay because Williams failed to say enough "nice things about San Diego"). The president of NBC News, Reuven Frank, addressed the

1971 convention of Sigma Delta Chi—a journalistic society that will not admit professional PR men as members—and told his fellow newsmen that they ought to improve their own public relations.

No matter how much they disdain it, the major media are dual users of public relations. They have their own PR or promotion departments, and they are the willing beneficiaries (or compliant prey) of the PR man on the outside.

For example, the Gannett newspaper chain (it prefers to be called "group") engages in PR by publishing an attractive employe publication called *The Gannetteer*. Gannett's amiability toward PR was also revealed when *Today,* its Cocoa, Florida, newspaper, hailed the opening of the Disney World amusement park near Orlando. *Today* airlifted 25 staffers to Disney World, armed with assignments for 22 opening-day stories. The result was eight full pages of Disney stories, including page one.

Fashion, real estate, sports, travel, recreation, financial, and drama pages are fertile ground for the publicist. Even food editors, whose major duty on most newspapers is to fill the columns of space around the grocery ads, are wooed with tours, conferences, and prizes by food processors. One food editor won a free ride on the "Kraft Salad Safari" to Denmark by giving the best English translation of *golbord,* a Danish word for smorgasbord. Her winning entry was "buffet." When the Senate Subcommittee on Consumers revealed that breakfast cereals are not especially nutritious, the story made the front pages—but not the food pages. However, two months later, when a paid consultant to the Cereal Institute announced that breakfast cereal was healthful after all, the food editors reported his speech in depth.[23]

What is happening is that public relations has become an integral part of the nation's information system. This is so, according to Scott M. Cutlip, a leading scholar of PR, because:

> 1. Our media's news values unduly emphasize the negative and conflictful and thus require balancing for a constructive democratic dialogue;
> 2. Our news media do not have the manpower, either in terms of depth or in terms of specialized knowledge, to adequately or accurately cover today's broadened, complex news spectrum.

Though PR may be unduly cheerful or self-seeking, its intrusion has value. Even if the PR man is a maker of images, he may do so in a good cause. And though he plants stories, they may richly deserve cultivation. In 1960 writer Tom Mahoney was approached by a PR firm that represented the Hickok Manufacturing Company of Rochester, New York. Hickok wanted a story written for *Reader's Digest* that would enhance its sales. Mahoney wrote the story, *Reader's*

Digest bought it, and Hickok's sales skyrocketed. Is this bad? Hickok manufactured automobile seat belts, and had underwritten basic research on their effectiveness at Cornell University. Despite their demonstrable value, seat belts were not popular and not required by law even though the U.S. Public Health Service, the American Medical Association, and the National Safety Council were urging their adoption. In short nothing much happened until Hickok, through Mahoney and the *Reader's Digest,* made an excursion into public relations. Within two months of the article's appearance, the state of New York enacted the nation's first safety belt legislation, auto manufacturers agreed to begin installing belt anchors, and the scene was set for Ralph Nader and other auto safety crusaders.[24]

The dependence of news media on PR as a reporter is indicated in a study by the American Institute for Political Communication, which found that "analysis of 22 key papers, which publish in eleven major metropolitan areas representing every sector of the country, reveals that one-fifth of the stories published in both the foreign affairs and health, education, and welfare fields are traceable in whole or in part to formal releases or statements issued by Executive agencies involved."[25]

In a study of publicity usage by Milwaukee media, William Schabacker found that the prestigious Milwaukee *Journal,* during a one-week period, in its nonwire, nonsyndicated editorial content, relied upon public-relations-generated releases or memos for more than 44 percent of its stories. The Milwaukee *Sentinel* based 52 percent of its local stories on PR material. That same week, 14 percent of WTMJ-TV's news stories were traceable to PR, as were 12 percent of WTMJ radio's. On the Wisconsin wire of the Associated Press that same week, 12.3 percent of items had their origins in PR.[26] This is not all bad. A good news medium will edit the puffery out of PR handouts and transmit only the worthwhile news, and alert editors will use news releases as tips for further investigation—sometimes of affairs that the PR man would rather not have ventilated. These studies do indicate, however, a high degree of mutual reliance between the PR man and the newsman.

The depth of PR's intrusion into the newsroom is suggested by the growth of paid publicity wire networks, whose teletypes clatter alongside those of the AP and UPI in major newspaper offices. One of these, P.R. Newswire, was founded in 1954, and by the 1970s it served more than 230 media in 50 cities. The media rarely mention these PR wires. As Cutlip has remarked, "The news media are quite contradictory in their attitudes toward the public relations function. They condemn public relations with lusty editorial voices but eagerly scoop up its handouts with their reportorial arms."[27]

The media are not alone in feeling ambivalent toward PR. Practitioners themselves are often apologetic about their profession—and some refuse to call it that. The Associated Press Managing Editors Association is truculent toward PR—and yet formed its own "Image Committee." Newsmen disparage publicists as freeloaders, and yet themselves accept—and even seek—free tickets, free meals, and free transportation. Scholars profess to be above the grime of huckstering and yet pay dues to professional organizations that lobby ardently.

We're reminded of a student of ours who barged into our office and asked for some information on public relations. He had decided to teach a course on the evils of PR at a nearby "free" university, and he wanted some ammunition. We mentioned Vance Packard's *The Hidden Persuaders* and a few other horror stories, and he thanked us profusely. As he turned to leave, he had a sudden thought. "By the way," he said in all sincerity, "can you give me any tips on how to promote the Free University?"

for further reading

Bernays, Edward L. *Crystallizing Public Opinion.* New York: Liveright, 1961.
Boorstin, Daniel. *The Image: A Guide to Pseudo-Events in America.* New York: Harper & Row, 1964.
Cutlip, Scott M., and Allen H. Center. *Effective Public Relations,* 4th ed. Englewood Cliffs, N.J.: Prentice-Hall, 1971.
Johannesen, Richard L., ed. *Ethics and Persuasion: Selected Readings.* New York: Random House, 1967.
McGinniss, Joe. *The Selling of the President, 1968.* New York: Trident, 1969.
Nimmo, Dan D. *The Political Persuaders.* Englewood Cliffs, N.J.: Prentice-Hall, 1970.
Raucher, Alan R. *Public Relations and Business, 1900–1929.* Baltimore: Johns Hopkins University Press, 1968.
Ross, Irwin. *The Image Merchants.* Garden City, N.Y.: Doubleday, 1959.
Simon, Raymond, ed. *Perspectives in Public Relations.* Norman, Okla.: University of Oklahoma Press, 1966.
Stephenson, Howard, ed. *Handbook of Public Relations,* 2nd ed. New York: McGraw-Hill, 1971.

law

the heavy control

John Stubbs or Stubbes was a very zealous Puritan who in 1579 published a protest against the project of a marriage between the Queen and the Duke of Alençon. He, his publisher Page, and his printer Singleton were condemned to have their right hands cut off, and the sentence on Page and Stubbes was carried out on November 3, 1579. When it was over, Stubbes waved his cap and shouted, "God save the Queen!"
—*The Fugger News-Letters,* Second Series, letter dated Nov. 22, 1579

Customers walking up to the box office of a Manhattan movie house saw parked alongside the curb a mobile home converted into a "sexmobile" where "free sex tests" were offered. The public assumed it was just a publicity gimmick cooked up by the producer of the film, something called *Is There Sex After Death?*

So did the theatre manager, who would also have acknowledged the need for some kind of gimmick to boost attendance. But a few months later, the producer filed a $1 million lawsuit against the theatre, claiming that ticket sales were underreported. He knew this, he said, because inside the "sexmobile" were observers who counted the number of ticket purchasers. Not to be outdone, the theatre owner, who happened to be Hugh Hefner of Playboy, filed a countersuit claiming the suit against him was another publicity gimmick. Hefner asked for $12 million in damages.[1]

In Charleston, North Carolina, the city council was so distressed about the nudism creeping up on their city that they decided to hit smut in the pocketbook. They enacted a special tax of $500 on any female "entertainer, dancer, employee or model" performing topless, bottomless, or both, live or on film.[2]

In Washington, a Chicano group from New Mexico went to Federal court to force the Federal Communications Commission to reveal financial figures on individual stations in Albuquerque, in order to try to see whether the stations had been adequately programming for local needs.[3]

In 1966, the American Broadcasting Company owned 399 theatres in 34 states, five television stations, 12 radio stations, a television network, record production and distributing companies, an international film distribution business, three agricultural papers, and numerous other businesses. International Telephone and Telegraph, which sought to merge with ABC, was the ninth largest industrial corporation in the world, with 433 separate boards of directors in at least 40 countries. It was involved in consumer finance, life insurance, investment funds, small loans, car rentals, and book publishing, in addition to its primary business in electronic equipment. The FCC, which by law was required to approve the merger, as the deal required transfer of ABC's broadcast licenses to ITT, said the merger was in the public interest. The U.S. Department of Justice said it was not, since ITT would be placed in the position of dealing with foreign governments with one arm and interpreting those dealings to the American public with the other. Justice asked the FCC to reconsider. The FCC did, and again approved the merger. Justice went to Federal court to try to block the deal. While the case was pending, ABC and ITT decided to call the merger off.[4]

These four illustrations suggest how the law works with respect to the media. Citizen may take on citizen. Government may take on the media, or individuals within the media. Citizens may seek to use the law to force government to shape up the media. And government may get in a squabble with itself over the media.

It's the age of the lawsuit. When Senator Barry Goldwater was running for President against Lyndon Johnson in 1964, *Fact* magazine ran an issue titled "The Unconscious of a Conservative: A Special Issue on the Mind of Barry Goldwater." Using an array of techniques which a jury later held to be in reckless disregard of the truth, publisher Ralph Ginzburg alleged that Goldwater "shows unmistakable symptoms of paranoia," and in other ways questioned his sanity. Goldwater sued for $2 million, and was awarded $75,000.[5]

That was peanuts compared to the 1967 suit filed by a retired general, Edwin Walker, when the Associated Press linked him with a Custer-like charge against Federal marshals during an integration riot at the University of Mississippi. He sued everyone he could think of, from the AP to the papers that carried the dispatch, for a total of $23 million. That was whittled down to $500,000 at the trial, and when the case reached the Supreme Court, even that was tossed out. At about the same time, the *Saturday Evening Post* ran a story accusing Wally Butts, the former University of Georgia athletic director, of conspiring to fix a football game with Alabama. Butts sued the *Post* for $10 million, and walked away with nearly half a million dollars.[6]

If these sums are scary, and they are (what editor would deliberately invite a $20 million lawsuit, even if he was sure he would win?), they at least represent a method of redress a trifle more civilized than the way things were settled in the old days. During the middle years of the last century, the editors of the Vicksburg (Mississippi) *Sentinel* had to be as fast with a gun as with a pen—as they engaged in endless combat on the streets. Four editors were killed, one drowned himself, one was imprisoned, and others were wounded. Mark Twain wrote engagingly of the period in a piece called "Journalism in Tennessee." In it the editor, who has just shot one man, is leaving the office for awhile. He instructs his new assistant:

> Jones will be here at three—cowhide him. Gillespie will call earlier, perhaps—throw him out of the window. Ferguson will be along about four—kill him. That is all for today, I believe. If you have any odd time, you may write a blistering article on the police.[7]

And even earlier, things were worse. In 1623 William Prynn printed a rather fanatical book in which he attacked play-acting as a Devil's device, and wound up his case by asserting that lewd women and whores were accustomed to take parts in plays. That might not have been so bad, except that England had a queen just then, and she liked plays, and had even played a part in one at her court a short time before. Prynn's book was construed as seditious criticism of the Queen. He was fined £ 10,000, given life imprisonment, branded on the forehead, had his nose slit and both ears cropped off. Later Parliament decided his trial had been illegal and released him, but by that time, they had even burned his book.[8]

the law is slow, limited, and negative

Settling disputes by resort to the law may be more genteel, but it is also slower. When the Federal Trade Commission decided in 1960 that advertising agency Ted Bates and Company had produced a misleading television commercial for Colgate-Palmolive, the FTC asked that the commercial be removed from the air. It was a pretty silly commercial, purporting to show that Palmolive Rapid Shave "out-shaves them all." Rapid Shave was applied to a sheet of sandpaper, which was immediately shaved clean by a single stroke of the razor. Actually, Rapid Shave could no more shave sandpaper than porcupine. The agency had used sand sprayed on glass to simulate sandpaper. The FTC decided this was misleading to the viewer, but Ted Bates and Colgate insisted it was just legitimate dramatizing of the wetting properties of the cream. To settle whether the practice was deceptive, the FTC and Colgate went through hearings and rehearings, in and out of court, finally all the way to the Supreme Court. More than three years elapsed, during which time the commercial's natural life ended, and others were developed for the shaving cream.[9]

Not only is the law slow, it is limited in what it can do. In 1964 the Times Mirror Company, publisher of the Los Angeles *Times,* sought to buy the San Bernardino *Sun,* published in a nearby city. What Times Mirror really wanted was the color printing facilities owned by the *Sun,* but the acquisition of the newspaper would have given the *Times* a near monopoly in the area. The U.S. Justice Department opposed the sale on the grounds that it would create an impenetrable barrier to the entry of another newspaper in the area, should someone desire to start one. Justice took Times Mirror to court, and won, but what did it win? The owners of the *Sun* now had to find another buyer willing to put up $15 million, and there were not too many of those around. The Pulitzers of St. Louis were interested, but the *Sun*'s proprietors did not care for their liberal Democratic politics. Finally, along came the Gannett Co. Gannett publishes 54 (at last count) daily newspapers, and has a number of other businesses, including broadcasting. The *Times* has a competitor worthy of its bank account, but the both of them together still have more than enough cash reserve to keep out competition.

Not only is the law slow, and limited in what it can accomplish. It is negative. Thou-shalt-nots outnumber thou-shalts in roughly the same proportion that losers exceed winners at Las Vegas. The Federal Communications Act of 1934 charges the FCC with enacting, from time to time, rules and regulations regarding broadcasting "in the public interest, convenience, or necessity." But it has always been much easier to say what is not in the public interest than what is. As a result, we know that fraudulent contests carried on over the air are forbidden, that disk jockeys may not make smutty remarks on their shows, and that Tea Leaf Kitty from Jersey City is no longer allowed to tell fortunes on the radio.

The advertising of cigarets on the air has been illegal since January 1, 1971, but the law said nothing about cigars that are packaged, advertised and smoked the same as cigarets.

But if the law is slow, limited, and negative, it is also handy. A free press, a wag once said, is a good wind that blows someone ill all the time. And when it blows cold on government, or any other power, there will likely be a backdraft. The range of legal restrictions is so wide that even a brief survey of the major ones shows how important the media are to society. Why? Because we spend so much time trying to restrain them.

licensing

The first control to hit printing in a systematic fashion, licensing for a long time was required in advance before books or other publications might be circulated. It is now obsolete in the U.S. and other Western countries, at least regarding print media. It continues in broadcasting, where it is considered necessary in order to free up the channels of communication. The FCC licenses not only radio and television stations, but ham operators, commercial shortwave systems such as those used by taxicab companies, airlines, and others.

Film licensing still goes on in this country and elsewhere, though it has been finding tough sledding here in recent years. One after another, the state licensing boards have been knocked off by the Supreme Court in cases that have shown censors acting peremptorily, without consideration for due process, or without allowing judicial review. For years one man kept films he didn't like out of Memphis, Tennessee, simply by refusing to license their showing. As chairman of the Board of Censors, Lloyd Binford filtered out Negro entertainers lucky enough to make it into films. Any song sung by Lena Horne was deleted "because there are plenty of good white singers." *Brewster's Millions* was banned because Jack Benny's Rochester was "too familiar."[10]

Chicago had a film licensing board consisting of a police sergeant, a patrolman, and, in the words of the sergeant, "five good little women." The sergeant was convinced that "one booklet or movie can undo what doting parents have accomplished in 10 years regardless of what the press thinks." The Swedish film *I Am Curious (Yellow)* flunked a licensing try in Maryland in 1969, and was still trying to get by three years later, long after other such movies, including *I Am Curious (Blue)* and *Sexual Freedom in Denmark* were licensed. How to explain it? Caprice of the licensers.[11]

When the idea of licensing began, a censor was lucky to get a book a week to judge. In a 10-year period ending in 1962, the New York state censorship board had to view nearly 13,000 films, or an average of 25 a week. It is thus clear that the work of the censor brings its own punishment. It should also be clear that licensing, or prior censorship, does not work very well. The chief reason is that society has never yet been able to devise a competent censor. Of course, dangerous ideas and thoughts ought to be censored, observed Ben Franklin, the question is, whom do we trust with the job? In a free society, every man is his own censor, and not his brother's.

Nevertheless, formal licensing will undoubtedly continue in the area of broadcasting and probably with certain kinds of films. Cable TV systems are licensed as franchises, with the city granting the franchise receiving a cut of the profits. Furthermore, the FCC has a voice in what may be carried over the cable, and no doubt will continue to have, since the Federal government has as legitimate interest in this new kind of mass communication as in the traditional kind.

censorship

If we cannot control the media through licensing, can't we just snip out the parts we don't like? The answer is, sometimes. Not in newspapers or magazines (unless it is wartime—and we do have press censorship laws on the books, should the Commander-in-Chief invoke them). Not in books. We can in movies, if we think they are obscene. We can in broadcasting, if the words are offensive. It's an interesting point, though, that prior censorship is not permitted in broadcasting. Instead, the law says this: Don't say bad words on the air; if you do, the FCC may decide you are not operating in the public interest, and lift your license. So, the prior censorship is carried out by the station licensee, or his agent the network. The end effect is the same, and sometimes worse. A survey of TV writers showed that 86 percent found from personal experience that censorship exists in television.[12] They were not talking about legally sanctioned censorship, but about the self-censorship of networks, stations, advertising agencies, production companies, and God knows who else.

Sometimes people get so disturbed by this kind of informal censorship that they propose formal, legal censorship instead, holding that at least we would *know* our media are being censored, whereas at present we are not sure. The way it works now we don't know the ground rules, which tend to be established at the whims of the sponsor, who fears giving offense to potential customers. A TV writer was invited to submit a story idea for "The FBI." It was just after four little black girls had been killed by a bomb in a Birmingham church. He told the producer he would submit a fictionalized version of that event. The producer checked the story through the sponsor (Ford Motor Company), through the FBI, through the network (ABC), and reported back that they would be delighted to have the story, provided the church was in the North, no Negroes were involved, and the story did not deal with civil rights.[13] And the writer had no idea which power center had issued which edict.

seizure of offending materials

If we can't license the media, and if we can't effectively snip out what we don't like, suppose we let them go ahead and print their nastiness, and then snatch it before they distribute?

From the point of view of would-be suppressors, the problem with this method of control is that it will never be completely efficient. It is applied far too late in the communication process too keep all circulation from taking place. Nevertheless, as licensing of print has been out since 1690, we have to make do with other means. And, if we can get away with it, they will be enough.

During the 1968 Democratic National Convention in Chicago there occurred what was later described in a report to the National Commission on the Causes and Prevention of Violence as a "police riot." In the violence that ensued, pitched battles were fought between police and demonstrators protesting the Vietnam war. Newsmen who sought to observe, record, and photograph the events were themselves set upon. Documented cases of some 49 newsmen being hit, Maced, or arrested by the police, apparently without reason, were submitted to the Commission. In 10 of the incidents, photographic or recording equipment was deliberately broken.[14]

A WDIO-TV (Duluth, Minnesota) photographer filmed two burglary suspects being arrested in the spring of 1971. Police seized his camera, though they returned it and the film next day. WDIO filed suit to contest the action. A year later, a federal judge ruled the police had acted illegally, adding that a newsman working in a law-abiding manner must not be interfered with in that way. To do so, said the judge, was a "prior restraint on free expression."[15]

Still, in the U.S. during the 20th century, seizure has been one of the most popular forms of control. In the 1920s the U.S. Customs Service seized a reproduction of Michelangelo's Sistine Chapel art, claiming it was obscene. A Harvard French professor ordered a shipment of Voltaire's *Candide* for his students, and a Boston customs official, noting they were labeled "unexpurgated," seized them on the grounds they therefore had to be obscene. In 1907 an issue of the *American Journal of Eugenics* was seized by the U.S. Post Office because it carried an ad for a book called *The History of Prostitution.* The book "from its very name is clearly indecent and unfit for circulation through the mails," wrote the Solicitor of the Post Office. Consequently, any magazine advertising it was also nonmailable.[16]

Sometimes seizure seems the only way to prevent materials from coming into a country or area where, for various reasons, they are not wanted. If the Customs Service were not allowed to seize bootleg books, no author would be able to retain property rights in his books, since book pirates could import editions printed with cheaper labor and materials, without paying royalties to the author. Textbooks might be cheaper, but writers soon would be discouraged from writing them. Seizure may keep out large-scale importation, but it is far too clumsy to prevent all items from slipping through, and it never stops an idea.

Moreover, the Customs Service must sometimes wonder whether it's all worth it. *Variety,* in its wonderfully deadpan, it's-all-show-biz way, has been reviewing skin flicks for years. In its critique of the movie *Sexual Customs in Scandinavia,* the tradepaper noted that while ostensibly filmed in Denmark, the hardcore material was "obviously shot stateside, since U.S. Customs are not yet that liberal."[17]

injunctions against publication in all or part

Sometime in the spring of 1971, the New York *Times* came into possession of a 47-volume study, classified top secret, entitled *History of the U.S. Decision-Making Process on Vietnam Policy.* This was a study undertaken at the order of Robert McNamara when he was secretary of defense and wondering just how the U.S. got into the Vietnam war in the first place. In June, the *Times* began to publish a series of nine articles based on the study. Some 48 hours later, Attorney General John Mitchell asked the *Times* not to publish any more articles, on the grounds that they would "cause irreparable injury to the defense interests of the United States." When the *Times* refused to stop the series, the attorney general sought and obtained a court injunction prohibiting further publication. For the next 15 days the *Times* was prevented from publishing articles, until the Supreme Court ruled on the matter, and decided the government had not shown publication would harm the country's interests.[18]

Going to court and asking for an injunction against publication is certainly a more civilized method of restraining the press than licensing, chipping material out of printing plates, or breaking reporters' tape recorders. At least it gives the publication a chance to defend itself, and requires the person or agency seeking the injunction to prove some kind of case. It is fairly easy to obtain a temporary injunction but difficult to make it stick. Long before Howard Hughes became a gleam in Clifford Irving's eye, the billionaire was on the lookout for what he considered threats to his privacy. *Look* magazine published three articles on Hughes in 1954. In 1965, apparently learning of a biography in the works, Hughes organized a company, Rosemont Enterprises, to buy the copyright on the articles. When writer John Keats and Random House decided to publish their biography of Hughes, Rosemont cried copyright infringement, sought and obtained an injunction stopping them. Random House had to go clear to the U.S. Circuit Court of Appeals in order to have the injunction overthrown.[19]

compulsory disclosure of authorship and ownership

Paul Branzburg, a writer for the Louisville (Kentucky) *Courier Journal,* produced an illustrated story with the headline THE HASH THEY MAKE ISN'T TO EAT, which ran in the paper on November 15, 1969. In the article Branzburg described how marijuana was converted into the more potent drug hashish. He had been allowed to watch the process while it was carried out by two producers, on his pledge that he would not reveal their identities. This was too much for the Jefferson County Grand Jury, which hauled Branzburg into court and demanded that he name the drug producers. Branzburg said he would not, that he was protected by Kentucky's "shield law," which allowed newsmen to withhold the "source of information" from the law.[20]

In July 1970, Paul Pappas, a newsman for WTEV-TV (New Bedford, Massachusetts), spent a night in the Black Panther headquarters in anticipation of a police raid, which never occurred. He was admitted only after promising not to report anything he heard or saw besides the raid. He was ordered to tell all by a grand jury investigating the Panthers, and refused. Massachusetts has no "shield law"; only 17 states do.[21]

After the CBS documentary "The Selling of the Pentagon" was broadcast in 1971, CBS President Frank Stanton refused the order of a Congressional subcommittee to produce all the "outtakes" and all notes made by reporters during the production of the program. Stanton didn't just say "No"; he said "Hell no." And, finally, he got away with it.

These current cases, and there are many more to look at, illustrate a very fashionable way of seeking to restrain the press. For if newsmen were required to reveal all their sources at the whim of government, little might be published that did not meet the government's approval. And a lot of information—possibly harmful to the government—might never reach the public.

But the issues—to force newsmen to reveal their sources, or not—are not easily resolved. Despite the fact that Kentucky has a law allowing reporters to protect news sources, a Kentucky court ruled that Branzburg should tell all. So he, and Paul Pappas, and Earl Caldwell, a New York *Times* reporter covering the Black Panthers in California, all appealed to the Supreme Court, which had no easy time reaching a solution that was, when it came, highly criticized by members of the press. The Court said there is no Constitutional protection granted by the First Amendment to reporters who wish to keep secret the names of news sources.[22] Reporters, said the Court, are just like everybody else. They have the same rights and no more than any other citizen. Critics of that decision pointed out that while the state obviously has an interest in obtaining information to use in protecting itself and its citizens, sometimes that information can come only if sources are free to remain anonymous. Otherwise reporters simply become agents of the government, and their sources will dry up.

The arguments in favor of a newsman's right to protect the confidence his sources have given him seem persuasive—until the other side is considered. Suppose, observed supporters of the Court's decision, a television station had film showing that what newspapers had declared a riot begun by demonstrators firing the first shot actually started when police opened fire first? Would not the public interest require that the film be made public, despite the station's desire to keep it secret? The law should move very carefully in considering whether to grant today something that may be questionable tomorrow, they argued.[23]

If we look at this control from the viewpoint of what it has to offer the consumer, there are areas in which compulsory disclosure clearly offers public good. The Federal Trade Commission has begun an advertising substantiation campaign in which it asks to see the evidence supporting claims made in advertising. When the FTC received the evidence from the automobile industry, some interesting "substantiation" turned up:

• A General Motors ad said Chevelle had "109 advantages to keep it from becoming old before its time." The substantiated list included such things as automatic choke, balanced wheels and tires, "up to four interior color choices," and—one by one—the safety features required by Federal law for all cars.

• Toyota advertised that its 1971 Corona "accelerates faster, has a higher top speed." Than what? Than the 1970 Corona.

• Ford, in substantiating its claim that its cars were quieter than expensive foreign imports, submitted results of a test of a new Ford against, among others, a 1963 Daimler with 37,000 miles and a 1964 Jaguar with 20,000 miles.[24]

The FTC publicized the "evidence," announced it was being studied for possible deception, and shifted attention to other industries. Is the consumer aided in his difficult work of choosing between products advertised in fulsome terms? Yes, if he is willing to take the time to inspect the evidence obtained under this new program. To do so he can either ask the National Technical Information Service for copies of the evidence (at about $3 per company), or go into a regional office of the FTC. Ralph Nader, who proposed the policy to the FTC, did his bit to publicize the results, but mostly the public remained unaware of the new program.[25]

postpublication criminal penalties for objectionable matter

British novelist John Galsworthy reported visiting Russia not long after the revolution of 1917. He came across a street-corner speaker criticizing the new government to a crowd that was getting angrier every minute. Finally, they made a move to rush the speaker, only to be halted by one of their fellows. "Comrades," he shouted. "You know we now have freedom of speech. We must hear our comrade out. But comrades, when he's finished, we'll bash his head in!"

The idea of letting a person—or a newspaper—speak freely, and then holding him accountable for what he says, is not new. The English jurist William Blackstone, who died in 1780, had great influence through his *Commentaries* on the form law took in the United States. Perhaps his chief contribution to freedom of the press was his working out of the theory that freedom of the press consists chiefly in laying no prior restraint upon publishers, that a man may say and print what he wishes, being responsible only for the consequences of his words.

Blackstone's idea is at once democratic and inefficient. It is democratic because it makes government wait until some ill effect of speech is shown, and it is inefficient because it allows hated opinions to be spread rather freely, instead of permitting them to be stamped out early. Anthony Comstock, perhaps the greatest censor this country has ever known, was a scourge of pornographers for the last half of the 19th century. In 1913, two years before his death, he bragged to an interviewer: "In the forty-one years I have been here [in New York] I have convicted persons enough to fill a passenger train of sixty-one coaches, sixty coaches containing sixty passengers each and the sixty-first almost full. I have destroyed 160 tons of obscene literature."[26] If Comstock had been able to work with benefit of a prior restraint or censorship before publication law, he not only would have been able to put away more than his 3650 persons, he would not have had to bother with the 160 tons of literature. He could have headed it all off at the licenser's office. As it was, he dealt out a lot of misery, but he really stopped very little.

There are only four of five generalized reasons why governments make it a crime to say certain things, or to advocate certain courses of action. And each reason contains a trap which over hundreds of years has become clear, so that the clear trend in the U.S. this century has been to reduce criminal penalties applied to those who utter "the hated opinion."

One reason suppression of speech is allowed, or those who speak sent to jail, is that it is sometimes quite vividly imagined what will happen if the speech is allowed. Anthony Comstock's imagination led him to browbeat Congress into passing a law that endures today. Charles H. Keating, Jr., head of Citizens for Decent Literature, also sees vividly the dangers of pornography: "We believe that pornography has an eroding effect on society, on public morality, on respect for human worth, on attitudes toward family love, on culture."[27]

If what Keating says will happen does in fact happen, then the state clearly has an interest in suppressing pornography. But the trap is twofold: one man's pornography is another man's masterpiece, and, as porno publishers are fond of saying, no one has ever yet shown that a girl was seduced by a book. Lack of real evidence as to what obscenity is and what its effects are has led the courts to draw back from convicting people on just anyone's say so. In three years, the City of Phoenix, Arizona, pressed more than 150 obscenity prosecutions. Finally in May 1971, a conviction was obtained for a grainy little 1000-foot skin flick called *Captain Peter.* Comstock would hardly be pleased at the percentage.[28]

A second reason for making speech a crime has to do with a longing for unity. We have some national ideal or purpose, and must not allow speech that might divert us. This mood comes on strongly in times of stress, usually in wartime. Abraham Lincoln felt its tug when he wrote a New York Democrat, "Must I shoot a simple-minded soldier boy who deserts, while I must not touch a hair of a wily agitator who induces him to desert . . .?"[29] His argument appealed so strongly that he commanded the arrest of the proprietors of the New York *World* and New York *Journal of Commerce.* But the trap is, if a country has to throw people in jail to obtain its unity, it may not be a national purpose at all.

Why bother to protect anything that is not worthwhile? This third argument for suppression has its trap, too, since carried to its logical extreme, it permits the lynch mob. This argument is accompanied by great confidence on the part of the people who make it. They invariably assume they will always be among those who will decide what is worthwhile and what is not. And, just as invariably, they wind up on the outside looking in. That is what happened to Robespierre, who helped lead the French revolution and who liberally applied the guillotine to enemies of the state, and then was guillotined himself.

The last big reason for making words a criminal offense is to prevent them from ripening into acts. A group of priests and nuns talk about kidnaping a high government official. That is a crime, says the government, because they might have gone ahead and done it. The fear of what might have happened makes such conspiracies illegal. The trap is this: if we begin jailing people for their thoughts instead of their deeds, who among us is safe?

postpublication civil suits
for damages

The criminal law of words takes care of enemies of the state and, occasionally, of the public good. When a citizen is harmed by a publication, he has recourse to law also. Mostly we mean he can seek compensation for the harm that has been done his good name, but sometimes it is not his reputation that has suffered but his privacy.

New York magazine published an article in which the writer asserted that Abkco Industries was making a profit out of the record album *Bangla Desh,* despite announcements that proceeds from the album's sale would go to starving children on the Indian subcontinent. The head of Abkco filed suit for $150 million against the magazine and the writer. To win that lawsuit, the Abkco head would have to establish that he was identified in the article, that the article was indeed published, and that he was defamed in some way, or held up to hatred, contempt, ridicule, or somehow lowered in the esteem of others. And all of this would have to be shown before the question of how much compensation it was worth could be considered.[30]

On the other side, the magazine and the writer might throw up a long list of defenses. They might seek to prove what they said was true (in which event they win). They might try to establish that the Abkco executive was a public figure and therefore had opened himself to criticism, harsh though it might be, under rules that permit such criticism for society's ultimate benefit. They might try a number of other approaches that in effect would argue that whatever was said needed to be said and did not attack the man personally.

Or, the magazine and writer might even print a retraction, possibly admitting that what they said was untrue, but adding that they meant no harm, and hoped an apology would set things straight.

They might even try to settle out of court for a sum of money. In the state of Washington, a newspaper ran a flattering feature story about an outstanding couple who had just moved to town. Both husband and wife had earned advanced degrees and were employed in responsible jobs. They had helped each other through college, one working while the other finished, and along the way had raised a handsome family. But some smart aleck in the composing room had set the type, in a sentence reading "Mrs. so and so worked to put her husband through college," to read "Mrs. so and so whored to put her husband through college." The error got into print, and right away several things happened. A purge was conducted in the composing room and among the proofreaders, and a lawyer made a visit to the lady in question, with an offer of a cash settlement. It was all news to the woman, who hadn't even read the article yet.

The whole area of libel law is marvelously complex and inconsistent. Wisconsin courts held a man defamed who was called a "swine." Washington courts said it was all right to call a man a "hog." The enlarging area of freedom of speech concerning public issues and public figures makes almost anything go, as long as it is not uttered in "reckless disregard of the truth." And the definition of "reckless" used by the courts has been tough and is getting more so. The object is to permit the widest possible discussion of public affairs—not to protect the media.

But if mean things may be said about a person's public acts, there is a tendency to restrict things that may be said about his private life. Is there a right to be let alone? In today's mass society we often think there should be. Without a privacy law, cameras might follow us anywhere, recorders might tape our most private conversations, computers might transmit our most intimate financial details to every bank and business in the land. Miss Norma Yoeckel had the misfortune to enter a tavern whose proprietor was a camera bug. While she was in a stall in the restroom, a flashbulb went off. When she returned to the main room, she found the bartender showing pictures of women he had photographed in similar circumstances. Feeling her privacy had been invaded, she sued. She failed to win her case, for the state it happened in had no privacy law.[31] Few states do, though this is unquestionably an area where more law will be made in the future.

discrimination in access to news sources and facilities

We hear of this control perhaps most often in connection with a newsman's ejection from the Soviet Union or some other controlled society. But it works in the United States, too.

In a way, denial of the "right to know" is the most effective censorship. If you can close off the news sources, you do not have to worry about chopping off the writing hands, jailing the editors who print disturbing news, or chase about trying to round up all the photocopies of some secret document.

Mounting pressure against concealment led Congress in 1966 to pass a Freedom of Information Act, which required the Federal government to open its records unless they were specifically exempted by the law. How well has the law worked? Better than no law at all, though you only need pick up a copy of any media trade journal, such as *Editor & Publisher* or *Broadcasting,* to read accounts of official refusal to give information. Moreover, the real problem exists at the state and local level, where relatively great secrecy still exists. In Madison, Wisconsin, for example, the chief of police in 1970 issued press cards to representatives of the local press. Two downtown dailies were given the cards, which permit holders to cross police lines in pursuance of their duties. A conservative student paper, the *Badger Herald,* was issued a pass. But the *Daily Cardinal,* which for some 60 years was the only student paper on the University of Wisconsin campus, was pointedly denied passes.

denial of the use of distribution facilities

If we must let them print it, maybe we can head them off at the mailbox. After all, we have at our disposal the entire postal system, other channels of interstate commerce such as the railway express, newsstands and other local commercial distributors, and even street-corner types who create a littering problem.

For a long time during the 1950s and 1960s, the word was that the Post Office was keeping a list of persons receiving mail from Communist countries. It didn't matter, really, what if anything the Post Office planned to do with that list, or even if such a list actually were being compiled. A threat was there.

For several years prior to the outbreak of hostilities in 1861, Southern postmasters seized newspapers and magazines dealing with the abolition of slavery.

The Postal Service, very belatedly, has been bowing out of the old interference-with-circulation routine. Law today says the receiver of the mail, not the carrier, should decide whether he wants to receive it or not. But assistant district attorneys and police inspectors sometimes have a way of suggesting to newsstand owners that a certain magazine may be obscene, and just to be on the safe side, better remove it.

interference with buying, reading, or listening

In Moose Jaw, Saskatchewan, a Danish film called *Threesome* was scheduled for (what else?) a three-day run. But it never got a screening. The theatre manager withheld the film after he was told by police that they had received complaints about newspaper advertising of the film.

The manager said he realized the police had acted in good faith by advising him of the complaints. "It takes only one person to see a film, find it objectionable and make a complaint," he observed. "Then the film is seized and the theatre is faced with a charge of showing an obscene film."[32] Meaning, in short, legal fees, time spent in court, loss of reputation, and other harassments.

In Massachusetts, a law was proposed which would prohibit drive-in movies from showing X-rated films where such movies are visible from public places. Drive-ins either would have to give up that kind of movie or build high fences.[33]

In 1972 the CBS television network decided to show an X-rated movie, *The Damned,* on its late-night movie series. Boston, Denver, Jacksonville, Lincoln, and many other cities declined to carry the movie, despite the fact that all the touchy scenes had been deleted to make the thing acceptable to the network. So the audience's viewing of that movie was interfered with by (1) Warner Brothers, who owned the film and cut it, (2) CBS, who insisted on the cuts, (3) stations that elected not to carry it, and (4) the chairman of the Senate subcommittee on copyright, who had a very interesting question. How is it, asked Senator John McClellan, that if all those nude scenes have such "redeeming social significance" and are crucial to the story in the first place, you can cut them all out to sell the picture to television?[34]

and that's really not the half of it

The list of controls on content that are based on law or grow out of provisions of the law is a very long one. We have only mentioned a few of the most popular here. But we could go on and on. There was the time Huey Long had Louisiana pass a special tax on newspapers with more than 20,000 circulation. There were 13 in Louisiana then, and 12 of them were editorially opposed to Long. That, said the Supreme Court, was a discriminatory tax. (In the fall of 1972, President Nguyen Van Thieu of South Vietnam required all the country's daily newspapers to post a $47,000 "deposit" in order to publish. From the money, fines would be deducted for "undermining national security." Rather than face this type of control, 13 of the country's 42 daily papers ceased publication, which is probably what the government wanted anyway.)

There have been discriminatory subsidies of newspapers and magazines, granted to friendly publications by political parties in control of the state's pursestrings.

There have been cases of labor unions, through legally valid contracts, hamstringing news operations, such as when an enterprising Chicago television station got the idea of videotaping videophone conversations with Illinois Congressmen in Washington, a sort of instant press conference. However, the union protested that the contract said when an interview was taped, a camera crew had to be there. In New York a newspaper that had been born in the aftermath of a strike was itself put to death after a life of eight months when the publisher decided he could no longer meet the demands of the contract between the typesetters and the paper.

On the other side, newspaper publishers in 22 cities argued that due to competition they were in poor economic condition, in danger of failing. What they wanted was to be allowed to retain the "joint printing operations" including common advertising and circulation departments which they had formed and which the U.S. Justice Department said was in violation of the antitrust laws. Despite the fact that none of the newspapers had actually put themselves up for sale (something a business generally does before it fails), the Congress duly enacted a 'Newspaper Preservation Act' that permitted these combinations to continue. Possibly the 22 cities will thus keep their competing newspapers; certainly an economic barrier has been raised to the entry of new papers in those markets.

In wartime, newspapers published in the United States by U.S. citizens have been banned because they were printed in the language used by, among others, the current enemy. During World War I, some 75 newspapers either lost their mailing privileges during the first year of the Espionage Act, or kept them only by agreeing to say nothing further about the war. In World War II, a Philadelphia German-language newspaper, the *Herold,* was barred from the mails. And Japanese papers published on the West Coast were stamped out ruthlessly.

Freedom from legal controls? Certainly we have it, probably in greater measure than most countries. But there is no such thing as absolute freedom for the media. There never has been, and probably never will be.

for further reading

Chafee, Zechariah, Jr. *Free Speech in the United States.* Cambridge, Mass.: Harvard University Press, 1947.

————. *Government and Mass Communications: A Report From the Commission on Freedom of the Press,* 2 vols. Chicago: University of Chicago Press, 1947.

Clark, David G., and Earl R. Hutchison, eds. *Mass Media and the Law: Freedom and Restraint.* New York: Wiley, 1970.

Gillmor, Donald, and Jerome A. Barron. *Mass Communication Law: Cases and Comment.* St. Paul, Minn.: West Publishing Co., 1969. Supplement issued in 1971.

Hachten, William A. *The Supreme Court on Freedom of the Press: Decisions and Dissents.* Ames, Iowa: Iowa State University Press, 1968.

Hutchison, Earl R. *Tropic of Cancer on Trial: A Case History of Censorship.* New York: Grove Press, 1968.

Levy, Leonard W., ed. *Freedom of the Press From Zenger to Jefferson.* Indianapolis, Ind.: Bobbs-Merrill, 1967.

Nelson, Harold L., ed. *Freedom of the Press from Hamilton to the Warren Court.* Indianapolis, Ind.: Bobbs-Merrill, 1968.

Nelson, Harold L., and Dwight L. Teeter. *Law of Mass Communications: Freedom and Control of Print and Broadcast Media.* Mineola, N.Y.: Foundation Press, 1969.

what the citizen can do

consumption, contribution, and criticism

And how many owners of TV stations could have suspected what the survey indicates—that roughly four out of ten Canadians actually *talk out loud* to their radio or TV sets?
—Canadian Special Senate Committee on Mass Media, 1970

In the English comedy film *Doctor in the House,* a gruff old professor of surgery shepherds his students on rounds of the charity wards. They stop at the bed of a haggard old man and the surgeon unceremoniously yanks away the covers. He asks a student for a diagnosis.

"Appendicitis," the student guesses.

"Good," says the surgeon. "And just how would you make the incision?"

The student makes a nervous little sketch on the old man's belly.

"Bah," shouts the surgeon, "that's peephole surgery. Do this." He describes a swath from the old man's rib cage to his hipbone.

The charity patient, who has been watching with increasing apprehension, emits a groan and nearly faints.

"You keep out of it," snaps the surgeon. "This has nothing to do with you."

Too often mass communication is something like that: media, government, and assorted experts haggle among themselves about the needs of the consumer, whose well-being, like that of the charity patient, is none of his own business.

Mass communication is a strong, steady stream in which drifting is easy but swimming is hard. Collectively the audience has some power to modify the stream, to erect a levee here, to open a new channel there, but individuals tend to founder in the inexorable currents. Still, the receiver of mass communication can cope in various ways, and we suggest three: careful consumption, contribution, and criticism. Each has its possibilities—and failings.

be intentionally selective

Some publishers and broadcast executives are fond of telling critical consumers to "read another paper," or to "switch us off." This is not bad advice, though it's a little like telling a junkie to find another source—and we're all media addicts.

To gauge the extent of your involvement with mass communication, try to avoid it for, say, three days. We and our students have attempted this, and the experience is both alarming and enlightening. Immediately one finds that mass communication, like dandruff, can only be avoided with luck and effort. One can scarcely walk or drive any distance without confronting outdoor signs, and there's no escaping direct-mail advertising this side of the grave. Within homes a radio or TV beckons at every turn, and newspapers, magazines, and books lie enticingly at hand. We are accustomed to beginning our days in the company of a favorite disk jockey (who also rides to work with us), and ending them with the late-night TV talkers.

Withdrawal from media is so painful that it is used as punishment in prisons (and in some homes). Those who participated in our experiments found themselves jarred out of orbit. Some began to eat more heavily because they didn't have to rush off to a movie or be distracted by a TV program. On the other hand, a few ate less because without the diversion of a morning paper and radio they were suddenly struck by the ghastliness of breakfast cereal. Most sought out conversations with acquaintances but found themselves short of things to say. At night some couldn't sleep because they were accustomed to drowsing over a book.

For many there was a dawning realization that Dr. Marcus Welby could remove gallstones without spectators and that the next Clint Eastwood flick might not differ profoundly from its predecessors. Media-deprived persons discover some virtue in silence, in doing domestic chores, and in having to compose their own thoughts.

Upon returning to media consumption, most attempted to make up for their loss selectively—by reading the main pages of newspapers, scanning the tables of contents of magazines, and tuning to specific programs instead of taking potluck.

Though the audience is too commonly regarded by the media as a vast swamp that needs filling, the receivers of mass communication need not contribute to this image; they don't have to be passive. Indeed, the audience has some responsibility in the communication process: to accept what is good and to skip the rest, to use the media and not be used by them.

This is a tricky responsibility, for the media are adept at making themselves attractive and easy to take. Although, as we pointed out earlier, the receivers of mass communication have certain natural defenses against the media onslaught—selective perception, attention, and retention—these defenses are also a burden to the responsible consumer because he must not only overcome the barrage of messages but his own biases and laziness as well.

There is no inherent evil in watching the eighth rerun of *Red River,* a very good movie, but it should be recognized as a donation of time and attention to the broadcasting, film, and advertising industries, and that there are other recreations—if not duties.

Obviously the discriminating receiver must be a shrewd user of indexes and guides, and in their eagerness to please, the media provide them. *TV Guide,* for example, is a synoptic index to television programming. A book called *Movies on TV* performs a similar function for old films. The National Association for Better Broadcasting annually publishes candid evaluations of network and syndicated TV series.[1] New films are more of a problem because newspaper and magazine reviewers cover only a fraction of those offered (reviews over radio are too brief and too smart-alecky to be helpful), and movie advertising is a spurious gauge of content. However, *Consumer Reports* presents a monthly list of current films together with a consensus of critic and audience ratings. Reviews of records, especially classics, are relatively easy to find; pop music reviews are a bit suspect as to objectivity. Program guides are usually available from radio stations that have progressed beyond newsflashes and bubble-gum rock music. By the way, a decent AM radio is capable of bringing in signals from a considerable distance, especially after dark—something we tend to forget. And then there is shortwave, which yields English-language services from around the world as well as broadcasts in other languages.[2] As for the print media, it is not necessary to submit to the foregone conclusions and computerized billings of the Book-of-the-Month Club as long as there are libraries and bookstores—and intelligent critics to tell you what's in them. For their part, newspapers and magazines employ consistent and convenient formats and provide indexes. If you crave specialized news and have a long purse, you can choose from among 5000 newsletters that circulate in the United States, including one called *Newsletter on Newsletters.* Some are very specialized indeed: in 1972, Ward's Communications, Inc., began a biweekly, $100-a-year newsletter devoted entirely to information about the Wankel engine.

roll your own

Another way to cope with the media is to become a mass communicator yourself. You need only talent and money—and sometimes little of either. If you want to buy a middle-sized television station, be prepared to pay $18 million, as Lee Enterprises did in 1971 for WMAZ-TV in Huntington-Charleston, West Virginia, the nation's 36th largest broadcast market. About the same time, the Gannett Company laid out $14.6 million for the 45,000-circulation Fort Myers, Florida, *News-Press,* which became Gannett's 52nd daily. Or as an alternative to ownership, perhaps you can simply buy an advertisement. A prime-time TV slot may cost more than $50,000 for one minute—enough time for about a hundred words and a few scenes—plus the cost of shooting the commercial. A full-page color advertisement in *Reader's Digest* costs about the same. On the other hand, a classified ad in the Boscobel, Wisconsin, *Dial* costs only 75 cents if you pay cash.

Some people are not fazed by the big numbers. Not long ago Dora Hall, a blonde, seventyish grandmother, decided to make a show-biz comeback after more than 40 years as a housewife. She had sung to the doughboys during World War I and later went on the Pantages theatrical circuit with a group called the Harmony Maids, but she quit in the 1920s and married a businessman named Leo Hulseman. In 1971, when Miss Hall discovered that the networks were not exactly avid for singing grannies, Mr. Hulseman obliged her by renting a studio from NBC and hiring a producer, director, crew, a 13-piece orchestra, 10 dancers, and a supporting cast that included Frank Sinatra, Jr., Phil Harris, Rich Little, Oliver, Ben Blue, and Rosey Grier. The one-hour show cost him $400,000. Fortunately, Mr. Hulseman owned the Solo Cup Company and was worth millions.[3]

Although one doesn't acquire a flourishing station or publication for peanuts, there are plenty of intriguing success stories, especially in the print media where a good idea can attract capital and an audience. The founding editors of *Reader's Digest* and the *New Yorker* began with little money of their own. The Los Angeles *Free Press,* the most successful underground newspaper, was started in a garage in 1964 with only $15 capital; six years later it had about 100,000 paid circulation. Hugh Hefner founded *Playboy* with $600 of his own and $10,000 more that he borrowed or begged. In 15 years he was king of a $127 million-a-year empire that embraced publishing, nightclubs, resorts, and film-making, and owned an all-black jet plane with a white bunny painted on its tail.

Despite these triumphs, the odds are dangerous, even for such an experienced editor as Clay Felker, who in 1967 paid $6757 for the title of *New York* magazine. He then raised a whopping $2.7 million from wealthy New Yorkers—and he needed it, because in its first year the magazine lost $2.1 million.[4] Even Hefner, who has remarked proudly that "we have a phenomenal record where it counts," dropped $1 million on *Trump,* a short-lived satire magazine, in 1957, and *Show Business Illustrated,* which succumbed after eight issues in 1962.

Although few members of the media audience aspire to ownership, many would like to participate in other ways. Entry to media employment is aided by courses of instruction offered by colleges, universities, and technical schools across the nation. Practically every college gives instruction in creative writing and drama, and at least 175 universities and colleges offer degrees in broadcasting. Nearly 1300 provide some form of journalism education, and about 220 four-year institutions award degrees in journalism. Increasingly the media seek college-educated men and women as employes.

And for every employe of the media, there must be dozens of would-be contributors. Professor William L. Rivers has estimated that a quarter of a million free-lance magazine articles are written every year. About 90 percent of them are rejected, but despite the odds free-lance writers relentlessly pursue success because the awards are highly pleasing: pride of publication, a degree of fame, entrée to important places and persons, freedom, expertise. Alvin Toffler, a free lance who wrote an article on the problems of adapting to rapid change, suddenly found his knowledge in demand. He expanded his research into a best-selling book, *Future Shock,* made several public appearances, and was hired by American Telephone & Telegraph as a consultant on the future. Ollie Stewart, a free lance who chooses to live in Paris and sell articles to U.S. magazines, has observed, "Freelancing means freedom to write what I enjoy writing; freedom to get up or to stay in bed; to booze and chase broads, to feel rich one month and worry about rent the next."

Then there is the lure of money. It seems laughably easy to jot down one's memories of Aunt Hazel and send them off to *Reader's Digest* in exchange for $3000. But such major free-lance markets as *Life, Look, Saturday Evening Post, American,* and *Woman's Home Companion* have all died in recent years. These were brutal losses to free-lance cartoonists and authors. "When the *Post* went out," writer Richard Gehman said, "it put a whole lot of us in terrible trouble." In 1969 a *Writer's Digest* survey of 64 members of the Society of Magazine Writers indicated that only eight earned more than $30,000 a year from free lancing and 11 made less than $10,000.

As a consequence, some free lances have increased their output (and, where they are paid by the word, their windiness). Though most of the big family magazines have been put to death by television, a wild variety of specialized publications solicit contributions at modest rates. *Office Supervisor's Bulletin* pays $25 per printed page, and *Intimate Story* rewards its confessants at the rate of three cents a word. A Chicago pie company called Virginia Hardy's Oven prints short stories on its cartons. It pays contributors fifty pies per story.[5]

Many full-time free lances don't feel very free. As their own boss they find they must pay their own medical bills, office expenses, retirement, and fringe benefits. Every minute away from the job is lost time and therefore lost money. Many seek part-time work in editing, public relations, for ghost-writing for the sake of security.[6]

The free-lance market is not going to disappear, if for no other reason than that magazines find it cheaper to buy "over the transom" material than to hire more staff writers. An editor of *National Geographic* has noted that while his magazine pays $2500 to $3500 for a contributed piece, it's a bargain: "There isn't a good man on the staff making less than $25,000 a year, and he has a secretary and does about three pieces a year."

Even though writing is fiercely competitive and financially insecure, many prospective authors doggedly await their Big Break. The late Wolcott Gibbs, who in his 30 years with the *New Yorker* probably contributed more words to that magazine than anyone else, made it sound easy:

> As much as anything else, I guess, I would have liked to instruct an endless succession of beautiful young women to play tennis. The only trouble with that was that I didn't really play tennis very well. Magazine writing, I suppose, simply occurred to me as the next easiest way

to make a living, and I applied to an obliging relative who happened to have access to an editor for such employment. It was simple as that.[7]

Other beginners, less amply blessed with talent and relatives, find the going rougher. Some are willing to pay hard cash to reach the first rung in the rickety ladder of success by enrolling in mail-order writing schools such as the Palmer Writers School, Writer's Digest School, or the Hollywood School of Comedy Writers.

One of the better-known correspondence courses is offered by the Famous Writers School of Westport, Connecticut, whose 15-member "guiding faculty" includes such worthies as Faith Baldwin, Bruce Catton, Red Smith, and Rod Serling. Not long ago Jessica Mitford, herself a famous if skeptical writer, looked in on the Famous Writers School.[8]

She found, first of all, that the famous writers of the guiding faculty don't have much to do with the Famous Writers School, whose brochures have promised that "on a short story or novel you have at hand the professional council of Faith Baldwin ... all these eminent authors in effect are looking over your shoulder as you learn." Miss Baldwin told Miss Mitford, "Oh, that's just one of those things about advertising. ... Anyone with common sense would know that the fifteen of us are much too busy to read the manuscripts the students send in." She asked Bennett Cerf how many books by Famous Writers students his Random House had published. "Oh, come on," Cerf said, "you must be pulling my leg—no person of any sophistication, whose books we'd publish, would have to take a mail-order course to learn how to write."

Money is the motivation of correspondence schools. Famous Writers is a child of Famous Artists Schools, which also owns Famous Photographers, Welcome Wagon, Evelyn Wood Reading Dynamics, and other enterprises. In the 1960s, the organization increased its total revenues from $7 million to $48 million annually. (After the Mitford article and other investigations, its revenues plunged sharply.)

The bulk of this comes from tuition, which, Miss Mitford learned, amounts to $785 for the 24-lesson course if the enrollee pays a lump sum; however, most pay installments totalling $900. About 800 salesmen around the country act as registrars and work on a straight-commission basis.

Student work is graded by two full-timers, Miss Mitford found, and by about 40 pieceworkers who are mostly Westport housewives. (One Famous Writers advertisement promised that "every one of our instructors is an accomplished writer or editor who has made his mark as a professional.") An executive of the school, Gordon Carroll, told her,

"We never hire professional teachers, they're too *dull!* Ph.D.'s are the worst of all."

Perversely, the backbone of mail-order instruction is not success, but lack of talent and failure. The entrance exams—aptitude tests —do indeed disclose lack of ability, but the grading is generous to a fault. Once enrolled, the student is under contract to pay whether he completes the course or not. The higher the dropout rate, the higher the profits. Miss Mitford estimated that 90 percent of Famous Writers students fall by the wayside. (The school itself was chary of releasing financial details.)

Obviously, home study has great merit for shut-ins, rural residents, and others who are unable to receive classroom instruction, and for those who prefer to work at their own speed. Highly introverted persons may also like to study privately. One mail-order writing school offers to send lessons in plain envelopes—and a Famous Writers advertisement capitalizes on modesty: "Are you one of the 'quiet ones' who should be a writer? Often it's the quiet ones who have the most to say." Then again, maybe the quiet ones have nothing to say.

Before signing a contract with a correspondence school, the would-be writer ought to consider five questions suggested by *Writer's Digest:*

1. Can you set a regular period each week to work on your "lessons," and can you stick to it?
2. Can you work by yourself without face-to-face contact with a teacher or other student?
3. Can you learn from the printed word as well as from a visual demonstration or spoken lecture?
4. Do you realize that in most cases your application blank is a legal contract and that if you give up the course, after a certain period of time, you must still pay the full tuition—just as a university student who drops out in the middle of a term usually receives no refund?
5. Do you accept the fact that the completion of any home study course does not guarantee your future success in a field?[9]

Another point: one could take a writing course, at very little cost, through the extension service of a state university.

If some people will mortgage themselves to correspondence schools, does it follow that some will also pay to have their work printed? It does. The process is known as subsidy or vanity publishing.

Ordinarily a book publisher serves as a broker between author and audience by selecting worthy manuscripts, performing useful editing, hiring a printer, and then selling the product to book dealers. In the case of a novel, the publisher typically pays a new author a 10 percent royalty on the retail price of every book sold. The percentage may increase as sales rise; above 5000 copies the author may get 12 percent. And if the novel is resold to a book club, to a paperback publisher, or to television or the movies, the author and his publisher evenly split the extra proceeds (a division that is distressing to many writers).

Unfortunately, chances are that only the printer is going to make much money from a first novel, which, *Writer's Market* estimates, typically sells only 500 to 2000 copies. So if the public buys only 1000 at $6 apiece, the author receives but $600 for what may have been a year or more of work.

Given these odds, regular publishers cultivate successful authors and are finicky about accepting new ones. The rejection rate of book manuscripts is about 90 percent. This leaves a good many unpublished and unhappy writers.

Enter the subsidy publisher, such as Exposition, Vantage, and Pageant. "Even though you may be a new or unknown writer, and may have been rejected by other publishers, do not be discouraged," says a Vantage Press advertisement. "History proves that publishers have made many mistakes in turning down books that later become critical or financial successes."

Naturally the subsidy publisher is cheerful, for his risk is nil —the author is going to pay all the bills. And pay well. According to *Writer's Market,* typical charges are $900 for 500 copies of a 48-page book of poetry and $3360 for 3000 copies of a 176-page novel. Fees can go higher, much higher. Usually the subsidy press attracts authors who can write nothing more interesting than a personal check, but this is talent enough for the vanity publisher, who showers the prospective writer-customer with encouraging comments on his manuscript. "It's unnecessary to tell them lies," says Edward Uhlan of Exposition Press. "I tell them things like 'your manuscript is indicative of your talent,' and that's enough for them."[10]

The vanity author is ordinarily promised high royalties—usually 40 percent—but he finds that aside from a handful of admiring (or morbid) friends and relatives, no one buys his book, and his royalties are a pitiful rebate of his own money, perhaps $15 or $30 against a cost of $1500.

He also learns that vanity publishers are strictly obedient to contracts. If the agreement says that 2000 are to be printed, the publisher does just that: he *prints,* but doesn't necessarily *bind,* that quantity. When sales rapidly plunge to oblivion, the vanity publisher offers to sell remaining copies to the author. Otherwise, the publisher warns, they will be gnawed into pulp by cruel machines. "Some of these authors wind up paying for their books a second time," says David Dempsey, a magazine columnist and long-time critic of vanity publishers, "and finish with 2000 copies crowding their back porch."[11]

The Federal Trade Commission has frequently scowled at vanity publishers, but their business is not illegal, although the ethics of encouraging a patently hopeless author to part with his savings is open to question. Subsidy publishing serves the fundamental need to communicate, and in a way it is democratic because it removes the formidable criterion of talent and substitutes that of money (which, while not altogether democratic, does permit a good many people— about 1000 a year—to buy a ticket to ride). Many subsidy authors have felt deep satisfaction in seeing their work in print and were under no illusions about producing a best-seller, becoming famous, and making money. They purchased a kind of immortality, and found the price reasonable.

The Federal Trade Commission urges the potential subsidy author to ponder these questions before signing a contract:

> 1. Am I counting on recovering all or a substantial part of my investment through the sale of my book?
> 2. If the book sells only a few copies, can I afford the loss of my investment?
> 3. If I contract for a specified number of copies of my book, will that number be printed and bound or is the publisher obligated to bind only those books for which a bona fide order is received?
> 4. Will the publisher deliver to me, at no extra cost, all unsold copies of the book at the termination of the contract?
> 5. What do bookstores, book reviewers and librarians in my community think about books published by the vanity press?
> 6. Will I have to do most of the promotion of my own book?
> 7. Could I have my book edited, printed and bound locally for the same or lower charges than those quoted by [a vanity house]?[12]

tell them what you think

An amateur author reported enthusiastically to *Writer's Digest* that he had found a new market for his work:

> I've just hit a way to air my writing talent. I write letters to newspapers and magazines. Two of my irate letters have appeared in *The Village Voice,* and *The East Village Other* in New York City. It gives me a chance to use a style and slam home an opinion.

His discovery was hardly news. Every year, without benefit of writing courses or the vanity press, 8 million Americans sensibly cope with mass communication by writing a letter to an editor on matters as varied as the nature of democracy and the mating habits of the rufous hummingbird.

What's more, editors like letters. The New York *Times* once grandly commented:

Letters to the editor are a valued part of every newspaper. Their variety of topic is endless. They correct—and make—errors. They reflect on a multitude of views and moods. They abound in curious information. They constitute a debating society that never adjourns, in which everything knowable is discovered. A sodality of voluntary correspondents, approving, wrathful, critical, philosophical, humorous, full of admonition, reproof, instruction, miscellaneous knowledge, has succeeded the long-winded Publicolas and Catos of our long-suffering ancestors.[13]

Only a handful of journals ignore letters. *National Geographic* prints none, and the *New Yorker* and *Reader's Digest* only rarely. In its second issue, *Scanlan's* announced that it would *charge* for letters at the rate of 25 cents a word. Most editors are eager for letters because of their high readership. *Playboy,* which prints about 100 per issue, sends advance copies of articles to leading experts, requesting their comments. The Providence *Journal and Bulletin* annually holds a banquet for the hundred or so writers of what it judges are the best letters of the year. Some newspapers give an award of a few dollars for outstanding letters of the month.

Of course major publications draw many more letters than they can accommodate. *Time* prints one in 50 and the New York *Times* in 1971 reproduced only about 6 percent of the 45,000 it received. Otherwise the *Times* would drown in correspondence, according to Associate Editor Clifton Daniel, who estimates that the 18 million words it receives each year from readers could completely fill at least 135 weekday issues.

An editor is not required to print a letter, and all have some criteria of what to publish. For one thing, a newspaper or magazine is vulnerable to lawsuit if a letter is defamatory. Insane or obscene letters are rejected (the Atlanta *Journal* once estimated that about one-fourth of the letters it receives are from crackpots, and the Indianapolis *Star* makes a similar estimate). Other grounds for rejection are unfairness, self-promotion, exhausted subject matter, bad writing, duplication, repetition, and lack of space. For the most part, letters are selected for aptness, clarity, variety, and wit, and they are edited only for brevity. Most newspapers apply a word limit, and some ration their more compulsive correspondents to one or two letters a month (the *Times* will print no more than two letters from one person a year).

An editor will usually refuse to print anonymous letters, though many will withhold the author's name at his request. Careful newspapers attempt to verify a writer's authenticity. A few years ago *Time* was embarrassed when it printed a letter believed to be from four persons from India; actually the names were obscene Hindi words.[14]

Letters to the editor are not particularly representative of public opinion. Those who write letters to the above-ground press tend to be older, richer, better educated, more rooted in their community, and more conservative than the general population.[15] Needless to say, underground papers attract their own kinds of correspondence.

Broadcast media—some stations, at least—have rough equivalents to letters in the form of call-in shows, which have proved to be inexpensive and attractive programs. The views expressed are often widely varied; the participants need no more equipment than a telephone and some patience. Unfortunately, the deejay moderators often try to hype the conversations with strained arguments and caustic rejoinders; opinion, rather than thought, prevails. Cable television systems are beginning to provide "soap box" channels over which ordinary citizens may speak their minds free of charge.

In the past few years, several newspapers and a few broadcast stations have experimented with "action lines"—a service that solves problems for readers or viewers. For example, a reader who is having trouble receiving mail-order merchandise calls the action-line number. The newspaper investigates the complaint, seeks redress, and reports the results in a daily column. A few of these columns—which appear under such names as "Trouble Shooter," "Help," "Do-It Man," and "Gotta Gripe"—also publish a paragraph or two of opinion supplied by readers. Unfortunately, not all action-line inquiries are acknowledged or investigated.

doing criticism

One day in 1900 a disgruntled lawyer named W. W. "Plug Hat" Anderson strode through the swinging doors of "The Bucket of Blood"—the red-walled office of a pair of rakehells who owned the Denver *Post,* Harry H. Tammen and Fred G. Bonfils. A pistol bulged in Anderson's pocket. As he and Tammen exchanged opinions of each other's integrity and ancestry, a sob sister named Polly Pry noticed the gun and screamed.

Bonfils leaped forward, slugged Anderson on the cheek, and flung him out of the room. Anderson returned for a last word. He shot Bonfils in the shoulder and chest and Tammen in the wrist and arm.

Polly prepared to wrestle him for the gun, but Anderson was so mollified by the sight of his adversaries lying prostrate and bleeding that he cheerfully departed for city hall, where he surrendered. The publishers survived. Colorado Governor Charles Spaulding Thomas is said to have sent a bouquet to Anderson's cell with this note: "I congratulate you upon your intention, but must condemn your poor aim."[16]

Assaults upon journalists are by no means passé. In 1968, Dan Hicks, Jr., editor of the Madisonville, Tennessee, *Monroe County*

Democrat, who had won major awards for exposing what he described as local "machine politics," was beaten, shot at twice, and his equipment stolen and held for ransom, and his office set afire.

Clobbering journalists is one way to deal with mass communication, but it is not only discourteous, it also seldom has the desired effect. Tammen and Bonfils recuperated and blithely continued their raucous brand of journalism. Hicks armed himself with two guns and sandbagged his office. He announced, "Whatever happens, we are not going to leave and we are not going to stop printing the truth."[17]

There is a need for media criticism, though not of the violent kind. A major source of it should be the audience, the anonymous, information-hungry mass in whose name the media claim their freedom and on whose behalf they profess to be responsible.

On one end of the critical spectrum are the Canadian viewers cited at the beginning of this chapter who confessed to muttering at their TV sets. On the other is the bilious correspondent who wields his pen like a white-hot poker. Somewhere between is a better path, and it is not well marked. Although numerous volumes have been written on criticism of fine art, literature, film, music, and drama, not much exists to guide the layman who wishes to talk back to the popular media. Some signposts ought to be erected, and we offer these:

1. *Pay attention to what you criticize.* This courtesy to your subject requires that, at the very least, you send your irate letter to the *right* newspaper. One should not be like the religious person who wrote a letter to a television game show, one of whose quiz categories was "potpourri," and denounced its reference to "popery" as "ridiculing the head of one of the great religions of the world."

2. *Criticism can include praise as well as blame.* Studies show that letters to the editor tend to be negative, no matter the topic. This dyspepsia is understandable; people are driven to scratch what irritates them, and they accept pleasures more casually. But it is wise to praise the media for what they do well, because this reinforces their better tendencies.

3. *Offer suggestions.* A general criticism of shallow coverage may be warranted, but shouldn't the critic also propose some means of improvement? In one Midwestern city, a civic-minded young couple praised the local editor for his support of charities but chided him for lack of investigation. How much money is collected? Where does it go? What are the campaign expenses? The newspaper responded with an in-depth story. The critics did not say that fund-raising campaigns are crooked, only that they ought to be reported as much as promoted.

4. *Provide evidence, and do not overstate your case.* If for no other reason than to make clear what you are talking about, cite examples of good or bad performance by the medium in question. Not long ago a reader wrote the editor of a Wisconsin weekly, "It is apparent you are a mean, little, biased, uninformed, ignorant nincompoop." Maybe so, but the nincompoopery, *et alia,* were not proved. As E. B. White once wrote, "When you overstate, the reader will be instantly on guard, and everything that has preceded your overstatement as well as everything that follows it, will be suspect in his mind because he has lost confidence in your judgment or your poise."[18] The media strew evidence of their performance for all to see or hear. We grant that difficulties arise in knowing what the media fail to show, and in discerning their standards of performance. (In the next chapter we will cite some media codes.) The most telling criticism tests a medium's performance against its own ideals. If you cannot determine these standards, ask the editor or station manager or movie exhibitor; this in itself is healthy criticism because it requires introspection.

5. *Recognize the natural constraints upon the media, and behold the motes and beams in your own eye.* The constraints are mainly those of time, money, and expertise. The late A. J. Liebling, a press critic and reporter, once sketched a foreign correspondent's problems:

> To understand perfectly a new country, new situation, the new characters you confront on an assignment, is impossible. To understand more than half, so that your report will have significant correlation with what is happening, is hard. To transmit more than half of what you understand is a hard trick, too, far beyond the task of the so-called creative artist, who if he finds a character in his story awkward can simply change its characteristics. . . . It is possible, occasionally, to get something completely right—a scene, or a pattern of larceny, or a man's mind. These are the reporter's victories, as rare as pitchers' home runs.[19]

The media critic cheers the home runs, doesn't expect them too frequently, but does demand many more hits than misses. Richard Graf, news director of WNBC-TV, New York, once said, "If you're going to criticize us, do it for what we are, not for what you think we should be." This is too strict, for if the audience has low expectations, the media may not rise above them.

About critics' blind spots, Eric Sevareid once said of TV critics who write for newspapers, "While they compose columns and editorials deploring TV's 'wasteland' of trivia, let them measure the column space devoted to astrology, moronic comics, advice to the lovelorn, liquor ads—none of which appears on TV." Wes Gallagher, general manager of the Associated Press, once said of critics: "Most pressure groups who criticize the news media today do not want reporters. They want advocates or, better still, outright propagandists of their point of view." The hardest thing for the critic is to adhere to the same high standards he demands of the media: accuracy, adequacy, fairness, sensitivity, and wisdom.

does it do any good?

Can an individual make a dent in the massive media? Every day there are quiet successes—quiet because the media, tender about charges of untoward influence and proud of their freedom, do not herald changes that owe to outsiders. Letters *are* read, even if not published or acknowledged. And in the media, as in other large institutions, change comes slowly—too slowly for many impatient critics, who turn to group action and who seek leverage.

Nicholas Johnson, *enfant terrible* of the Federal Communications Commission, wrote:

> You *can* fight city hall, the "little man" *can* do effective battle with massive corporate and governmental institutions, the government *can* be made responsive to an individual citizen's desires. The individual's frustration in our institutionalized society comes only from ignorance, not impotence.[20]

Johnson cited the case of John Banzhaf, a young lawyer who set out to do something about cigaret advertising on television. Banzhaf grabbed a potent lever—the FCC's "fairness doctrine," which requires broadcasters to present all sides of "controversial issues of public importance." Banzhaf argued that New York's WCBS (and by implication all other stations) presented only the favorable side of smoking by running cigaret commercials. To the surprise and irritation of the television and advertising industries, the FCC agreed and invoked the fairness doctrine. Soon a flood of antismoking commercials made their appearance. Later all cigaret advertising was banished from the air.

During the 1960s, citizen groups drew a bead on television's tenderest spot, the license renewal process. As mentioned in Chapter 4, in 1964 the Office of Communication of the United Church of Christ joined with two black civil rights leaders in Jackson, Mississippi, to file a petition to deny renewal to station WLBT-TV on grounds that it had systematically excluded Negroes from access to its facilities, had promoted segregationist views, and had denied presentation of opposing views. Up to then the FCC had not permitted private citizens to enter the renewal proceedings—only incumbents and applicants had "standing." After lengthy hearings before the FCC and appeals to the courts, the U.S. Court of Appeals in 1969 revoked the license, rebuked the FCC for its balkiness, ordered additional applications, and gave standing to citizen groups. This decision, together with increased consumer activism, led to the birth of such groups as the National Citizens Committee for Broadcasting, Action for Children's Television, Black Efforts for Soul in Television, and an organization led by John Banzhaf called Terminating Unfair Broadcasting Excesses.

In the face of numerous renewal protests, broadcasters turned to Congress for protective legislation. They also became more attentive to community interests and eager to negotiate with citizen groups that threatened action to deny renewal. Marsha O'Bannon Prowitt of the Office of Communication of the United Church of Christ put it this way: "Many groups have used both persuasion and legal action in their campaigns with considerable success: it often has been the case that the *ability* to take legal action at the FCC if necessary has been the prerequisite to successful non-legal negotiation with a station or network."[21]

One of the more spectacular examples of negotiation arose after the Citizens Communications Center filed a petition in 1970 with the FCC opposing the sale of radio and television stations in three cities to Capital Cities Broadcasting Corporation, on grounds that Capital Cities had ignored the public interest during purchase transactions. While the FCC was mulling over the sale, Capital Cities agreed to negotiate with Citizens Communication Center and to consult minority groups in the three cities affected—Philadelphia, New Haven, and Fresno. The result was a pledge by Capital Cities to spend $1 million over a three-year period for programming that reflected the views of black and Spanish-surnamed Americans. Capital Cities also promised to form community advisory groups to help plan programming and to recruit minority employes. When this was put into writing and became part of the transfer-of-ownership documents, Citizens Communications Center withdrew its petition and the FCC approved the transfer.

In a pioneering case, United Church of Christ in 1969 entered into direct bargaining with KTAL-TV of Texarkana, Texas, after filing a petition to deny renewal of KTAL's license. The outcome was a statement attached to the renewal application and filed with the FCC in which the station promised, among other things, to recruit minority-group employes, to publicize the rights of poor persons and to "inform public opinion about the problem of poverty and the steps that are being taken to alleviate it," to "cover the entire range of religious thought" in its religious programming, and to "consult with all substantial groups in the community regarding community taste and needs."

Nicholas Johnson has said of local negotiations, "This immensely significant development may herald a new technique of community influence over the media, in which concerned citizens negotiate directly with their local stations to seek reforms with the complicated and costly legal proceedings required before the FCC and the courts."

In short, community groups win concessions, the station receives its license, and the FCC and the courts are spared endless litigation.

So is everyone happy? Not entirely. Richard W. Jencks, president of the CBS Broadcast Group, raises some serious questions about deals between broadcasters and protest groups:

> Probably the most fundamental demand ... is that a large percentage of the station's weekly schedule be programmed with material defined as "relevant" to the particular community group—usually an ethnic group—making the demand. ... For ethnic minority groups the idea of "relevance" seems to mean that the programming is relevant to the needs of the black person, for example, only if the programming deals directly with the black experience.
>
> It seems possible that there is a strong thread of racial separatism in the demand for relevance. Like the demand of some black college students for segregated dormitories, it may be regarded in large part as a demand for segregated programming. ...
>
> Television can be said to be the only remaining mass medium which is capable of reaching most of the people most of the time. Is it important to preserve television as a mass medium? I think so, particularly when I consider the racial problem in this country.
>
> For the importance of television as a mass medium has not been in what has been communicated *to* minorities as such—or what has been communicated *between* minority group leaders and their followers—but in what has been communicated *about* minorities *to the general public.* ...
>
> If audience fragmentation to meet the special requirements of minority groups would destroy television as a *local* mass medium, it would, by the same token, of course, make impossible the continuance of network television as a *national* mass medium. ...
>
> The *means* used by community groups may have an even more important impact on the nature of American broadcast regulation, and in particular upon the FCC. ...
>
> *Should* private groups be encouraged to do what official law enforcement bodies are "unable or unwilling to do"? In particular, should they police a licensee by means of exploiting the power of that very regulatory agency which is said to be "unable or unwilling" to do so?
>
> It would seem that to ask the question is to answer it. ...
>
> In the second place, private law enforcement is hard to control. ... A medium which can be coerced by threat of license contest into making such concessions to black or Spanish-speaking groups can as readily be coerced by a coalition of white ethnic groups. ...
>
> Clearly, there is at the heart of this matter a broad question of public policy—namely, whether public control of licensee conduct should be supplemented by any form of private control. ...

So far the effectiveness of community group strategy has rested upon the willingness of the Commission to tacitly support these groups and their objectives. Indeed, it might well be argued that where groups are successful in obtaining concessions, they can really be called *governmental action.* . . .

I suggest it would be far more in the public interest for the Commission to do these things than to permit them to be done covertly by private groups.[22]

In answer to Jencks it could be said that these groups are scarcely covert in their activities—most, in fact, are fairly noisy. And local programming and local control of broadcasting have been FCC ideals from the beginning. And if licensees accede to things the FCC is "unable or unwilling" to impose, it is the fault of timorous broadcasters and not of citizens' groups.

Still, nagging questions remain as to the extent and quality of a citizen's involvement in control of mass communication, as as to his means of exercising it. Which pressures are unwarranted and unwholesome? Which groups? Is it fair for a private group to use the threat of government intervention as leverage? Could it be successful otherwise? Can a medium meet its responsibilities by sharing them with private groups? Could it be responsible otherwise?

These problems are not new. In 1815 John Adams wrote a friend:

If there is ever to be an amelioration of the condition of mankind, philosophers, theologians, legislators, politicians and moralists will find that the regulation of the press is the most difficult, dangerous and important problem they have to resolve. Mankind cannot now be governed without it, nor at present with it.

for further reading

Adler, Mortimer J. *How to Read a Book.* New York: Simon & Schuster, 1940.

Byrne, Robert. *Writing Rackets.* New York: Lyle Stuart, 1969.

Cirino, Robert. "I Had to Publish It Myself," *Grassroots Editor,* September-October 1971, pp. 4–6, 18.

Green, Daniel St. Albin. "Dear Mr. Editor, You Fink: Masses of Letters Deluge Nation's Newspapers as Readers Speak Out," *Quill,* July 1970, pp. 16–19.

Handbook for Film Societies. New York: American Federation of Film Societies, 1959.

Jensen, Jay W. "A Method and a Perspective for Criticism of the Mass Media," *Journalism Quarterly* 37 (Spring 1960), pp. 261–266.

Lichty, Lawrence W., and Blankenburg, William B. "Challenging a TV License: The Madison Story," *Chicago Journalism Review,* October 1972, pp. 10–13.

Liebling, A. J. *The Press.* New York: Ballantine Books, 1961.

Milam, Lorenzo. *Sex and Broadcasting: A Handbook on Starting Community*

Radio Stations. Los Gatos, Calif.: Dildo Press, 1971.

Prowitt, Marsha O'Bannon. *Guide to Citizen Action in Radio and Television.* New York: Office of Communication, United Church of Christ, 1971.

The Public and Broadcasting: A Procedure Manual. Washington, D.C.: Federal Communications Commission, 1972.

Rivers, William L. *Free-Lancer and Staff Writer: Writing Magazine Articles.* Belmont, Calif.: Wadsworth, 1972.

Sayre, Nora. "How Free Is the Free-Lance Writer?" *Mademoiselle,* March 1968, pp. 66–177.

Seigel, Kalman. *Talking Back to the New York Times: Letters to the Editor, 1851–1971.* New York: Quadrangle, 1972.

Shamberg, Michael, and Raindance Corporation. *Guerrilla Television.* New York: Holt, Rinehart and Winston, 1971.

Shayon, Robert Lewis. *Open to Criticism.* Boston: Beacon Press, 1971.

Uhlan, Edward. *The Rogue of Publishers Row.* New York: Exposition Press, 1956.

what the media can do

a few beginnings

The nut that is easy to crack is often empty.
—Charlie Chan, *Murder Over New York*

Not long after Vice President Spiro Agnew delivered his 1969 oration on network news bias, Honolulu station KHVH aired a spunky editorial that began, "Do you want the government to choose your news for you?" It concluded with an invitation to the audience: "Intimidation is implicit in this situation, and the current administration seems willing to take advantage of it. This is a situation that Americans should not tolerate, not at the hands of any administration, be it national or municipal. We want your support. Let us know."

The audience responded, all right—in favor of Agnew. Five

days later a highly chastened KHVH reported, "We have just found out that we don't know our audience . . . and our audience doesn't know us —that's a shock for any medium."

Shocks were felt elsewhere. A poll taken by ABC after the Agnew speech revealed that of 559 adults interviewed, 51 percent agreed with the Vice President that TV news was biased, 33 percent disagreed, and 16 percent didn't know or had no opinion. Around the same time, a station in the Southwest was visited by two separate pairs of men who were interested in beating the hell out of anti-Agnew newsmen.

In another survey, the CBS New Election Unit found that:

> The majority of adults in America seem willing to restrict some of the basic freedoms constitutionally guaranteed by the Bill of Rights. Specifically, about three-fourths (76%) of the 1,136 people interviewed in the telephone survey believe extremist groups should not be permitted to organize *demonstrations* against the government, even if there appeared to be no clear danger of violence. Moreover, well over one-half of the people (54%) would not give everyone the right to *criticize* the government, if the criticism were thought to be damaging to our national interest; and a comparable number (55%) felt newspapers, radio, and television should not be permitted to *report* some stories considered by the government to be harmful to our national interest (wartime censorship was excluded in the question).[1]

Badly nettled but never at a loss for words, the media promptly discerned a "crisis of confidence" between themselves and their audience. The diagnosis was especially painful because it came at a time when the old flint-skinned media merchants and their public-be-damned attitudes were, most of them, safely in their graves. Their successors speak in more socially conscious terms; here is Otis Chandler, publisher of the huge and powerful Los Angeles *Times:*

> What concerns me . . . is the vast group of about a million daily subscribers who are not at all homogeneous. . . . I am concerned with keeping and expanding our circulation among all of them. And I am just as concerned with what we say to them, how we say it, and the effect it has upon them—the socio-political effect it has upon them. I am concerned, most of all, with the role and methods of a mass circulation daily newspaper in a time that can only be described as revolutionary—a time, that is, of very radical change. And how, in such a time of change, my newspaper can maintain a posture that will enble it to be an influencing factor in seeking the more perfect nation, the more perfect city, the more perfect world.[2]

The modern mass communicator at least knows the litany of responsibility. He is not certain what to do about it. The familiar aches and pains of competition, technology, economics, and regulation can be treated with time-honored remedies that include greater efficiency, further mechanization, more enticing content (including a dash of sensationalism), more passionate wooing of advertisers, some judicious rate-cutting, another new pitch to the youth market, and a fending-off of bad regulation while lobbying for favorable legislation. But the problems of public confidence and responsible performance have no ready solutions.

How can the media meet the goal of responsibility, with freedom, in service to a distant and huffy public? Again, Otis Chandler: "I am going to confess, candidly, that I do not know and I doubt that anyone in journalism really knows the answers, and knows none of the answers exactly." This is not as glum as it sounds, because an acknowledgment of fallibility is the beginning of wisdom.

constructing and following guidelines

The idea of formulating a code of conduct is simple: the wisest heads of the industry get together and lay down a set of standards against which all performance can be measured. But who is to decide? Who is to enforce the code? What are the penalties for nonconformity? And what about freedom of expression?

The eminent journalist and iconoclast H. L. Mencken once observed that "journalistic codes of ethics are all moonshine. Essentially they are as absurd as would be codes of streetcar conductors, barbers, or public jobholders." Mencken had a point, and yet even if we grant that media codes—and there are many—are not something that Moses lugged down a mountain, they do represent a manifestation of media responsibility.

There have always been individual journalists with high standards of performance, but it was not until the industrial revolution that responsibility became an institutional concern of mass communication and other fields. By the turn of the century, mass-produced communication was the work of many hands. It cut across class lines, trod on many toes, and purveyed broad (and not always lofty) content.

The progressive-reformist impulse of the first decade of this century, followed by the great collective effort needed to win World War I, inspired a rash of self-regulatory codes in business, trades, and professions. By 1924 some 130 business and trade codes had been established.[3] Among them were the Canons of Journalism, adopted by the American Society of Newspaper Editors (ASNE) in 1923. Only a few hundred words long, the Canons speak in positive, idealistic language. Canon I sketches the concept of responsibility:

The right of a newspaper to attract and hold readers is restricted by nothing but considerations of public welfare. The use a newspaper makes of the share of public attention it gains serves to determine its sense of responsibility, which it shares with every member of its staff. A journalist who uses his power for any selfish or otherwise unworthy purpose is faithless to a high trust.[4]

The remaining canons treat the topics of freedom, independence, sincerity, truthfulness, accuracy, impartiality, fair play, and decency. They prescribe no punishment for media miscreants: "Lacking authority to enforce its canons, the journalism here represented can but express the hope that deliberate panderings to vicious instincts will encounter effective public disapproval or yield to the influence of a preponderant professional condemnation." Early in its existence, the ASNE attempted to expel the roguish Fred G. Bonfils of the Denver *Post* who was accused of blackmailing oil magnate Harry Sinclair in connection with the Teapot Dome scandal. Running true to form, Bonfils showed up with a lawyer and announced he would sue everyone in sight. He was permitted to resign.[5]

Codes such as the Canons of Journalism—simple, broad, and idealistic—are *prescriptive.* Bruce A. Linton, a scholar of media regulation, distinguishes them from codes that are *proscriptive:* full of specific prohibitions and negative in tone. Most codes have a mixed character, with those of entertainment media tending to be the more proscriptive.[6]

If a code acquires some teeth of enforcement, mass communicators begin to worry about the shalt-nots than the shalts. This happened with the Motion Picture Production Code, which eventually gained the power to put a film to death. Almost every producer paid close attention to it. By contrast, the Canons of Journalism have not changed, remain couched in positive generalities, and are virtually unknown to working journalists.

Movies came under fire as soon as they grew popular. In 1909 the People's Institute of New York created the National Board of Film Censorship—later to be called the National Board of Review—to inspect films for cleanliness. It was supported by the powerful Motion Picture Patents Company, which did not want this task to fall into the more potent hands of government. Yet municipal and state censorship boards sprouted like crabgrass, and when the threat of Federal control became acute in 1922, the industry hired Postmaster General Will Hays to become head of the Motion Picture Production Association (later Motion Picture Association of America). Among other things, Hays decided which plays and books were fit for filming and reviewed all scripts for naughty content. He also staved off major threats of

Federal and state regulation in the 1920s. By 1930 Hays had devised a Production Code that was chock full of "don'ts" and "be carefuls" and covered a whole swamp of indecencies, ranging from profanity to immodest costuming.

The Production Code had little clout until 1934 when, in response to threats from the newly formed Catholic National Legion of Decency, the major producers agreed not to exhibit any film that lacked the Production Code seal. In the 1950s and 1960s the code was gutted by several forces: the rise of television, the importation of unblushing foreign films, a general relaxation of moral strictures in entertainment, and antitrust actions that separated the major companies from their chains of theatres.[7] In 1968 the MPAA resorted to film ratings, G through X.

Broadcasting codes—which have much to say about advertising as well as entertainment—bear a strong family resemblance to the old movie Production Code. Their motivations are similar: fear of outside regulation. Sponsored by the National Association of Broadcasters, the Radio Code first appeared in 1929 and underwent several reincarnations according to the way the winds blew from Congress and the networks. The first Television Code was adopted in 1952. After the payola and quiz-show scandals of the late 1950s, the National Association of Broadcasters established a new Code of Good Practices and set up a Code Authority to interpret its provisions, to review programs and commercials for acceptibility, to hear complaints, and to keep tabs on governmental menaces. Station membership in the NAB and subscription to the broadcast codes are voluntary and separate. In 1970, 51 percent of the radio stations belonged to the NAB and 34 percent subscribed to the Radio Code; the figures for television stations were 86 and 65 percent, respectively.[8]

As long as subscribing stations adhere to the code, it has some teeth. The producer or advertiser whose material is not compliant runs the risk of having his programming rejected by subscribing stations.

The broadcast codes also have been successful in holding government at bay—or so many broadcasters believe. As Thad M. Sandstrom, vice president and general manager of WIBW in Topeka, remarked at an NAB symposium, "It seems to me that the Radio and Television Codes are the strongest weapons we as broadcasters have for the preservation of our free enterprise system of broadcasting in this country. To me the Code is the only answer because if we don't do it ourselves, then Big Brother is going to do it for us."[9]

Each month the Code Authority issues *Code News,* a newsletter that keeps stations up to date on the meaning of the code and the acceptability of advertisements and sponsor-packaged programs. One recent advertisement that "raised questions" was a 30-second TV commercial for the film *B.S. I Love You.* The Code Authority said it was acceptable for scheduling only during "adult viewing hours." The reasons:

> This recommendation is made in light of scenes #5 (Girl in bra and panties, lying on bed), #7 (Girl in bed beckoning to man), and #8 (Man in hallway of an apartment. He is dressed in under shirt and under shorts. He tries to push a girl into a bathroom before he can be noticed, but an older man sees him), which through highlighting out of context raise concerns under Television Code Sections IV–27 and IV–28 ("costuming of performers . . . etc.").[10]

In addition to supporting the NAB codes, the networks impose "continuity acceptance" or "standards and practices" policies of their own. About a hundred network "program policy editors" (they prefer to be called anything but censors, though that is their function) review all entertainment and advertising before it is transmitted to affiliated stations. Because revision of finished material can be expensive, the censors are consulted at all stages of production, beginning with story ideas. There is considerable haggling with producers, who are canny adversaries. The *Wall Street Journal* describes an interlude between George Schlatter, executive producer of "Laugh-In," and Sandy Cummings, an NBC censor:

> On some shows the censor rules by fiat. But decisions on the big comedy shows generally are reached by negotiation. Mr. Schlatter heads the Laugh-In negotiating team. The censors concede that he is a formidable bargainer. Taking a call from Mr. Cummings, he leans his big frame back in his chair, tilts his beard toward the ceiling and begins on a conciliatory tack.
> "Sandy, baby, you're beautiful," he says. "Did you know we've just spent all morning softening up show number 11 just for you?" But soon he moves to the offensive. "I saw five Polish jokes on the Bob Hope show last night, Sandy," he says. "I trust this means a change in network policy."
> Ethnic humor, particularly Polish jokes, is a frequent bone of contention. The Chicago-based Polish-American Guardian Society rumbles about suing "Laugh-In" and NBC over alleged defamation of the Polish people. . . .
> Mr. Cummings patiently explains to Mr. Schlatter that there hasn't been a change in network policy on Polish jokes. However, there may be relaxation of censorship for certain performers. . . . Bob Hope gets more leeway on topical humor than do most comedians, as does Dean Martin, who "has a roguish image that allows him to say things innocently that, coming from someone else, might be offensive."
> Mr. Schlatter offers a suggestion that contested words be removed by "blooping" them—cutting them out of the sound track. Mr. Cum-

mings declines. Another censor explains, "The audience will always imagine the worst possible meaning for the word you take out, often far worse than it really was." Also, the censors hate to have their handiwork evident.[11]

The censor's posture is ungainly. He is squeezed between authors, producers, directors, performers, advertisers, network executives, pressure groups, regulatory agencies, lawyers, and the great American audience. He is often called a silly blue-nose—a "Priscilla Goodbody," in Johnny Carson's words. Presumably his reward is the satisfaction of protecting the public. If so, what is he to make of this letter from a viewer?

> We ... do not particularly care for those overly-personal advertisements such as a laxative. [But] ... don't pay any attention to any cards or letters that complain about too much violence or immodesty on the regular programs. I believe that you must face the facts of life and that includes murders, robberies, beatings, and divorces, rapes and sexy dolls. Keep these on.[12]

Are media codes worth the bother? They can be attacked on many grounds. The prescriptive codes are high-minded but vague and forgettable. Proscriptive codes are specific, perhaps too much so, and can delude a mass communicator into believing that avoidance of petty sins is equivalent to sainthood.

Economically marginal media find it hard to turn down paid material even if it fails to meet code—or personal—standards. At the other end of the scale, some strong-minded media people regard a code as no more wholesome than government regulation. Certainly there are producers and advertisers who see little difference between being shut out by code adherents or by governmental censors. Codes without sanctions seem frail and windy, but enforceable codes can constrict freedom of expression.

The answer, if any, is that a code that is thoughtfully composed, voluntarily accepted, wise in its prescriptions, slender and flexible in its prohibitions, and attentive to the public's needs is *probably* more good than bad. At their best, codes are signs of conscience and points of reference for mass communicators and their audiences alike.

professionalism and its problems

In a speech to the National Press Club, psychiatrist W. Walter Menninger, who had been a member of the National Commission on the Causes and Prevention of Violence, reviewed the responsibilities of mass communication and offered a modest proposal:

In other professions with a public trust—medicine, law, education— laws for licensure and certification assure the public that the practitioner has fulfilled minimum standards, met certain requirements for training and demonstrated competence in the profession. The public is entitled to similar safeguards for the quality of the practitioners of this most important cornerstone of our democratic society.

Other critics of the media are struck by the fact that while a broadcast engineer must pass a formal FCC test before operating even a small transmitter, disk jockeys, newscasters, and entertainers have to undergo no such examination even though they have the attention of a huge audience many hours every day.

Take the case of a young woman who wishes to teach third grade and compare her requirements, as Nicholas Johnson did, with those of a broadcaster:

The applicant may have to have a college degree from a school of education. She must be qualified under standards established by the state for a teacher's certificate. She must meet the standards of the local school board. She probably must have spent some time as a supervised practice teacher. She may be compelled to continue to take in-service training. She must meet these standards because she is going to spend time with a group of perhaps twenty-five children for several months out of the year. . . .

Contrast these concerns and standards, if you will, with those we associate with broadcasters, with their access to *millions* of young minds for far more hours every year.[13]

The answer of mass communicators to suggestions that they be licensed is swift and angry. Long-time newspaper editor Basil "Stuffy" Walters growled, "This Menninger is a great doctor and better stick to doctoring."[14] Frank Angelo, managing editor of the Detroit *Free Press,* said Menninger's suggestion was nonsense: "Who is going to determine who should be licensed? It is almost impossible to set up criteria to license newsmen that wouldn't lead to some form of control."[15]

It is not hard to find the source of journalistic fears. In countries that license newsmen, the press is dead or docile, and the public suffers accordingly. The limited licensing we do have in this country grew from practical, rather than ideological, concerns: broadcast stations are licensed to use specific channels so that their signals do not interfere, and all media enterprises are subject to routine business licensing. Reporters are accredited by authorities to work in certain areas—war zones, for example—where there are limited accommodations or certain dangers. A free press recognizes the need for such regulations, but even these have a way of getting out of hand. Military commanders have used disaccreditation as punishment for critical newsmen, and municipal governments have invoked sanitation and fire-protection ordinances to harass local mass communicators, especially producers of avant-garde stage plays.

In one form or another, licensing has long been a characteristic of the traditional professions, and it's not surprising that it occurs to Menninger, a doctor, and Johnson, a lawyer. By most definitions, a "true" professional makes his services available to the public, usually on an individual basis, after mastering a special body of knowledge (which must be continually upgraded) and after passing qualifying examinations. He is subject to disbarment for unprofessional or incompetent behavior. Although journalists like to call themselves professionals, the term doesn't quite fit. There is no unique body of knowledge peculiar to journalism, there is no single professional organization to enforce standards (like a medical society or bar association), and the practitioners of mass communication, for the most part, are not self-employed. And the right of free expression squarely collides with a licensing scheme for mass communicators.[16]

In the case of mass communication, even the requirement of formal education has some drawbacks. Stuffy Walters cites an example: "One of the greatest reporters was Eddie Lahey. I don't know how far he got along in school, he wasn't a high school graduate, but he was a checker of freight cars out of the yards in Chicago, counting the cars and getting the numbers down, and he saw a reporter out there one day, and he said, 'I'd like to be a reporter.' He went down to Henry Justin Smith and got a job. And he was one of the great reporters of our times. Now he could never have passed the Menninger test when he applied for a job."[17]

This is not to discount education, because all competent mass communicators are educated—but in widely varying ways. The major media seek employes who have both a college education and practical experience. Specialties within mass communication demand education in depth, and *all* journalism requires a breadth of education or experience that permits a reporter to make sense of what he observes. As do the formal professions, journalism increasingly recognizes the value of continuous learning. Harvard University has for many years offered Nieman fellowships for working journalists who wish to return to campus to study whatever they feel they need. More recently similar programs have been supported by the Ford Foundation on other campuses.

Some observers call the field of mass communication a "quasi-profession," and the term is apt.[18] While mass communication has some earmarks of a true profession it cannot accede to restrictions on entry and the power to disbar. (And these powers have not completely rid medicine and law of quackery and venality.) What is needed in mass communication is a spirit of professionalism—a duty to public service —without constraints that impair freedom.

cure thyself

The media are not famous for their receptivity to criticism, but who is? Harry Ashmore recalls that the American Society of Newspaper Editors greeted the Hutchins Commission book, *A Free and Responsible Press,* by "huddling rumps together, horns out."

Animosity toward outsiders is understandable, but it's a hallmark of professionalism to give and take criticism *within* the profession. Consider this example from medicine, written by an intern:

> Any death in the house is hashed out in open meeting [of the hospital staff], and everyone has a chance to say what they think was right or wrong about the treatment. I guess they get pretty critical sometimes, too. I know back in May someone had a patient who ruptured her uterus, and the doctor mishandled the case. The woman survived, but the case came up at the staff meeting, and a resolution was passed to censure the doctor for his handling of the case, and the record of the censure vote was sent to . . . the surgical and OB divisions of the hospital, for entry into the hospital records.[19]

So even if mass communicators are leery of outside evaluations, they should be somewhat amenable to intramural criticism. This has not always been the case, but times are changing. A. J. Liebling observed a few years ago that "newspapers write about other newspapers with circumspection. The two surviving press associations, whose customers are newspapers, write about newspapers with deference. Newspapers write about themselves with awe, and only after mature reflection."

Were he still living, Liebling would be both astounded and pleased by the home-grown journalism reviews that have appeared in major American cities. The first was the *Chicago Journalism Review,* conceived by reporters who were disgusted with the regular Chicago papers' coverage of the 1968 Democratic Convention. Since then, reviews have appeared in New York, Providence, Atlanta, Honolulu, Denver, St. Louis, and elsewhere, written and edited by local journalists on their own time.

These reviews share with the national *Columbia Journalism Review,* founded by the Graduate School of Journalism at Columbia University in 1961, a zest for dissecting such journalistic infirmities as reliance on "official sources," coziness with advertisers, and susceptibility to freeloading and handouts.

Like the media they criticize, the reviews are occasionally

errant, superficial, and prone to righteousness. But the reviews frequently display a sense of humor and are not always above confessing their own blunders.

The reviews have received mixed greetings in their home towns, and the established media tend to ignore the upstarts. Denver's review, *The Unsatisfied Man,* wryly reported its own birth notices: "A new publication has reared its snooty head in Denver. . . . How do we know about the local press drudges' superego trip? We read it in *Time,* where else? We note, as critics, that the national magazine scooped the local papers on this one."

The same current of activism that inspired the journalism reviews has given rise to a growing demand by reporters for autonomy —a say-so about the handling of their copy, and a voice in policy-making.

For many years the editorial staffs of some leading foreign newspapers, notably in Scandinavia and France, have achieved independence by contract from the ownership of the publications. More recently in Germany, newsmen have negotiated "statutes"—actually house agreements—that guarantee a share of control over executive appointments, access to financial and editorial planning, and the right not to be forced to write anything contrary to their consciences or to be penalized for refusing to do so.

Even though there are employe-owned newspapers in the United States, staff influence remains largely informal. When Professor Bryce Rucker urged greater employe power in an article in the *Bulletin* of the American Society of Newspaper Editors, the response from news executives was apoplectic. *Editor & Publisher* reported that:

> The consensus [of executives] was that—regardless of how well it may work at *Le Figaro, Le Monde* and other European and Canadian newspapers—it would definitely bring chaos and not improvement to American newspapers. Some felt it would lead to anarchy in Journalism. All believed that in the final result American newspapers are under control of the "working press"—that good reporters with administrative ability become editors, and that control—somebody saying "yes" or "no"—is essential to any enterprise, including the newspaper business.[20]

Actually, the majority of American newspapers do possess some mechanisms for internal criticism, though not of employe control. These include staff meetings, personal conferences, memoranda, and employe publications. Sometimes these methods tend to be one-sided— not the sort of mutual criticism envisioned by professionalism. In response to a survey by the ANPA News Research Center on internal criticism, an editor said of his staff, "I like to call 'em over to my office and give 'em hell." Crudely used, internal criticism can be a thumbscrew to enforce policy and may lead to what editor Edward T. Fairchild of the Athol, Massachusetts, *Daily News* deplores as "factory management in news departments." But the same survey revealed, contrary to stereotype, that a great many editors are solicitous of reporters' feelings and sensitive to their comments.[21]

Despite some uneasiness, a few American newspapers are acquiring more policy participation by editorial employes. The 1970 contract between the American Newspaper Guild and the Denver *Post* contained provisions for an advisory ethics committee composed of three editorial employes and three executives. (Another provision stipulated that the *Post* could not print any correction or retraction of a story without first consulting the reporter who wrote it.) About the same time, the Rochester *Times-Union* and *Democrat and Chronicle* voluntarily expanded its editorial policy board to include two reporters. The Bangor, Maine, *Daily News* and Plainfield, New Jersey, *Courier-News* began similar practices.

No doubt some publishers agree to greater policy involvement by newsmen in order to thwart an alarming (to them) attempt by the inmates to take over the asylum. Other executives, taking a longer view, share the rationale of H. Doyle Harvill, managing editor of the Tampa Florida, *Times:*

> The reporter is usually more informed about his community, particularly in his area of responsibility, than is the editor or editors.
>
> The "ignorance" of some editors, in my experience, has dampened the enthusiasm of young journalists, and in some extreme cases, driven them into the arms of public relations firms with higher salaries and more luxurious working conditions.
>
> Reporters today, even the very young, are better educated, more enthusiastic, see journalism as a force to change old institutions, and are very susceptible to advice and guidance from an older and wiser head, if the counsel is fair and informed.
>
> The young reporter must be informed about the decisions of the newsroom management, so that he may feel a part of the organization.
>
> In order to make of him a real news person, we at the Tampa *Times* solicit his or her opinions both individually and in groups, formally and informally.
>
> We forthrightly tell the reporter that he is the "boss" in his area of work, and place the responsibility squarely on him for accuracy, fairness, taste, personal behavior and professionalism generally.
>
> If he fails to accept the responsibility placed upon him, he is dismissed after notice by me that he has not measured up to what we expect of reporters on the Tampa *Times.* I might add that few are dismissed. Turnover is slight.
>
> Meetings of the editors are held in my office almost daily. We critique the paper, quite often in hypercritical tones, and reporters are asked often to sit in on the meetings.

Planning sessions on special sections, series and other in-depth projects by the Tampa *Times* include reporters.

Reporters are urged to criticize headlines, captions and editing of their copy by the city desk editors.

An example of how we allow freedom of thought and expression among reporters was recently illustrated by one of the women on my staff. I was mildly critical of her failure to follow up on a previous story. She replied, "Cool it, boss. The story's in the works."[22]

ombudsmen and press councils

In mid-1967 the Louisville *Courier-Journal* and *Times* ran a large advertisement picturing a burly, balding man who wore an optimistic grin. The caption said, "This is an Ombudsman. His name is John Herchenroeder. His job is to help you."

The term "ombudsman" is Scandinavian. In Sweden he is a government official empowered to hear complaints from the public and to do something about them. After A. H. Raskin of the New York *Times* suggested that newspapers might profit from the services of an ombudsman, the Louisville newspapers took up the idea and appointed Herchenroeder, a veteran newsman and editor, to look into reader grievances.

During his first two years, Herchenroeder handled about 900 complaints, suggestions, and questions from Louisville readers, many of whom mangled his name and title but still appreciated the chance to talk back. In some cases the complaints resulted in corrections, changes in news policies, and deeper coverage. In others Herchenroeder gently told readers they themselves were in error.

Other newspapers, too, have experimented with ombudsmen, including the Lafayette, Indiana, *Journal & Courier,* the St. Petersburg *Times* and *Evening Independent,* the Utica *Observer-Dispatch,* the Rockford *Morning Star* and *Register* and the Washington *Post.*

Ombudsmanship is not confined to newspapers. For several years Mike Shapiro, general manager of WFAA-TV in Dallas, has appeared on a weekly half-hour program called "Let Me Speak to the Manager" in which he fields complaints, explains policies, and interviews visiting broadcast officials and performers. Shapiro says his program has a quarter-million viewers and a number-one rating in its time slot. Not many other stations have attempted a similar program, but Shapiro has advice for those who care to try:

> In order to prevent the program from being a weekly or monthly promotion session for your operation, you must discuss all stations, all networks, and all programs. Call letters or channel numbers must be revealed in these discussions, else the whole point is lost. Unless each letter is openly and candidly handled—even to the point of

laboring over a problem involving the opposition—the show will never get off the ground.[23]

Unfortunately for his own serenity, the ombudsman is in an excellent position to catch flak from all sides. The audience may find his responses weak or unsatisfying, and his colleagues may accuse him of fouling his own nest. Wherever he stands, the footing is slippery. Richard Harwood served as the Washington *Post*'s first ombudsman in 1970 and 1971, then returned to his earlier position as national editor. His departure broke few hearts among reporters and editors. "Everybody liked the experiment," executive editor Benjamin Bradlee said afterward, "but when an individual got into Dick's sights, they liked it less."[24]

One value of the ombudsman is his merger of two important streams of criticism—the public and the professional—that are necessary to develop media responsibility.

Another way of encouraging more public participation and remedying the one-wayness of mass communication is local press councils, groups of laymen who meet regularly with newspapermen and broadcasters to evaluate media performance and to discuss their communities' information needs. By the early 1970s, more than a dozen such councils were operating, under a variety of names, in cities across the country. These councils have no power beyond giving advice, and the mass communicators who listen to it need not accept it

The need for systematic feedback was sharply revealed in the 1960s when the National Commission on the Causes and Prevention of Violence noted an enormous communications gulf between the media and minority groups, and a failure to cover the underlying problems of social unrest. The commission urged establishment of a privately funded Institute of Urban Communications. Among other things, the proposed institute would review media performance regarding riots and racial issues. Echoes could be heard of the 1947 Hutchins Commission's suggestion for a "new and independent agency to appraise and report annually upon the performance of the press."

Late in 1972, the New York-based Twentieth Century Fund announced plans to create a 15-member council to monitor the performance of the national news media and investigate public complaints. The council would have no coercive power. Reactions from the media were mixed, with a majority of executives opposed. Arthur Ochs Sulzberger, publisher of the New York *Times,* said a national press council "would simply be regulation in another form." But John Hughes, editor of the *Christian Science Monitor,* said he welcomed the council idea. In its broad outlines, the proposed United States council resembled the British press council, which began in 1953 and presently consists of 20 members from journalistic organizations and five laymen.

A General Purposes Committee of the British council deals with positive aspects of performance, such as protection of freedom of the press from censorship, and a Complaints Committee considers grievances brought by members of the public against individual media. Of 446 cases adjudicated in recent years, the council upheld readers in 247 cases—more than half the time[25]. When it finds a newspaper at fault, the council issues an admonition or, in more serious cases, censure. There is no punishment beyond publicity (the complaining member of the public has to waive his right to sue before he is permitted to approach the council). In only a handful of instances has the offending newspaper failed to publish council judgments.

Other foreign councils are not so respectful of freedom—some have powers of censorship and expulsion—and for this reason American journalists have shied away from the press council idea. Many American newsmen also believe that the British model does not translate easily into the American idiom: we do not have a national newspaper system of the scope and following of England's. Our newspapers are essentially local, and the logistics of scanning the U.S. press could be enormous.

The British model has misled Americans in some important respects. First, because the British council is national, it is assumed that all councils must be national. Second, the British council is best known for its grievance proceedings, and this has left the impression that every council must be judicial (and at least faintly punitive) in style. Overlooked are the British council's nonadjudicative opinions on the nature of responsibility and the fact that if media are local, press councils too can be local and perhaps ought to be heavily manned by members of the audience.

Few local councils were attempted in this country until 1967 when the Mellett Fund for a Free and Responsible Press sponsored four advisory groups in California, Oregon, and Illinois for newspapers, and two multimedia councils in St. Louis and Seattle. The latter concentrated on problems of minority groups.

The mass communications industry viewed these experiments with wary fascination. Two of the publishers who volunteered to sit with councils received a letter from an executive of the *Wall Street Journal,* who asked, "Why are you giving up your press freedom?" Neither intended to give up a blessed thing, and told their councils as much. Later, when they found their lay advisers less than sinister and frequently insightful, the publishers grew appreciative of the experience.

Ray Spangler of the Redwood City, California, *Tribune* reflected that "a press council establishes a communications link with the public—valid to the extent that the council is a cross section of the community—which could well feed new ideas into tired newspaper minds." The Illinois publishers agreed that their newspapers became more aware of and responsive to community needs and that press council members gained a better understanding of the newspaper's role and the problems it faces. None of the participants felt swindled of his freedom.

To a visitor, a meeting of a community press council might seem excessively casual. The resident newsman at the end of the table taking notes is not bruised and bleeding, and there is a good deal of banter among the members. Their discussion sounds trivial—they talk about letters to the editor, look over a special section devoted to advertising, and make comments on the society page. Yet each of these topics is only a half-step away from some of the deep and troublesome problems of mass communication we've discussed: the right of access, the influence of advertisers, racism and chauvinism. And just by *being there* a press council encourages a healthy self-consciousness among mass communicators, who are ordinarily barricaded from their audiences by the bulky machinery of their industry.

More press councils have been formed, some as a result of the Mellett examples and some for indigenous reasons. In early 1970 Dr. Jim Richstad of the University of Hawaii and the Reverend Dr. Claude Du Teil arranged a conference on the badly deteriorated relations between Honolulu Mayor Frank Fasi and the *Star-Bulletin.* An outcome was the founding in May 1970 of the Honolulu Community-Media Council. Not long after, another council was begun in Hilo.

The first regional press council—covering the state of Minnesota—was founded in 1971 by the Minnesota Newspaper Association, which patterned its venture on the British press council. Its grievance procedures require the complainant first to meet face-to-face with the editor of the newspaper that allegedly did him wrong. If this meeting fails to resolve their differences, the council's grievance committee makes a preliminary investigation. The committee holds a public hearing if the complaint appears valid and if the plaintiff waives his right to legal action. The Minnesota council, composed of nine journalists and nine laymen, decided its first case in early 1972, when it found the St. Paul *Union Advocate,* an AFL-CIO journal, at fault in its coverage of a meeting between a state legislator and a lobbyist. The decision held that the *Union Advocate*'s report "was not an accurate presentation of everything alleged to have occurred and there was not a fair journalistic presentation in the news story." Ironically, the editor of the *Union Advocate* was one of the founding members of the press council.[26]

It is unlikely that hundreds of local press councils are going to spring up overnight, but it is clear that media attitudes toward them are changing. The media are troubled by the depth of public indifference and distrust, and deeply disturbed by any threat of statutory sanctions. In a full-page essay in the Miami *News,* editor Sylvan Meyer said in part:

> To consider outside review and the possible censorious consequences thereof looms as a major departure from traditions. One tradition is that of a free press. The other is confidence in Americans' ability to figure out things for themselves without reliance on specially anointed powers to do it for them.
>
> Nevertheless, it is obvious such confidence is waning. Attacks on the press, whether justified or not, are finding a strong public response. The press must act, not defensively, but by seeking to provide means where legitimate protest can be expressed and reasonable grievances satisfied. . . .
>
> Any review of the press might be more dangerous to liberty than it would be worth. On the other hand, widespread public distrust of the press could undermine freedom by making people unsure of the information upon which they rest their judgments of public institutions and office holders.
>
> The press itself must take the initiative either to find a method or to prove that no method is feasible. Otherwise, government or other special interest or self-protecting groups may try at great risk to freedom.[27]

The question of how to secure responsibility *with* freedom is not an easy nut to crack. Criticism, thoughtfully given and carefully considered, seems the most rational path.

No single method of encouraging criticism—ombudsmen, codes of ethics, letters to the editor, press councils—is completely satisfactory, just as there is no neat set of criteria to define professionalism in mass communication. Professionalism and responsibility must be pursued freely and cooperatively. As NBC correspondent Edwin Newman remarked in one of his radio commentaries, "The American news business needs criticism from the outside, *and* it needs to criticize itself, *and* its component parts need to criticize each other."

for further reading

Balk, Alfred. "Minnesota Launches a Press Council," *Columbia Journalism Review,* November-December 1971, pp. 22–27.

Broadcast Self Regulation. New York: Code Authority, National Association of Broadcasters, 1971.

Childs, Marquis, and Douglass Cater. *Ethics in a Business Society.* New York: Harper, 1954.

"Ethics and the Press: Conflicts of Interest, Pressures Still Distort Some Papers' Coverage," *Wall Street Journal,* July 25, 1967, p. 1.

Gerald, J. Edward. *The Social Responsibility of the Press.* Minneapolis, Minn.: University of Minnesota Press, 1963.

Hill, Norman. "The Growing Phenomenon of the Journalism Review," *Saturday Review,* September 11, 1971, pp. 59–60.

Isaacs, Norman E. "Why We Lack a National Press Council," *Columbia Journalism Review,* Fall 1970, pp. 16–26.

Levy, H. Phillip. *The Press Council: History, Procedure, and Cases.* New York: St. Martin's Press, 1967.

Murray, George. *The Press and the Public: The Story of the British Press Council.* Carbondale, Ill.: Southern Illinois University, 1972.

Lange, David L., and Sandra J. Ball, eds. *Mass Media and Violence,* Vol. IX of *A Report to the National Commission on the Causes and Prevention of Violence.* Washington, D.C.: U.S. Government Printing Office, 1969, pp. 384–393.

"The New Press Critics: Local Journalism Review Sampler," *Columbia Journalism Review,* May-June 1971, pp. 29–36.

Press Councils and Press Codes, 4th ed. Zurich: International Press Institute, 1966.

Rivers, William L., William B. Blankenburg, Kenneth Starck, and Earl Reeves. *Backtalk: Press Councils in America.* San Francisco: Canfield Press, 1972.

Schwoebel, Jean, and Edwin Diamond. "The Coming Newsroom Revolution," *Columbia Journalism Review,* Summer 1970, pp. 8–18.

whither media?

a look at the crystal ball and other gadgets

As all visible objects are impressed upon our senses by differing quantities of light, it will be understood that when these variations of luminous rays can be duplicated at the distant end of an electrical conductor we shall in effect *see through the wire.*
—Charles H. Sewall, *Harper's Weekly,* December 29, 1900

Sir William Preece, chief engineer of the British Post Office a hundred years ago, was asked if he had any comments on the newest American invention, the telephone. He replied: "No sir. The Americans have need of the telephone—but we do not. We have plenty of messenger boys."

Sir William was so wildly wrong that we are tempted to lunge in the other direction and predict, for example, that the ultimate medium of communication will be the biochemical pill, which will transfer information and implant memory by genetic means. Or that psychosurgery will permit our brains to interact directly with computers.

Both prospects seem improbable, but first steps have been taken. Scientists are speaking of transmitting memory, IQ, and certainly ability to learn through genetic control. Animals have been successfully connected to electronic brain simulators which have ordered muscle movement—and been obeyed.[1]

This seems a quantum leap beyond mass communication as we know it today, and not very closely related to the media. Yet technology is taking us to a place where mediated communication is less one-directional, and where the distinctions between interpersonal and mass communication—and among the media themselves—are less clear. These developments could have deep meanings for individualism, society, democracy, and power. Will they happen?

Change in the media may come slowly at first, but it can pick up speed rapidly. Often the communications specialist himself is fooled into being too optimistic about the short run, and overly pessimistic about the long. The reason, science writer Arthur C. Clarke has asserted, is simple. "The human mind tends to extrapolate in a linear manner, whereas progress is exponential."[2]

If the technician is impatient with the takeoff, the media consumer is disarmed by its slowness. We welcome novelties like radio and television, and it may be some time before we realize that a new medium has not only rearranged our furniture but our lives.

Also disguising change in communication processes are certain constants. The fundamental need to communicate will be with us and so will two basic technical functions of the media: the conveyance and storage of information.

People find additional uses for media, and when the modes of storage and transmission change, some important social balances are tipped. In an earlier chapter we noted the impetus given the Reformation by Gutenberg's invention, which allowed knowledge—and power—to slip from the control of the Roman Catholic Church. Ben H. Bagdikian adds a more recent example:

> Part of the past stability of Negro oppression in the South was due to strict local control of information. The typical pattern was that local newspapers, radio stations, libraries, and schools did not give out information that would disturb existing racial patterns. . . . National television was more difficult to control locally. By the time of mass TV ownership, race relations had become a dominant theme in the news, especially after the Supreme Court school decision of 1954 (which was not routinely reported in all Southern papers). . . . The mobilization of Negro rejection of their three-hundred-year status, and the comprehension of this by the white majority, is attributable in significant part to the failure of traditional social controls over news media that used to be typical of the American South.[3]

New technology can also upset economic balances. Research indicates that the amount of audience money available for mass communication is fairly constant. If a new medium enters the field and attracts customers, the economic pie does not grow larger—it is sliced thinner.[4] The old media take losses in those functions the new medium performs better. The growth of television came at the expense of motion pictures (which suffered from the visual and convenience aspects of the new medium), of radio (which lost its programming to TV), and mass consumer magazines (which lost their audiences for fiction).

Not only would it be gross error to assume the media will continue to have the same forms they have today, there is ample evidence that entire media come and go as their functions are replaced by others. Beginning about 1860, there grew up a visual mass medium that became extinct by 1920, and remains today only a novelty, mostly for children. It was the stereograph, or stereopticon, and during its heyday more than 5000 photographers offered more than four million different three-dimensional views to the American public. Featuring for the most part sheer entertainment in sitcom format, the stereographs also offered the parlor viewer scenes of national dignitaries, floods, fires, train wrecks, all the what-have-you of a modern news and picture magazine. But as technology permitted more and better photography in newspapers and magazines, and as the entertainment media of films, recording and broadcasting burst onto society, interest in the fixed world of the stereograph declined. No other medium could offer 3-D—then—but it did not seem to matter.[5] If you wish a more recent example, ask anyone over 40 what he remembers about newsreels.

The economic and social consequences of media technology are never clearly foreseen in the early stages, not even by the inventors, let alone anyone else. In 1931, General C. McK. Saltzman, a member of the Federal Radio Commission, told the National Association of Broadcasters:

> It often occurs when a new invention or technical development with revolutionary possibilities is launched on the world, that unscrupulous persons or companies take advantage of the interested public. Such companies sometimes have large bales of freshly printed gilt edged stock certificates for sale which will make the purchaser fabulously rich before Saturday. Personally, I do not intend to invest any of the Saltzman millions in television stock this week.[6]

Who's to blame him? In those days television was little more than a laboratory demonstration, fraught with technological problems, short of capital, and faced with entrenched competition and an unknown audience.

the cable medium

And now another new medium is upon us—cable communication, an outgrowth of community antenna television, or CATV. Like other media before it, cable has been variously met with enthusiasm, hostility, and indifference. Its beginnings, like those of its predecessors, were charmingly casual.

In Astoria, Oregon, late in the 1940s, Grace Parsons heard about television and decided she wanted some pictures with her radio. She told her husband Ed to go out and find some. Unfortunately, the nearest TV station was 125 miles away in Seattle, well out of normal range. But Ed Parsons, an old hand at radio, promised to hunt all over Clatsop County for a good place to put up a big antenna. He didn't go far—just up to the roof of the John Jacob Astor Hotel, a few feet above his and Grace's apartment.

The antenna brought in a fairly decent picture—and more visitors than Grace could abide. At first she served snacks to friends who just happened by to watch TV. This got to be expensive, and by Christmas of 1948 Ed and Grace had to lock their door and pretend they weren't home. Ed solved the problem by running a wire down to the hotel lobby and then out to Cliff Poole's music store. Before long he connected private homes to his magical wire for a charge of $100. He also sold TV sets.

Around the same time, when residents of Lansford, Pennsylvania could not receive Philadelphia TV because they were on the wrong side of a mountain, an enterprising repairman named Robert J. Tarlton climbed the mountain, put up a few experimental antennas, and then formed the Panther Valley Television Company to build a tall master antenna. He strung coaxial cable from the mountain to Lansford and neighboring communities. These pioneers recognized that cable television does two things very well: it provides pictures of high quality and it can bring them from long distances. Later it became apparent that cable could have enormous channel capacity, could carry other kinds of information besides television entertainment, and could make piles of money. And there is more, as we shall see.

A prospective cable-system operator begins by seeking a franchise from a city to cross its streets and alleyways with his wires. He must also negotiate with an existing utility—the telephone or power company—to rent space on its poles. The old days of hanging wires willy-nilly are now past, and cities charge annual franchise fees for the privilege. Because cable is a natural monopoly, competition is fierce for franchises; the president of one large cable company was indicted for bribing city councilmen.

The system itself begins with a large, carefully engineered

antenna aimed toward broadcast signals. More distant signals are imported through microwave relays. The captured signals are piped a short distance to a distribution center, where they are adjusted for strength and clarity before retransmission along trunk and lateral lines to subscribers' homes. Amplifiers are placed at intervals along the lines to keep the transmissions strong and clear. It costs about $4000 a mile to lay wire where the going is easy, and perhaps 10 times as much in crowded areas where streets must be trenched.

The coaxial cable itself is not much larger than a telephone wire. It consists of a center copper wire, a surrounding layer of polyethylene foam, and an outer sheath of braided copper or seamless aluminum. It can carry dozens of channels—the estimates rise almost daily (though amplification problems have temporarily kept the practical number in the low twenties).

By 1972 there were about 2750 cable systems in the United States serving about 6 million subscribers who paid, on the average, $4.95 a month for the service. The typical system had about 2000 subscribers—the largest was New York's, with just over 50,000—and offered 10 channels.

Although only 10 percent of American homes were wired, the growth of cable, especially since 1964, had been vigorous, and some experts believe this was only the early rumblings of a volcano. Early in 1972 a bullish advertisement for Research Institute Investors Service appeared in the business section of the New York *Times:*

CABLE TV STOCKS

Why we now project some 1000% growth
of CATV revenues in the 1970's

A monumental change in Federal regulations of Cable Television now promises to unleash the surging expansion of the still-infant industry into the nation's 100 biggest and richest TV markets ... where, for several years now, CATV growth has been virtually locked out.

For stock market investors, the mushrooming of cable TV into a *major* new communications industry may represent one of the classic ground-floor growth opportunities of this decade. Solid evidence suggests that CATV earnings may even challenge the *combined* earnings of *all three* nationwide broadcast TV networks.

The "monumental change" in FCC regulations was a set of rules that became effective March 31, 1972, allowing limited importation of distant signals into the hundred largest television markets.[7]

The new rules represented a compromise between cable and broadcast interests, and marked another crabwise step in the FCC's meandering history of regulation.

In 1959 the FCC had decided it lacked jurisdiction over CATV, but under pressure from Congress and broadcasters, it gradually changed its mind. By 1966 it assumed broad authority over cable and prevented importation of out-of-town signals into the major markets. This decision favored broadcasters, who feared that importation would dilute the local audience and thereby reduce advertising revenues, which are pegged to viewership. The audience, which might revel in the diversity that goes with dilution, was not consulted. Because the hundred largest markets comprise about 90 percent of the nation's population, large-scale growth of cable TV was successfully halted.

By 1971 about 35 percent of cable systems were owned by broadcasters and another 8 percent by newspaper publishers (AT&T and the broadcast networks are substantially prevented from owning cable systems), and this cross-fertilization helped break the freeze on the top hundred markets. The March 31, 1972, rules set narrow limits on importation and granted certain exclusive program rights to broadcasters, but on the whole the cable industry was happy and felt that at last it had something extra to sell the public in big cities. Some experts predicted that by 1980 half the nation's homes would be wired and that the industry would have revenues of over $4 billion (compared with $300 million in 1970) and a net worth of about $15 billion.

"Community antenna television" is no longer an adequate title for the new medium—cable communications is better—which by law and inclination will also originate programming. Other uses, too, are forecast, and the future will doubtless yield applications that elude contemporary imaginations.

While the backbone of cable communication will be commercial entertainment supported indirectly through advertising or directly through program fees—a kind of pay-TV—there is sufficient channel capacity for many other uses. At present about 40 percent of cable systems offer continuous transmission of weather and news by means of automated scanning. There could also be local and neighborhood cablecasting. Cable is prodigal enough to permit trivial uses, as, for example, a channel devoted entirely to showing tropical fish in living color. Or, as cable operator Morton David has proposed, there could be mood pictures as background to living-room conversations—Pictures to Ignore Television By.

Several touted uses of cable depend on its two-way capability, which could allow consumers to shop and bank from their homes, to attend lectures of their choice, to vote, to use electronic libraries, and to have their utility meters read automatically. A home could have a device that looks like a cross between a TV set and a typewriter. Such machines, involving cathode-ray tubes for display of data, are now widely used by stockbrokers, newspapers, and in many industries.

Much depends on joining cable systems with computers and converting existing information from printed form to electronic data. The costs are high and the processes are not perfected. Moreover, methods of indexing need considerable improvement before it becomes as easy to pull desired information out of storage as it is to tuck it away.

Where will all the money come from? Ultimately from the public, and at the expense of other forms of communication—including mass communication—which will see their functions taken over and performed more efficiently by the new medium. Consider the U.S. postal system, our modern equivalent of Sir William Preece's corps of messenger boys. Cable some day might permit delivery of letters through dark of night, sleet, and all the rest—and on Washington's Birthday as well. The fact that letter carriers may be expected to resist this incursion into their livelihood suggests strong reasons why some applications of cable communication will move very slowly. And the economics of such developments will be formidable.

To existing media and their employes, cable represents both a threat and an opportunity. The newspaper or magazine of the future —one that does not arrive on paper, or that is reproduced in the home in facsimile—is a distinct possibility. Thousands of production and distribution workers could find their jobs outmoded. Reduced costs—or costs transferred directly to the subscriber—might be attractive to a publisher. But in using cable as a delivery system, the publisher will be operating through a regulated medium, which is contrary to his ideas of freedom. It would also mean obsolescence of his expensive manufacturing equipment. One reason technological change has come slowly to newspapers is the existing high investment in durable, reliable hardware.

Full development of the cable medium would change the nature of gatekeeping. In some respects the gatekeeper could become less important because the increased channel and storage capacities would reduce the need for whittling. On the other hand, his duties as a guide through the thickening jungle of information would increase. It would become more the editor's responsibility to assign, collate, and index the news—but less his responsibility to edit for what is sometimes subversively called "policy." More of the selection process—the winnowing and sifting of content—will fall to the reporter, who will have more freedom and responsibility. Newsmen could be more free from the constraints of time and space, and less ignorant of what the reader wants because they'll know what he's requesting. The journalist will also know that the customer has ready access to other sources and to background material.

some attractions
of common carriage

If certain principles of common carriage were imposed on cable communications, the ordinary citizen, as well as the professional communicator, would be more able to place his information and opinions into the stream of communication. Common carriage requires equal access at reasonable rates, and it presupposes a high-capacity system, such as cable. It distinguishes sharply between the carrier of content and the content itself, with the former having no control over the latter. Of course, common carriage does not guarantee an audience, but it does offer a chance to seek it. The professional would still have the advantage because of his packaging and indexing skills.

Common carriage ought to be congenial to right-of-access theorists such as Professor Jerome Barron. The restraints upon carriers would allay newsmen's fears of using channels owned by someone else. Under common carriage, cable operators would not be tempted to create an artificial shortage of channels to enhance their own programs, because they would be forbidden to program. Rather, they would be eager to rent and lease channels.

Unfortunately, the FCC has taken only minimal steps toward common carriage, and indeed it went the opposite direction by ruling that all systems having 3500 or more subscribers *must* originate programming. While this may be advantageous in the short run, helping to get cable off the ground, it could lead to the kind of vertical integration common to motion pictures a generation ago, when production, distribution, and exhibition were all in one corporate fold.

The cable operators themselves are antagonistic toward the idea of common carriage, perhaps because they anticipate the pleasures of monopoly or, more likely, because they fear rate regulation. Cable operators have tended to adopt ideologies of earlier media, just as broadcasters pilfered the motion-picture code of ethics. The National Cable Television Association has produced a code that borrows heavily from that of broadcasting. It says that cablecasters should "develop programs to foster and promote the commonly accepted moral, social, and ethical ideas characteristic of American life." This kind of thinking is peculiar to limited-capacity media, and is inappropriate to cable and contrary to the public interest. But it persists. Amherst Cablevision, a suburban Buffalo, New York, system with 3000 subscribers, early in 1972 admitted deleting a news story on school integration at the request of Amherst's chief school administrator. "We're just getting started," declared the cable company's program director, "and at this point I don't think we can afford to hurt our public relations in that way."[8]

some prospective worries

Any scenario for the wired nation must also include some apprehensions. Will everyone be able to afford these wonders? Will anyone wish to have his pulse taken by sensors instead of a sympathetic physician? Who's going to be watching the computer that's watching you?

Just about every advance in communication technology affects the right of privacy, and cable is no exception. We're fairly tolerant of blatant intrusions such as Muzak, third-class mail, billboards, and other people's transistor radios. We may not like these impositions, but at least we know what is going on. Clandestine invasions are more scary. Two-way cable raises the spectre of an unblinking eye in the parlor—or bedroom. For some time police have used closed-circuit TV to monitor traffic, and it has also been installed in lobbies and elevators to prevent crime.

It is unlikely that cable's intrusion will come as an icy stare. For the present, at least, direct surveillance can be done more efficiently through wiretaps, telescopic cameras, and various miniature sensors.

Cable could join with other technologies to make indirect monitoring more of a threat. Any device that automates transactions and remembers them makes computerized surveillance easier. If we shop and bank by cable, use it for voting or polling, have it record our household utilities, or ask it to play certain programs for us, we are creating data that can be stored and analyzed.

And, some fear, these data can be used against us. The dilemma is that many kinds of surveillance are desirable. We'd want our medical histories instantly retrievable if we were suddenly stricken by accident or disease. We'd like our credit ratings quickly available when we seek a loan. Rapidly retrieved data on our whereabouts could locate us in case of emergency. But obviously this information could also be used to our detriment.

We worry, too, that information about us might not be accurate and that, somehow, where there is no forgetting there is no forgiving. Of course, much information has already been collected. Its use, for good or ill, has been impeded by its cumbersomeness. But improved computer storage and more convenient access give new life to moribund data.

The problem is to retain the good uses of data banks and to prevent abuse. In the very least a citizen should have the right to examine whatever data are held on him, to add, and to challenge.

There are even deeper worries about media technology and the future of society. The forecasts are contradictory, but the concerns are sincere.

The coupling of communications satellites with cable systems and direct broadcasting from satellites could make intercultural understanding viable and could lay the foundation for a truly global society. Satellites have already led to international cooperation on channel allocations and the exchange of scientific information. But the idea of people speaking to people is not uniformly welcomed. Groups still exist in the United States that campaign to "get the U.S. out of the UN." The Berlin Wall has stood between people of a common heritage. Citizens of the Third World fear "cultural imperialism."

The other side of the crystal ball discloses a new individualism, with people becoming their own gatekeepers, choosing from vast warehouses of information, enjoying freedom from the monolithic voices of leaders who previously had prime access to the limited-capacity media. But in this forecast the individual would no longer *have* to interact with others, and could curl up in a womb of congenial information. He would only attend to what he liked, when he liked. Society would become more, not less, fragmented, with individuals easily ignoring the plight of others.

The question of whether everyone can afford cable may be largely beside the point. But then, not everyone could afford television when the decision was made to go ahead with that new medium. Today, one way or another, television is afforded by nearly all, and the poor make the heaviest use of it among all segments of society.

the response of institutions

The question of how other media will respond to the coming of cable communications is another matter, however. Implicit in cable is a threat to conventional broadcasting facilities. The new medium plus satellite communication has the capacity to leapfrog local stations completely. Holders of what may now be old-fashioned broadcast licenses are thus in the position of trying to restrain cable with one hand while grasping for cable franchises with the other.

Newspapers, Ben Bagdikian suggests, will pretty soon have to decide "whether they are printing factories or analysts of daily political and social information. . . . If present newspapers do not prepare to become research libraries for political and social information, then the inevitable demand by the consumer for a few subjects pursued in depth will be met by other kinds of organizations." Make that last read "cable companies." Beleaguered for some time now by competition from other media for the time of their readers and the dollars of their advertisers, newspapers face a future that will be challenging, to say the least. Cable could very easily offer the consumer not too far in the future a computer matched with the cable, and the consumer could ask the computer to produce the Washington *Post* national news review or a summary of local news from community supplier. (Already the New York *Times* has begun transferring its voluminous library of more than 20 million clippings into an information bank.)

And magazines, afflicted with rising production costs for years, complicated recently with postal rates increases, likewise face challenges, whether they recognize it or not. The magazine, perhaps more than any other medium, has been a child of the distribution system—up to now strictly physical—available to it. As the electronic age has taken hold, changes within the magazine industry have permitted, first, the dispersion of printing plants across the country to facilitate printing and distribution, and second, the insertion of regional advertising. Now, the historic form of the magazine may be about to change.

Forms may be changing, but not functions. At the turn of the century the automobile was seen as the perfect answer to urban pollution. It would replace horses, which at that time were depositing daily some 25 million pounds of manure and 60,000 gallons of urine in the streets of New York City alone.[9] The form changed but not the function. And the new form brought its own problems, as cable unquestionably will.

But if by the year 2000, cable plus computer plus satellite (and maybe lasers and holography) is to be the communications medium, displacing print, film, and broadcasting by performing their function more flexibly and cheaply, more will have to happen than simply heavy capitalization.

Institutions of government, built under the influence of paper with its implicit time lag between act and communication of the significance of the act, must revise themselves to cope with a world in which the people have the capacity to be as well and as quickly informed as government itself. The natural reluctance of us all to engage in self-reform will surely slow universal acceptance of the concept of the wired nation.

Law and legal institutions will have to undergo sweeping changes. Revision of the 1909 copyright law, enacted before broadcasting, before mass-produced phonograph records, before Xerox, has been stalled for years. And now copyright is widely ignored by everyone from college students and professors to foreign countries. Perhaps a whole new concept of how the author is to be remunerated for his work will be required. Privacy is virtually a Constitutional guarantee today, yet we have less and less of that commodity. Perhaps we shall return to the era of complete lack of privacy, where we were before architecture invented walls. And if what we want for our communication media is more freedom, the increasing governmental control from agencies such as the Federal Communications Commission, the Federal Trade Commission, the Justice Department with its antitrust division, plus the state consumer-protection agencies, would indicate that we may in fact have less. The questions of how much freedom, for whom, and with what kinds of controls will remain with us.

The media are what we make of them. They are, after all, extensions of man. They are avaricious and altruistic, sinners and martyred saints. They show us at our best, and at our worst. The ancient Chinese curse, "May you live in interesting times," seems to have been pronounced upon us. The media constitute the channels through which most of us receive the manifestations of that curse. Which is perhaps why we love and hate them at the same time.

for further reading

Bagdikian, Ben H. *The Information Machines.* New York: Harper & Row, 1971.

Baier, Kurt, and Nicholas Rescher, eds. *Values and the Future.* New York: Free Press, 1969.

Bretz, Rudy. *A Taxonomy of Communication Media.* Englewood Cliffs, N.J.: Educational Technology Publications, 1971.

Goldhamer, Herbert, ed. *The Social Effects of Communication Technology.* Santa Monica, Calif.: Rand Corporation, 1970.

Gribbin, August. "Insurance Firms Maintain Secret Data Repository," *The National Observer,* November 3, 1969, pp. 1, 4.

Jurgen, Ronald K. "Two-Way Applications for Cable Television Systems in the '70s," *IEEE Spectrum,* November 1971, pp. 39–54.

Le Duc, Don R. "A Selective Bibliography on the Evolution of CATV, 1950–1970," *Journal of Broadcasting,* Vol. 15, No. 2 (Spring 1971), pp. 195–234.

Mathison, Stuart L., and Philip M. Walker. *Computers and Telecommunications: Issues in Public Policy.* Englewood Cliffs, N.J.: Prentice-Hall, 1970.

Miller, Arthur R. *The Assault on Privacy.* New York: Signet, 1972.

Oppenheim, Jerrold. "Cable TV Comes to Clout City," *Chicago Journalism Review,* August 1971, pp. 3–8, 14.

Price, Monroe, and John Wicklein. *Cable Television: A Guide for Citizen Action.* Philadelphia: Pilgrim Press, 1972.

Sloan Commission on Cable Communications. *On the Cable: The Television of Abundance.* New York: McGraw-Hill, 1971.

Smith, Ralph Lee. *The Wired Nation: The Electronic Communications Highway.* New York: Harper & Row, 1972.

Toffler, Alvin. *Future Shock.* New York: Bantam, 1970.

notes

chapter 1. a mass communication system at work

1. The portrait of Miss Joplin in the ensuing pages was drawn from contemporary accounts published at her death. *Rolling Stone,* October 29, 1970, printed several lengthy stories on her death and its impact on various rock musicians and fans. Other accounts consulted appeared in *Jazz & Pop,* December 1970, and Deborah Landau, *Janis Joplin: Her Life and Times* (New York: Paperback Library, 1971).

2. University of Washington *Daily,* April 16, 1971, p. 15.

3. *Variety,* June 1, 1971, p. 1.

4. *Rolling Stone,* October 29, 1970, p. 16.

5. *Ibid.,* p. 7.

6. Arnold Shaw, *The Rock Revolution* (New York: Crowell-Collier, 1969), pp. 14–15.

7. Jonathan Eisen, *The Age of Rock: Sounds of the Great American Cultural Revolution,* Vol. I (New York: Random House, 1970), pp. 51 ff.

8. *The Rock Revolution,* p. 17.

9. *The Age of Rock,* Vol. I, p. 48.

10. *Billboard,* November 7, 1970, p. 1.

11. Danny Fields, "Who Bridges the Gap Between the Record Executive and the Rock Musician? I Do," in *The Age of Rock,* Volume I, pp. 153–169.

12. *Jazz & Pop,* January 1971, p. 35.

13. *Variety,* April 21, 1971, p. 1.

14. *Ibid.,* May 5, 1971, p. 55.

15. Myra Friedman, quoted in *Rolling Stone,* October 29, 1970, p. 6.

16. *Jazz & Pop,* November 1970, p. 10.

17. *Melody Maker,* August 17, 1968, p. 11; *Time,* August 9, 1968, p. 71; *Life,* September 20, 1968, p. 20; *New York Times Magazine,* February 23, 1969, p. 36; *Ramparts,* August 10, 1968, p. 74.

18. *Billboard,* November 7, 1970, p. 1.

19. Testimony of Richard W. Clark in *Responsibilities of Broadcasting Licensees and Station Personnel,* Hearings on Payola and Other Deceptive Practices in the Broadcasting Field before a Subcommittee of the Committee on Interstate and Foreign Commerce, House of Representatives, 86th Congress, 2d Session. Part 2, p. 1169.

20. *Ibid.,* pp. 1455–1456.

21. *Kaleidoscope,* November 22–December 5, 1968, pp. 15, 24.

22. *Rolling Stone,* February 4, 1971, p. 32.

23. Robert Masin, "Payola in America," unpublished paper for Professor David G. Clark, University of Washington, Spring 1971.

24. *Variety,* April 7, 1971, pp. 1, 35.

25. "First Tuesday," National Broadcasting Company, August 9, 1971.

26. *Variety,* April 7, 1971, p. 49; June 9, 1971, p. 45.

27. Paul M. Hirsch, "Sociological Approaches to the Pop Music Phenomenon," in *American Behavioral Scientist,* Volume 14, No. 3, January/February 1971, pp. 371–388.

28. Paul Johnson, in *New Statesman,* February 28, 1964, quoted in *The Age of Rock,* p. xii.

29. Gary Allen, "That Music: There's More to It Than Meets the Ear," in *The Age of Rock*, Volume 1, p. 212.

30. *Ibid.*, p. 207.

31. *Variety*, April 14, 1971, p. 1.

32. *Billboard*, November 7, 1970, p. 1.

33. *Variety*, June 2, 1971, p. 41.

chapter 2. presenting mass communication

1. Much of what is known about Gutenberg derives from legal documents. These are laboriously and lovingly gathered in Douglas C. McMurtrie, *The Gutenberg Documents* (New York: Oxford University Press, 1941). Other material on the first century of printing appears in Rudolph Hirsch, *Printing, Selling and Reading*, 1450–1550 (Wiesbaden: Otto Harrassowitz, 1967).

2. This definition follows that of Charles R. Wright, *Mass Communication: A Sociological Perspective* (New York: Random House, 1959), p. 13.

3. Precise data on the media are difficult to find and are always outdated by the time they are published. Those presented here are approximate and generally current to 1971 and derive from such sources as *The Statistical Abstract of the United States; Editor & Publisher International Year Book; World Almanac; Broadcasting Yearbook; The Film Daily Yearbook of Motion Pictures; Billboard International Buyer's Guide; N. W. Ayer & Son Directory; Newspapers and Periodicals; International Television Almanac; The Bowker Annual of Library and Book Trade Information;* Standard Rate & Data Service, Inc.; the Motion Picture Association of America; Record Industry Association of America; and the Outdoor Advertising Association of America.

4. The authors' students have estimated that start-up prices for an underground newspaper may range from $50 to $5000, depending on how much equipment is owned, rented, borrowed, or stolen. The figure of $2500 comes from Abbie Hoffman, *Steal This Book* (New York: Pirate Editions, 1971), p. 116. Most large cities have firms that deal in used printing equipment and provide price lists.

5. Many of the economic data on mass communication appearing in this chapter come from Ben H. Bagdikian, *The Information Machines: Their Impact on Men and the Media* (New York: Harper & Row, 1971), an incisive and long-needed study.

6. Dennis T. Lowry, "Agnew and the Network TV News: A Before/After Content Analysis," *Journalism Quarterly*, 48 (Summer 1971), pp. 205–210.

7. John Steinbeck, *Travels with Charley* (New York: Viking, 1962), p. 154.

8. Elihu Katz, "The Two-Step Flow of Communication: An Up-to-Date Report on an Hypothesis," *Public Opinion Quarterly*, 21 (Spring 1957), pp. 61–79.

chapter 3. man's need to communicate

1. Bernard Berelson, "What 'Missing the Newspaper' Means," in *Communication Research*, ed. Paul F. Lazarsfeld and Frank Stanton (New York: Harper, 1949).

2. Harold Lasswell, "The Structure and Function of Communication in Society," in *Mass Communications*, ed. Wilbur Schramm (2nd ed.; Urbana: University of Illinois Press, 1960), pp. 117–130. See also Charles R. Wright, "Functional Analysis and Mass Communication," *People, Society, and Mass Communications*, ed. Lewis Anthony Dexter and David Manning White (New York: The Free Press, 1964), pp. 91–109.

3. Desmond Morris, *The Naked Ape: A Zoologist's Study of the Human Animal* (New York: McGraw-Hill, 1967), pp. 108–109.

4. Many of the ideas and views of the ensuing paragraphs have been taken from, among other sources: Sol Tax, ed., *The Evolution of Man* (Chicago: University of Chicago Press, 1960); Harold Innis, *The Bias of Communication* (Toronto: Toronto University Press, 1951); and John Parry, *The Psychology of Human Communication* (New York: American Elsevier, 1968).

5. Eldridge Cleaver, *Soul on Ice* (New York: Dell, 1970), p. 42.

6. Alexander S. Weissberg, *The Accused,* trans. Edward Fitzgerald (New York: Simon & Schuster, 1951), p. 89.

7. Malcolm X, *The Autobiography of Malcolm X* (New York: Grove Press, 1968), p. 304.

8. The experiences of Byrd are cited in Charles A. Brownfield, *Isolation* (New York: Random House, 1965), pp. 13–17.

9. Alvin Toffler, *Future Shock* (New York: Bantam Books, 1970), pp. 343–367.

10. Richard L. Meier, *A Communications Theory of Urban Growth* (Cambridge, Mass.: MIT Press, 1962), pp. 43, 130.

11. Benjamin Lee Whorf, *Language, Thought, and Reality,* ed. John B. Carroll (New York: Wiley, 1956), p. 214.

12. Abbie Hoffman, *Steal This Book* (New York: Pirate Editions, 1971), p. iv.

13. *Straus Editor's Report,* June 7, 1971, p. 1.

14. Walter Lippmann, *Public Opinion* (New York: The Free Press, 1965), pp. 54–55.

15. William Small, *To Kill a Messenger* (New York: Hastings House, 1970), pp. 175–191.

16. S. E. Asch, "Effects of Group Pressure upon the Modification and Distortion of Judgments," *Readings in Social Psychology,* 3rd ed., ed. Eleanor E. Maccoby, Theodore M. Newcomb, and Eugene L. Hartley (New York: Holt, Rinehart and Winston, 1958), pp. 174–183.

17. Bruno Bettelheim, "Individual and Mass Behavior in Extreme Situations," *Readings in Social Psychology,* 3rd ed., ed. Eleanor E. Maccoby, Theodore M. Newcomb, and Eugene L. Hartley (New York: Holt, Rinehart and Winston, 1958), p. 308.

18. Raymond Bauer, "The Obstinate Audience," *American Psychologist,* Volume 19 (1964), p. 321.

chapter 4. broadcasting

1. *Variety,* September 22, 1971, pp. 25, 36.

2. Sources for the early history of broadcasting are many, but the principal ones used here include: Gleason Archer, *History of Radio to 1926* (New York: American Historical Co., 1938); *Big Business and Radio* (New York: American Historical Co., 1939); William Peck Banning, *Commercial Broadcasting Pioneer: The WEAF Experiment, 1922–1926* (Cambridge, Mass.: Harvard University Press, 1946); and Eric Barnouw, *A Tower in Babel* (New York: Oxford University Press, 1966).

3. Mayflower Broadcasting Corp., 8 FCC 333, 1941.

4. Opinion on Editorializing by Broadcasters, Docket No. 8516, 13 FCC 1246, 1RR 91, 201, June 2, 1949.

5. *TV Guide,* July 24, 1971, pp. 6–10.

6. Eric Barnouw, *The Image Empire* (New York: Oxford University Press, 1970), pp. 153–154.

7. *Ibid.,* p.151.

8. *Ibid.,* p. 152.

9. *Ibid.,* p. 154.

10. "Status Report, ABC-TV Network Entertainment Schedule," January 22, 1969, pp. 400–401 in *Violence and the Media,* Vol. 9–A, *A Staff Report to the National Commission on the Causes and Prevention of Violence.* Prepared by Robert K. Baker and Sandra J. Ball (Washington, D.C.: U.S. Government Printing Office, 1969).

11. *Variety,* September 8, 1971, p. 31.

12. This study, done by Boston University Professor F. Earle Barcus, was funded by Action for Children's Television, a citizens' group seeking to improve the quality of children's television. It is a good example of the kind of pressure group sometimes established in desperation as a goad both to broadcasting and government. Reported in *Variety,* September 8, 1971, p. 31.

13. See David G. Clark and William B. Blankenburg, "Trends in Violent Content in Selected Mass Media," Vol. I., *Media Content and Control,* of *Television and Social Behavior: A Technical Report to the Surgeon General's Scientific Advisory Committee* (Rockville, Md.: National Institute of Mental Health), pp. 188–243, for a discussion of the cyclical nature of programming trends.

14. The Nielsen method, the chief measurement device used today, is described in Les Brown, *Television: The Business Behind the Box* (New York: Harcourt Brace Jovanovich, 1971), pp. 32–35, and in *Nielsen Television Index in Action* (Chicago: A. C. Nielsen, 1962).

15. The Sparger affair is related in, among other places, *Broadcasting,* July 11, 1966, pp. 50–52.

16. See Norman M. Lobsenz, "Everett Parker's Broadcasting Crusade," in *Columbia Journalism Review,* Fall 1969, pp. 30–36, for a full account of the United Church of Christ campaign to shuck the license from WLBT-TV.

17. The Alfred I. duPont–Columbia School of Journalism annual *Survey of Broadcast Journalism* carries numerous accounts of suppression of programs and segments of programs at network and local levels. The 1971 edition was published by Grosset & Dunlap.

18. Complaint and Request for Declaratory Ruling by The Students Association of the University of New York at Buffalo, filed with Federal Communications Commission, October 7, 1971.

19. *Variety,* March 31, 1971, p. 42.

20. Ralph Blumberg, "A Broadcaster's Nightmare in Bogalusa, La.," *Quill,* April 1966, pp. 12–16; Blumberg, interview with David G. Clark, November 1969.

chapter 5. the movie business

1. John Gregory Dunne, *The Studio* (New York: Bantam, 1970), p. 80.

2. Ingo Preminger, "M*A*S*H Notes," *Esquire,* August 1970, p. 142.

3. Pauline Kael, *Kiss Kiss Bang Bang* (New York: Bantam, 1969), pp. 83 ff.

4. *Variety,* May 12, 1971, p. 4.

5. A recent exception: Directing *Happy Birthday, Wanda June,* Mark Robson rehearsed the full cast on complete sets for three weeks before shooting.

6. Dunne, p. 31.

7. Quoted in Kenneth Macgowan, *Behind the Screen* (New York: Dell, 1965), pp. 6–7.

8. *Ibid.,* p. 287.

chapter 6. the news ethic

1. Every author of a textbook for beginning reporters must deal with the question of how to define the content of news columns. See especially Phillip H. Ault and Edwin Emery, *Reporting the News* (New York: Dodd, Mead, 1959); Curtis D. MacDougall, *Interpretative Reporting* (New York: Macmillan, 1932), later titled *Reporting for Beginners* (1938, 1948, 1957); Mitchell V. Charnley, *Reporting,* (New York: Holt, Rinehart and Winston, 1959, 1966); and Grant M. Hyde, *Newspaper Reporting* (New York: Prentice-Hall, 1952). These writers appear to quote each other in substance if not in exact words, but in reality they are trying to explain for beginners the operation of the news ethic.

2. Willard G. Bleyer, *Newspaper Writing and Editing* (Boston: Houghton Mifflin, 1932), p. 30.

3. Victor von Klarwill, ed., *The Fugger News-Letters,* Second Series (London: John Lane The Bodley Head Ltd., 1926), p. 46.

4. Perhaps the most illuminating consideration of the influence communications systems have had upon form and function of government is Harold Innis' *Empire and Communications* (London: Oxford Press, 1950).

5. Lawrence C. Wroth, *The Colonial Printer* (New York: Grolier Club, 1931; Portland, Maine: Southworth-Anthoensen Press, 1938), pp. 144–145.

6. Alfred M. Lee, *The Daily Newspaper in America: The Evolution of a Social Instrument* (New York: Macmillan, 1937), pp. 98–99.

7. Population figures here are taken from B. R. Mitchell, *Abstract of British Historical Statistics* (Cambridge, Mass.: Cambridge University Press, 1962), p. 5, and from Fred Albert Shannon, *America's Economic Growth,* 3rd ed. (New York: Macmillan, 1951), pp. 136–140.

8. Frank Luther Mott, *American Journalism* (New York: Macmillan, 1962), p. 220; Willard Bleyer, *Main Currents in the History of American Journalism* (Boston: Houghton Mifflin, 1927), pp. 155–156.

9. New York *Sun,* July 4, 1834. Quoted in Mott, *op. cit.,* p. 223.

10. Bleyer, *op. cit.,* pp. 160–161.

11. New York *Sun,* August 25, 1835; Mott, *op. cit.,* pp. 225–226.

12. *Ibid.*

13. The portrait of Bennett and his contributions to the development of the mass circulation newspaper is drawn principally from Oliver Carlson, *The Man Who Made News* (New York: Duell, Sloan and Pearce, 1942); Bleyer, *op. cit.,* pp. 181–210; and Mott, *op. cit.,* pp. 228–238.

14. Gay Talese, *The Kingdom and the Power* (New York: World, 1969). Citation is to Bantam Books edition (1970), p. 410.

15. Harold Innis, *The Press: A Neglected Factor in the Economic History of the Twentieth Century* (London: University of London Press, 1952), pp. 6–7.

16. A quick glance at the *Moody's Industrials Annual* listing for any of these public stock companies will provide excellent evidence of the importance self-owned forests and mills have for today's publishing conglomerates.

17. William A. Hachten, "Journalism and the Prayer Decision," *Columbia Journalism Review,* Fall 1962, pp. 4–9.

18. Ben H. Bagdikian, *The Information Machines* (New York: Harper & Row, 1971), p. 275.

19. Wes Gallagher, "What Halo? We Never Had One," *Quill,* February, 1969, p. 42.

20. Otto Friedrich, "There Are 00 Trees in Russia," *Harper's Magazine,* October 1964, pp. 61–65.

chapter 7. the peculiarities of freedom

1. Raymond B. Nixon, "Freedom in the World's Press: A Fresh Appraisal with New Data," *Journalism Quarterly,* 42 (Winter 1965), pp. 3–14, 118.

2. Fred S. Siebert, Theodore Peterson, and Wilbur Schramm, *Four Theories of the Press* (Urbana, Ill.: University of Illinois Press, 1956), p. 9.

3. Fred S. Siebert, *Freedom of the Press in England, 1476–1776* (Urbana, Ill.: University of Illinois Press, 1952), p. 261.

4. Quoted in Ronald T. Farrar and John D. Stevens, eds., *Mass Media and the National Experience* (New York: Harper & Row, 1971), pp. 42–43.

5. *Ibid.,* p. 16.

6. Leonard W. Levy, *Freedom of Speech and Press in Early American History: Legacy of Suppression* (New York: Harper Torchbooks, 1963), pp. xxi–xxii.

7. Merrill Jensen, *The Making of the American Constitution* (New York: Van Nostrand, 1964), p. 150.

8. William Hocking, *Freedom of the Press: A Framework of Principle* (Chicago: University of Chicago Press, 1947), p. 55.

9. W. H. Ferry, "Masscomm as Guru," *Mass Communications,* ed. W. H. Ferry and Harry S. Ashmore (Santa Barbara, Calif.: Center for the Study of Democratic Institutions, 1966), p. 13.

10. Theodore F. Koop, *Weapon of Silence* (Chicago: University of Chicago Press, 1946), p. 270.

11. Siebert, *Freedom of the Press in England,* p. 10.

12. Dwight L. Teeter, *A Legacy of Expression: Philadelphia Newspapers and Congress During the War for Independence, 1775–1783.* Doctoral dissertation, University of Wisconsin, 1966, p. 261.

13. John P. Roche, *Shadow and Substance* (New York: Macmillan, 1964), p. 8.

14. Farrar and Stevens, *op. cit.,* p. 17.

15. Donald L. Shaw, "News Bias and the Telegraph: A Study of Historical Change," *Journalism Quarterly,* 44 (Spring 1967), pp. 3–12, 31.

16. The Irwin series has been reproduced, with commentary, by David G. Clark and Clifford F. Weigle, eds., *The American Newspaper* (Ames, Iowa: Iowa State University Press, 1969).

17. Commission on Freedom of the Press, *A Free and Responsible Press* (Chicago: University of Chicago Press, 1947), p. 22.

18. John Merrill, *The Press and Social Responsibility,* Freedom of Information Center Publication No. 001 (Columbia Mo.: School of Journalism, University of Missouri, 1965).

19. The remark is attributed to William Peter Hamilton of the *Wall Street Journal.* See Siebert, Peterson, and Schramm, *op. cit.,* p. 73.

chapter 8. what the media do to us, maybe

1. Alberta Engvall Siegel, "The Effects of Media Violence on Social Learning," in *Mass Media and Violence,* A Report to the National Commission on the Causes and Prevention of Violence, Robert K. Baker and Sandra J. Ball, eds. (Washington, D.C.: U.S. Government Printing Office, 1969), p. 282.

2. Commission on Obscenity and Pornography, *Report of the Commission on Obscenity and Pornography* (New York: Bantam Books, 1970), p. 616.

3. Wilbur Schramm, *Mass Media and National Development* (Stanford, Calif.: Stanford University Press, 1964), p. 246.

4. Herbert I. Schiller, *Mass Communications and American Empire* (New York: Augustus M. Kelley, 1969), pp. 109–110.

5. Marshall McLuhan, *Understanding Media* (New York: Signet, 1964), p. 280 and *passim.*

6. Harold A. Innis, *The Bias of Communication* (Toronto: University of Toronto Press, 1951), p. 31.

7. The hairy image comes from *Understanding Media,* p. 286: "The TV extension of our nerves in hirsute pattern possesses the power to evoke a flood of related imagery in clothing, hairdo, walk, and gesture."

8. Jonathan Miller, *Marshall McLuhan* (New York: Viking, 1971), p. 123.

9. Paul Lazarsfeld, Bernard Berelson, and Hazel Gaudet, *The People's Choice* (New York: Columbia University Press, 1944).

10. Joseph Klapper, *The Effects of Mass Communication* (Glencoe, Ill.: The Free Press, 1960), p. 8.

11. Bernard Berelson, "Communications and Public Opinion," *Mass Communications,* ed. Wilbur Schramm (Urbana, Ill.: University of Illinois Press, 1960), p. 531.

12. *Report of the Commission on Obscenity and Pornography, op. cit.,* pp. 29, 32. It should be noted that there were strenuous dissents to the majority position—they take up about one-third of the published report.

13. Wilbur Schramm, Jack Lyle, and Edwin B. Parker, *Television in the Lives of Our Children* (Stanford, Calif.: Stanford University Press, 1961), pp. 1, 2.

14. William R. Catton, Jr., "Mass Media as Producers of Effects: An Overview of Research Trends," *Mass Media and Violence, op. cit.,* p. 248.

15. Kurt Lang and Gladys Engel Lang, *Politics and Television* (Chicago: Quadrangle, 1968).

16. Paul F. Lazarsfeld and Robert K. Merton, "Mass Communication, Popular Taste and Organized Social Action," *Mass Communications, op. cit.,* p. 503.

17. Catton, *op. cit.,* p. 251.

18. Charles Sopkin, *Seven Glorious Days, Seven Fun-Filled Nights* (New York: Ace, 1968), p. 9.

19. Charles Siepmann, "Radio," *The Communication of Ideas,* ed. Lyman Bryson (New York: Harper, 1948), p. 196.

20. Quoted in Schramm, Lyle, and Parker, *op. cit.,* p. 158.

21. Lazarsfeld and Merton, *op. cit.,* pp. 501–502.

22. Seymour Feshbach, "The Catharsis Effect: Research and Another View," *Mass Media and Violence, op. cit.,* p. 467. A review of research on catharsis appears in the same volume, pp. 453–459.

23. *Television and Growing Up: The Impact of Televised Violence,* The Surgeon General's Scientific Advisory Committee on Television and Social Behavior (Washington, D.C.: U.S. Government Printing Office, 1972), p. 11.

24. "The Television World of Violence," *Mass Media and Violence, op. cit.,* p. 317.

25. Schramm, Lyle, and Parker, *op. cit.,* p. 77.

26. Catton, *op. cit.,* p. 254.

chapter 9: pop culture

1. Presumably Macdonald wishes us to realize that as "low" is the opposite of "high," what he really means is that there is high culture and low culture. Some writers see a high-, middle-, and low-brow triumvirate of cultures. One has even labeled them "refined," "mediocre," and "brutal." Needless to say, few of us assign the terms "brutal" or "lowbrow" to the particular form we espouse. See Ernest Van den Haag, "A Dissent from the Consensual Society," in *Daedalus,* Journal of the American Academy of Arts and Sciences, Vol. 89, No. 2, and Edward Shils, "Mass Society and Its Culture," in the same, both reprinted in Bernard Rosenberg and David Manning White, eds., *Mass Culture Revisited* (New York: Van Nostrand Reinhold, 1971), pp. 61–92.

2. This synopsis was taken verbatim from Patrick D. Hazard, ed., *TV as Art* (Champaign, Ill.: National Council of Teachers of English, 1966). It was written by David Boroff, a teacher of English at New York University. Mr. Boroff has been dead for nearly ten years. The kind of teleplay he was describing lives zestfully on. Is it art? The series was "The Nurses and the Doctors," *circa* the early 1960s.

3. *Variety,* February 2, 1972, p. 35.

4. David W. Rintels, "Will Marcus Welby Always Make You Well?" in New York *Times,* March 12, 1972, Section II, p. 1.

5. Aljean Harmetz, "Two Partridges in a Money Tree," New York *Times,* September 5, 1971, Sec. D, p. 11.

6. Gans' analysis may be found in *Social Policy,* Vol. 2, No. 1 (May-June 1971), pp. 34–36.

7. Erich Segal, *Love Story* (New York: New American Library, Signet, 1970), p. 16.

8. Jules Feiffer, *The Great Comic Book Heroes* (New York: Dial Press, 1965).

9. *Newsweek,* December 27, 1971, p. 43.

10. Robert J. Glessing, *The Underground Press in America* (Bloomington, Ind.: Indiana University Press, 1970), pp. 104–105.

11. Lee Preble, "The GI Antiwar Press: What It Says and Why." Unpublished M.A. thesis, University of Wisconsin, 1971, pp. 52, 65.

12. *Variety,* April 5, 1972, p. 92.

13. *Ibid.,* p. 48.

14. Michael Shamberg and Raindance Corporation, *Guerrilla Television* (New York: Holt, Rinehart and Winston, 1971), pp. 41, 61.

15. *Encyclopaedia Britannica* (Chicago: Encyclopaedia Britannica, 1970 edition), pp. 594–595; Frank Luther Mott, *A History of American Magazines,* Vol. IV, 1885–1905 (Cambridge, Mass.: Harvard University Press, 1957), pp. 377–380.

16. Vol. 19, August, 1895, p. 386, quoted in Mott, *op. cit.,* p. 378.

17. Mott, *op. cit.,* p. 379.

18. Nicholas Johnson and Kenneth Cox, *Broadcasting in America and the FCC's License Renewal Process: An Oklahoma Case Study* (Washington, D.C.: Federal Communications Commission, 1968), pp. 172–173.

19. *Technical Report of the Commission on Obscenity and Pornography,* Vol. III (Washington, D.C.: U.S. Government Printing Office, 1970), p. 123.

chapter 10. advertising

1. *Advertising Age* annually publishes a compilation of advertising agency demographics, listing details on billings of more than 600 top advertising agencies.

2. *New York Review of Books,* July 22, 1971.

3. Chandelor v. Lopus, Exchequer Chamber, 1603. Quoted in Frank Thayer, *Legal Control of the Press,* 4th ed. (New York: Foundation Press, 1962), p. 647.

4. In his *The Economic Effects of Advertising* (Chicago: Irwin, 1942), Neil H. Borden of the Harvard Graduate School of Business Administration concluded just that.

5. Association of National Advertisers, Russell H. Colley, ed., *Defining Advertising Goals for Measured Advertising Results* (New York: Association of National Advertisers, 1963), pp. 62–68.

6. American Tobacco Company, *"Sold, American!"—The First Fifty Years* (American Tobacco Company, 1954), p. 75.

7. Robert E. Dallos, Los Angeles Times Service, "Cigar Ads Aim at Young Swingers," in Madison (Wis.) *Capital Times,* August 19, 1970, p. 11.

8. *"Sold, American!"—The First Fifty Years,* p. 5.

9. Michael Knight, New York Times News Service, "The Smoke Shall Rise Again," in *Wisconsin State Journal,* February 13, 1972, Sec. 4, p. 8.

10. Quoted in *Editor & Publisher,* January 23, 1965, p. 11.

11. Los Angeles *Times,* February 19, 1972, Sec. 4, pp. 8, 10, and 12.

12. National Association of Broadcasters *Code News,* Vol. 3, No. 8, October 1970, p. 4.

13. *Ibid.*

14. Quoted in *Advertising Age,* February 22, 1971, p. 130, on the occasion of his address to the southeastern area conference of the American Association of Advertising Agencies.

chapter 11. relating with the public

1. David Yale, "Punching the Enemy in the Mouthpiece," *NUC-MLC Newsletter,* October, 1969, p. 10.

2. Frank Luther Mott, *American Journalism,* 3d ed. (New York: Macmillan, 1962), p. 235.

3. Daniel Boorstin, *The Image: A Guide to Pseudo-Events in America* (New York: Harper & Row, 1964), p. 207.

4. Alan R. Raucher, *Public Relations and Business: 1900–1929* (Baltimore, Md.: Johns Hopkins University Press, 1968), p. 11.

5. Robert B. Harper, *Reporting Social Strife in Five Labor Conflicts, 1914–1966,* M.A. thesis, University of Wisconsin, 1971, pp. 22ff.

6. *PR Reporter,* June 14, 1971.

7. Scott M. Cutlip and Allen H. Center, *Effective Public Relations,* 4th ed. (Englewood Cliffs, N.J.: Prentice-Hall, 1971), pp. 186ff.

8. Charles N. Stabler, "Changing Times: For Many Corporations, Social Responsibility Is Now a Major Concern," *The Wall Street Journal,* October 26, 1971, p. 1.

9. *Ibid.,* p. 29.

10. Roger E. Celler, *The Challengers* (Washington, D.C.: Public Affairs Council, 1971).

11. Jane Cracraft, "Kunstler Urges 'Imagination' in Trials," *The Denver Post,* July 30, 1971, p. 20.

12. *Chiropractic: Questions and Answers,* pamphlet distributed by Luedtke Storm Chiropractic Clinic, Madison, Wisconsin, 1966.

13. Joe McGinniss, *The Selling of the President, 1968* (New York: Trident, 1969), p. 125.

14. Jeffrey O'Connell, "Lambs to Slaughter," *Columbia Journalism Review,* Fall 1967, p. 22.

15. Curt Gentry, *The Last Days of the Late, Great State of California* (New York: Ballantine Books, 1969), p. 120.

16. James F. Chatfield, "Behind the Blue Flame," *Public Relations Journal,* August, 1971, pp. 22–25.

17. Boorstin, *op. cit.,* pp. 39–40.

18. *Public Relations News,* August 16, 1971, pp. 3–4.
19. Quoted in Theodore Peterson, Jay Jensen, and William L. Rivers, *The Mass Media and Modern Society* (New York: Holt, Rinehart and Winston, 1965), p. 191.
20. Nicholas Meyer, *Love Story Story* (New York: Avon, 1971), p. 20.
21. *APME Guidelines,* Associated Press Managing Editors Association, 1969, p. 42.
22. John Chancellor, NBC radio commentary, February 8, 1971.
23. Richard Karp, "Newspaper Food Pages: Credibility for Sale," *Columbia Journalism Review,* November/December, 1971, pp. 36–44.
24. Beatrice Schapper, ed., *Writing the Magazine Article* (Cincinnati, Ohio: Writer's Digest, 1970), pp. 179–199.
25. American Institute for Political Communication, *The Federal Government–Daily Press Relationship* (Washington, D.C.: The Institute, 1967), p. 108.
26. William Schabacker, *Public Relations and the News Media.* M.A. thesis, University of Wisconsin, 1963.
27. Scott M. Cutlip, "The Public Relations Practitioner and the Nation's Public Information System." Address to the Weekly Newspaper Conference, University of Wisconsin, November 6, 1971.

chapter 12. law—the heavy control

1. *Variety,* February 2, 1972, p. 4; February 16, 1972, p. 3.
2. *Variety,* May 5, 1971, p. 58.
3. *Variety,* February 9, 1972, p. 46.
4. The story of the proposed ABC-ITT merger has been told in several places, nowhere more clearly than in Nicholas Johnson, "The Media Barons and the Public Interest," in *Atlantic,* June 1968, pp. 43–51.
5. See Goldwater v. Ginzburg, 414 F. 2d 324 (2d Cir. 1969).
6. Both Walker and Butts were decided by the Supreme Court in one opinion, Curtis Publishing Co. v. Butts and Associated Press v. Walker, 388 U.S. 130 (1967).
7. Mark Twain, *Sketches Old and New* (New York, 1875), quoted in Frank Luther Mott, *American Journalism,* 3rd ed. (New York: Macmillan, 1962), pp. 309–310.
8. 3 Howell's State Trials 561 (1632–3), cited in Frank Thayer, *Legal Control of the Press,* 4th ed. (New York: Foundation Press, 1962), pp. 9–10.
9. Retold in David G. Clark and Earl R. Hutchison, *Mass Media and the Law* (New York: Wiley, 1970), pp. 352–359.
10. Quoted in Ira H. Carmen, *Movies, Censorship, and the Law* (Ann Arbor: University of Michigan Press, 1966), p. 207.
11. *Variety,* February 23, 1972, p. 25.
12. Testimony of David W. Rintels before the Senate Subcommittee on Constitutional Rights, reported in New York *Times,* March 5, 1972, Section 2, p. 1.
13. *Ibid.*
14. Daniel Walker, *Rights in Conflict* (New York: Signet Books, 1968), p. 295.
15. *Variety,* February 23, 1972, p. 44.
16. James C. N. Paul and Murray L. Schwartz, *Federal Censorship: Obscenity in the Mail* (Glencoe, Ill.: The Free Press, 1961), recount the fascinating history of customs and Post Office censorship in this country.
17. *Variety,* March 1, 1972, p. 20.
18. A brief but thorough recapitulation of the case has been done by Don R. Pember, "The 'Pentagon Papers' Decision: More Questions Than Answers," *Journalism Quarterly,* Autumn 1971, pp. 403–411.
19. Harold L. Nelson and Dwight L. Teeter, *Law of Mass Communications* (Mineola, N.Y.: Foundation Press, 1969), pp. 223–224.
20. 461 S.W. 2d 345 (Ky. 1970), quoted and discussed in Donald M. Gillmor and Jerome A. Barron, *Supplement to Mass Communication Law* (St. Paul, Minn.: West Publishing Co., 1971), pp. 63–64.
21. *Ibid.,* pp. 58–62.

22. See Branzburg v. Hayes, 92 S. Ct. 2646 (1972), and U.S. v. Caldwell, S. Ct. 2686 (1972).

23. For an especially thorough working out of this position, see Fred W. Friendly, "Justice White and Reporter Caldwell: Finding a Common Ground," in *Columbia Journalism Review,* September-October 1972, pp. 31–37.

24. United Press International, in *Wisconsin State Journal,* October 15, 1971, Section 3, p. 14.

25. The Federal Trade Commission News Summary carries monthly the latest developments. Full evidence submitted is obtainable from the National Technical Information Service, 5285 Port Royal Road, Springfield, Virginia 22151.

26. Heywood Broun and Margaret Leech, *Anthony Comstock: Roundsman of the Lord* (New York: Boni, 1927), p. 15.

27. *The Report of the Commission on Obscenity and Pornography* (New York: Bantam Books, 1970), p. 458.

28. *Variety,* June 2, 1971, p. 23.

29. Quoted in Harold L. Nelson, ed., *Freedom of the Press from Hamilton to the Warren Court* (Indianapolis, Ind.: Bobbs-Merrill, 1967), pp. 229–230.

30. *Variety,* March 1, 1972, p. 55.

31. Yoeckel v. Samonig, 272 Wis. 430, 434–5, 75 N.W. 2d 925, 927 (1956).

32. *Variety,* March 1, 1972, p. 16.

33. *Variety,* March 1, 1972, p. 18.

34. *Variety,* March 1, 1972, pp. 1, 33.

chapter 13. what the citizen can do

1. Information is available from The National Association for Better Broadcasting's office at 373 North Western Avenue, Los Angeles, California 90004.

2. The times, frequencies, and origins of shortwave broadcasts in English are listed in the *World Radio-TV Handbook,* distributed by Billboard Publications, 165 West 46th St., New York, N.Y. 10036.

3. Joseph Finnigan, "Hubby Spent $400,000 So Now Dora Hall Is Featured in a TV Show," *TV Guide,* August 21, 1971, pp. 10–11.

4. Stuart W. Little, "How To Start a Magazine," *Saturday Review,* June 14, 1969, pp. 52ff.

5. "The Mailbag," *Writer's Digest,* September, 1970, p. 6.

6. A. Kent MacDougall, "Going It Alone: Free Lance Writers Cite Long List of Woes but Like Independence," *Wall Street Journal,* August 7, 1970, p. 1.

7. Wolcott Gibbs, *More in Sorrow* (New York: Holt, 1958), pp. ix–x.

8. Jessica Mitford, "Let Us Now Appraise Famous Writers," *The Atlantic Monthly,* July 1970, pp. 45–54. Thanks largely to Miss Mitford's revelations, Famous Writers' profits took a tumble and the New York City Department of Consumer Affairs began an investigation of its own, with the result that Famous Writers tempered its advertising and agreed to make some partial refunds. See *Consumer Reports,* March 1972, p. 169.

9. "Learning by Mail," *Writer's Digest,* September, 1970, p. 31.

10. "The Vanity Press," *Newsweek,* December 23, 1968, pp. 83–85.

11. *Ibid.,* p. 85.

12. Quoted in " 'Vanity' Services: A Consumer Alert," *Publisher's Weekly,* March 2, 1970, p. 60.

13. Quoted in Irving Rosenthal, "Who Writes the 'Letters to the Editor'?" *Saturday Review,* September 13, 1969, p. 116.

14. A. Kent MacDougall, "Dear Sir. You Jerk! Letters to Editor Rise, and Beleaguered Press Gives Them More Room," *Wall Street Journal,* August 8, 1970, p. 1.

15. David L. Grey and Trevor R. Brown, "Letters to the Editor: Hazy Reflections of Public Opinion," *Journalism Quarterly,* 47 (Autumn 1970), pp. 450–471.

16. Described in Gene Fowler, *Timberline* (New York: Covici Friede, 1933), pp. 153–159.

17. Craig Tomkinson, "Editor Attacked Again," *Editor & Publisher,* January 24, 1970, p. 38.

18. William Strunk, Jr., and E. B. White, *The Elements of Style* (New York: Macmillan, 1959), p. 59.

19. A. J. Liebling, *The Press* (New York: Ballantine Books, 1961), p. 72.

20. Nicholas Johnson, *How To Talk Back to Your Television Set* (New York: Bantam Books, 1970), pp. 190–191.

21. Marsha O'Bannon Prowitt, *Guide to Citizen Action in Radio and Television* (New York: Office of Communication, United Church of Christ, 1971), p. 18.

22. Richard W. Jencks, "Broadcast Regulation by Private Contract: Some Observations on 'Community Control' of Broadcasting," address to the 1971 Broadcasting Industry Symposium, Washington, D.C., January 18, 1971.

chapter 14. what the media can do

1. Marvin Barrett, ed., *Survey of Broadcast Journalism 1969–1970* (New York: Grosset & Dunlap, 1970), pp. 31–39.

2. Otis Chandler, speech upon receiving the Honor Award for Distinguished Service in Journalism, University of Missouri, Columbia, Missouri, May 9, 1969. Reprinted in *Seminar,* September, 1969, pp. 12–14.

3. Bruce A. Linton, *Self-Regulation in Broadcasting* (Lawrence, Kansas: William Allen White School of Journalism and Public Information, 1967), p. 6.

4. William L. Rivers and Wilbur Schramm, *Responsibility in Mass Communication,* rev. ed. (New York: Harper & Row, 1969), Appendix A. Other media codes are reproduced in the same volume. Updated broadcasting codes can be secured from Code Authority, National Association of Broadcasters, 1771 N St. N.W., Washington, D.C. 20036.

5. Carl Lindstrom, *The Fading American Newspaper* (Garden City, N.Y.: Doubleday, 1960), pp. 53–54.

6. Linton, *op. cit.,* p. 8.

7. Kenneth Macgowan, *Behind the Screen* (New York: Dell, 1965), pp. 347–372.

8. Sidney W. Head, *Broadcasting in America,* 2d ed., (New York: Houghton Mifflin, 1972), p. 469.

9. Quoted in "Something of Value," brochure of the Code Authority, National Association of Broadcasters, 1966.

10. Letter to the authors from the Code Authority, August 31, 1971.

11. David R. Boldt, "Blue-Pencil Men: TV Censors Work Hard Screening Racy Humor of Bold Comedy Shows," *Wall Street Journal,* January 29, 1969, pp. 1, 10.

12. Linton, *op. cit.,* p. 31.

13. Nicholas Johnson, *How to Talk Back to Your Television Set* (New York: Bantam, 1970), pp. 169–170.

14. *Seminar,* September 1970, p. 12.

15. Kansas City *Star,* February 5, 1970, p. 4.

16. The Public Relations Society of America has an accreditation program that requires five years of experience, a six-hour written test, and an oral examination. More than 2000 PRSA members have been accredited since the program began in 1965—a small fraction of all practitioners in the country. There is no real penalty for those who do not seek accreditation or who fail to pass the test. See Kerryn King, "Accreditation Passes a Milestone," *Public Relations Journal,* November 1970, pp. 38–41.

17. *Seminar,* September, 1970, p. 12.

18. Linton, *op. cit.,* p. 4.

19. Doctor X, *Intern* (New York: Harper & Row, 1965), p. 165. See also Liz Roman Gallese, "Watching Doctors: Medical-Ethics Panels Are Set Up to Resolve Dilemmas on Research," *Wall Street Journal,* April 14, 1971, p. 1.

20. "Staff Control of Newspaper Policy? Symposium Finds Idea Off-Base," *Editor & Publisher,* January 17, 1970, p. 12.

21. Lenora Williamson, "Criticism of Press Begins in Newsroom," *Editor & Publisher,* June 20, 1970, p. 40.

22. Letter to the authors, April 20, 1970.

23. "Let Me Speak to the Manager," brochure, WFAA-TV, Dallas–Ft. Worth, Texas, undated.

24. Joseph Volz, "Post-Ombudsman," *(More),* January 1972, p. 3. Harwood was succeeded as ombudsman by Ben H. Bagdikian, who resigned 11 months later amid some bitterness. See J. Anthony Lukas, "The Limits of Self-Criticism," *(More),* September 1972, p. 3.

25. Donald E. Brown, "Press Council Rulings Serve as Guidelines for Journalists," *Editor & Publisher,* April 24, 1971, p. 17.

16. For an overview of American press council experience, see William L. Rivers, William B. Blankenburg, Kenneth Starck, and Earl Reeves, *Backtalk: Press Councils in America* (San Francisco: Canfield Press, 1972).

27. "A Time of Challenge for Freedom of the Press," Miami *News,* March 17, 1970, p. 16–A.

chapter 15. whither media?

1. Theodore J. Gordon, "The Feedback Between Technology and Values," in Kurt Baier and Nicholas Rescher, eds., *Values and the Future* (New York: The Free Press, 1969), pp. 179 ff.

2. Arthur C. Clarke, "Beyond Babel: The Century of the Communications Satellite," *Broadcasting from Space,* UNESCO Reports and Papers on Mass Communication No. 60 (Paris: UNESCO, 1970), p. 49.

3. Ben H. Bagdikian, *The Information Machines* (New York: Harper & Row, 1971), pp. 17–18.

4. Maxwell E. McCombs, "Mass Media in the Marketplace," *Journalism Monographs* No. 24, August 1972.

5. Robert S. Kahan, "The Antecedents of American Photojournalism." Ph.D. dissertation, University of Wisconsin, Madison, Wisconsin, 1968, pp. 43–60.

6. Speech to the National Association of Broadcasters, October 26, 1931, reprinted in *The Journal of Radio Law,* Vol. 2 (1932), p. 186.

7. The rules are reproduced in *Broadcasting Magazine,* February 7, 1972, pp. 17–36.

8. *Variety,* February 16, 1972, p. 31.

9. These remarkable data were compiled by *Newsweek;* see "Technology's Seers," March 6, 1972, p. 69.

index

in comics, 103–104
in news photography, 99
on television, 59–61, 125 ff.
   See also National Commission on
      the Causes and Prevention of
      Violence
Vogue, 151

Walker, Edwin, B., 187
Wall Street Journal, 117, 228, 237
Walters, Basil, 230–231
Warner Bros., 77
Washington *Post,* 111, 236, 251
WBOX, Bogalusa, La., 66–67
WDIO-TV, Duluth, Minn., 191
WEAF, New York, 56
Wealth and Power in America, 109
Webster, Noah, 152
Weissberg, Alexander Semyonovitch, 40
WFAA-TV, Dallas, 235
White, E. B., 216
Whorf, Benjamin Lee, 43
WIBW, Topeka, 227
Wiggins, J. Russell, 98
Wild Angels, 33
Wild Rovers, The, 74
Willard, 74

Willis, Ellen, 33
Wire services, 138
   and public relations, 183–184
Wisner, George, 88
WLBT-TV, Jackson, Mississippi, 64, 217
WMAZ-TV, Huntington-Charleston, 206
WNBC-TV, New York, 216
WNEW, New York, 149
Wolfe, Thomas, 7
Wolfe, Tom, 100
Woman's Home Companion, 208
Wood, Robert, 51
Woodbury soap, 158
Writer's Digest, 208, 210, 212
Writer's Market, 211
WTEV-TV, New Bedford, Massachusetts,
   193
WXOW-TV, La Crosse, Wisconsin, 29

Young, Whitney, 6

Z, 124
Zanuck, Darryl, 70
Zappa, Frank, 14
Zenger, John Peter, 106–107
Zip News, 152